00
S3/0714

C000277059

Documents of Medieval History 4

Advisory Editors

G. W. S. Barrow
Professor of Scottish History, University of Edinburgh
Edward Miller
Master of Fitzwilliam College, Cambridge

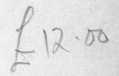

£12·00

CITY OF COVENTRY
W. LATHOME
COMPREHENSIVE
SCHOOL
EDUCATION COMMITTEE

The Crusades

Idea and Reality, 1095–1274

**Louise and Jonathan
Riley-Smith**

Edward Arnold

©Louise and Jonathan Riley-Smith 1981

First published 1981
by Edward Arnold (Publishers) Ltd
41 Bedford Square, London WC1B 3DQ

British Library Cataloguing in Publication Data

Riley-Smith, Louise
   The Crusades. – (Documents of medieval history; 4)
    1. Crusades – History – Sources
   I. Title II. Riley-Smith, Jonathan III. Series
   940.1'8   D151

ISBN 0–7131–6348–8

All rights reserved. No part of this publication may be reproduced, stored in a
retrieval system, or transmitted in any form or by any means, electronic,
photocopying, recording, or otherwise, without the prior permission of Edward
Arnold (Publishers) Ltd.

Typeset by Keyset Composition, Colchester, Essex, in 11/12 Bembo Linoterm.
Printed in Great Britain by Richard Clay (The Chaucer Press) Ltd, Bungay,
Suffolk

For Toby, Tammy and Polly

liberis nostris hoc libro couterinis

Contents

Contents

Contents

Foreword

Attitudes to the past are always changing. Forty years ago few historians would have considered translating many of the texts we present here. Although they recognized of course that in the past there were good and sincere men who were convinced that acts of violence were divinely authorized and meritorious and could therefore lead to salvation, the idea of sacred violence was so repulsive to them that they seem to have been reluctant to give the arguments used to support it serious attention or to concede that there was any intellectual force in them. Since 1945, however, there have emerged in nearly all the branches of Christianity militant liberation movements, the exponents of which propagate what is in fact sacred violence. We believe that theologians and historians should look again at the arguments for crusading and the experiences of crusaders, which are echoed in the beliefs and activities of some extremists today. Too many militant theologians, mistakenly convinced of the novelty of the premises they use, do not realize that Christians have been committed to an ideology of violence before, with very unfortunate consequences. We have tried to present the theological arguments used by the popes and preachers who promoted crusades and also to treat seriously the attitudes of those men and women who responded to their appeals to take the cross: the sources tell us a good deal about the piety and religious zeal which led so many of them to sacrifice and endure much.

Two-thirds of our texts have never been translated before and we decided to translate the others afresh. We have, therefore, few acknowledgements to make. We must thank Dr Edward Miller for inviting us to prepare a volume for the series, Pauline Wagg for typing a difficult script and our children, who have had to put up with quite a lot from us during the last few months. It is right that the book should be dedicated to them with our love.

L R-S
J R-S
Winkfield
December 1980

Abbreviations

PL   *Patrologiae cursus completus. Series Latina*
(J. P. Migne, 221 vols., Paris, 1841–64)

RHC Oc. *Recueil des historiens des croisades. Historiens occidentaux*
(Académie des Inscriptions et Belles-Lettres, 5 vols., Paris, 1844–96)

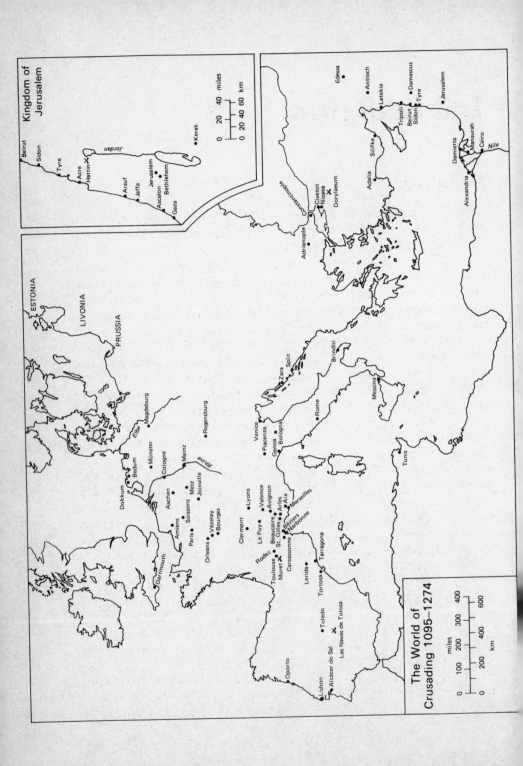

Kingdom of
Jerusalem

Beirut
Sidon
Tyre
Acre
Hettin ✗
Jaffa
Arsuf
Jerusalem
Ascalon
Bethlehem
Gaza
Kerak
Jordan

0   20   40 miles
0 20 40 60 km

ESTONIA
LIVONIA
PRUSSIA

Dokkum
Bedum
Münster
Cologne
Aachen
Mainz
Metz
Joinville
Amiens
Soissons
Paris
Vézelay
Bourges
Orleans
Clermont
Le Puy
Lyons
Valence
Avignon
Beaucaire
Arles
St. Gilles
Aix
Marseilles
Rodez
Béziers
Toulouse
Carcassonne
Narbonne
Muret ✗
Tarragona
Lerida
Tortosa
Oporto
Toledo
Alcácer do Sal
Las Navas de Tolosa ✗
Lisbon

Elbe
Magdeburg
Regensburg
Rhine

Dartmouth

Venice
Piacenza
Genoa
Bologna
Rome
Zara
Split
Brindisi
Messina
Tunis

Constantinople
Adrianople
Civetot
Nicaea
Dorylaeum

Édessa
Antioch
Latakia
Silifke
Adalia
Tripoli
Beirut
Sidon
Tyre
Damascus
Jerusalem
Mansurah
Cairo
Damietta
Alexandria
Nile

The World of
Crusading 1095–1274

miles
0   100   200   300   400
0 200   400   600
km

Introduction

Definition

A crusade was a holy war authorized by the pope, who proclaimed it in the name of God or Christ. It was believed to be Christ's own enterprise, legitimized by his personal mandate. Proposed, like all justifiable Christian violence, as a defensive reaction to injury or aggression or as an attempt to recover Christian territories lost to the infidels, it answered to the needs of the whole Church or of all Christendom, conceived of as one universal, transcendental state, rather than to those of a particular nation or region: many of the campaigns of the Spanish Reconquest, fought in the name not just of Spain but of Christendom at large and drawing recruits from all over western Europe, were crusades; the wars against the Turks of the sixteenth and seventeenth centuries, undertaken by alliances of individual states bound together in the face of a common threat, were not. A man became a crusader by making a public vow, which was not at first distinguishable from, and was always based on, the vow to make a pilgrimage, and crusaders and pilgrims had the same legal status, being temporarily subjected to church courts and enjoying ecclesiastical protection of their persons, properties and families. Crusaders, whether they were fighting against Muslims in the East or in Spain, pagans in the Baltic region, or heretics or schismatics or political enemies of the popes in the European heartlands, were also given indulgences; in fact the notion of the indulgence developed with its constant use in grants to crusaders.

Not everyone would agree with the definition we have just given. Some historians consider only expeditions for the liberation or defence of the Holy Sepulchre in Jerusalem to have been true crusades: for them all other campaigns which have been given the name of crusades belonged to another species of war and should be treated separately, or were perversions of the original ideal which did much harm, giving rise to disillusionment among the faithful and damaging the popes who preached them. They are inclined to use a narrower range of material than we are and they make different judgements on the success or failure of the movement. Indeed the continuing enthusiasm in the West in the fourteenth century is hard for them to explain, because, looking only to the East, they expect to find only disappointment and frustration after the reverses of the late thirteenth century.

It would, of course, be quite wrong to deny the unique place that Jerusalem had in the crusading movement: it cast a spell over the participants in the First Crusade and crusading to the East always had a special attraction; Jerusalem was, as the wording of many of the grants of indulgences to crusaders in Europe made clear, the touchstone against which all other crusades were tested. But there is good evidence that as far as popes, the Roman curia and canon lawyers were concerned crusades in Europe or on its frontiers had the same status as crusades to Jerusalem. It has been argued that the diversion of crusading elsewhere was a late development and attracted so much criticism that it cannot be regarded as being acceptable to most Latin Christians: moreover, that the Roman curia was not Christendom as a whole. This is untenable. The extension of the status of a crusade to the Spanish Reconquest dates from the pontificate of Urban II **(2 iv)**: in other words the diversion of crusading was contemporary with the First Crusade. Since any crusade depended for its legitimization on papal authority, moreover, the only way of knowing that a crusade was in train was because a pope had proclaimed it; a crusader could only be recognized because he had taken a vow, enforceable by church courts, had a certain legal status, which resulted from ecclesiastical protection, and enjoyed certain privileges, which had been granted to him on the pope's behalf. In fact the popes decided what were crusades and what were not. Nor is the argument that they were unrepresentative of Latin Christendom convincing. When one studies contemporary writers who criticized the dissipation of crusading efforts in areas other than the East or challenged the validity of the diversions one finds that there were not very many of them and that most of them came from regions that were in some way directly affected. It is not surprising to find someone in Palestine complaining that funds were being put to uses other than the financing of the war in the East, or inhabitants of south-west France opposing the Albigensian Crusade, or Italian Ghibellines and Germans criticizing crusades against the Staufen, or the French government banning the preaching of a crusade against Frederick II at a time when the king was in the Orient; France was later to support Charles of Anjou's crusade into southern Italy. And against the few critics one should weigh the actions of the thousands who answered the summons of the popes. The Spanish campaigns drew support from France, Italy, Germany and Britain as well as from within Spain; Bohemians, Poles, Danes and Englishmen fought with the Germans along the shores of the Baltic; Englishmen, Italians and Germans joined the French in the Albigensian Crusade; Frenchmen and Italians fought as crusaders against the Staufen, Aragonese and Ghibellines; and the wars against the Hussites involved crusaders from many parts of Europe. These thousands of individuals represented a 'silent majority'. Their motives may not all have been disinterested, but their presence is evidence that to a very large section of Christian opinion these enterprises were legitimate crusades.

The arguments of those who will only recognize crusading to Jerusalem are fundamentally weak and one cannot help feeling that often their attitude is based on the subjective conviction that it was somehow more acceptable to fight infidels in the East than fellow-Christians in the West. There were certainly those in the central Middle Ages who shared this view, but in fact in the traditions of Christian ethics the use of violence against Christians was justified in a way that it never was with regard to infidels. In canon law one was forbidden to force the faith on an infidel, born in error; one should seek to persuade him by reason. On the other hand, it had been argued by most Christian writers from the fourth century onwards that one was bound to use violence against an intransigent heretic – by definition a fellow-Christian – to direct him back on to the right path.

Background

The eleventh century was not a comfortable age for western Europeans. There was taking place a spiritual revival, affecting all sections of society, which was characterized by an obsession with the consequences of sin. It was obvious that little a man might do could justify himself objectively in the eyes of God and theologians accepted that there were in the Christian community the elect, predestined by God for heaven. But at the same time there was the belief that a man's actions, however unworthy, could help him to salvation: that in his mercy God would take account of what a man had done when he came to judge. Modern theologians of merit take a positive line, stressing the grace that is merited by good acts. But the eleventh-century theology of merit strikes one as being more negative in that there was a tendency to emphasize that every good deed would be weighed in the balance against previous sins, repaying some little part of man's debt to God; only Christ himself, man as well as God, and the saints had built up a credit balance in what was later to be called the Treasury of the Church. The theology of merit was strongly penitential and many good deeds were viewed as voluntary penances performed to reduce some part of the punishment imposed by an infinitely just God for sin. And a problem faced by most ordinary Christians was that it had traditionally been held that the best way of gaining merit was to renounce a flawed world by withdrawing into a monastery or religious house: love of God began by taking one's leave of earthly things and devoting oneself to a life of prayer.

The second of Christ's commandments, however, was that we should love our neighbour and to show such love was of course a meritorious act. It is not surprising that in the eleventh century there began what was to be a phenomenal growth in charitable activities: not only education and the care of the poor and sick, but also violence, certain expressions of which could be treated as acts of love. At the turn of the fourth and fifth centuries St Augustine had tried to reconcile the use of force with the demands of Christian love and his solution satisfied many generations of theologians. He found many instances, not only in the Old Testament but also in the New, of prophets and saints and even of Christ accepting the use of violence as a punishment for sin and as a means of defence against injury. To Augustine the key to this lay in an understanding of the intentions of these holy men, whose sanctity stemmed from their power of loving. They did not hate but only desired justice and the correction of those offenders who were the objects of their love: it was, in fact, often more loving to use force than indulgence. Augustine, therefore, justified the repression of heresy by physical force. It was a sign of love and mercy in imitation of Christ for a loving Church in collaboration with a loving state to compel heretics to foresake the path of error for their own benefit: he drew attention to the parable of the host at the wedding feast, who sent out his servant to force those in the highways to come to the banquet.

Augustine's arguments on force and love were not easy to come by, because they were scattered throughout his many writings, but just before the First Crusade they were made available to a wide readership in three important collections. In *c.* 1083 St Anselm of Lucca issued in books XII and XIII of his *Collectio canonum* a sample of the basic Augustinian texts on violence, including those on force and love, and in *c.* 1094 Ivo of Chartres made other collections in his *Decretum* and *Panormia*. Anselm and Ivo were writing for a purpose: the *Collectio canonum* may have been commissioned by Pope Gregory VII and the *Decretum* and *Panormia* by Pope Urban II. Augustine's justification of the use of force, particularly in the suppression of heresy, appealed to the party for ecclesiastical reform at a time when it was trying to free the Church from lay control and tended to see its struggle with temporal powers in terms of a fight against heretics and schismatics, or at least against disobedient men and excommunicates, to which Augustine's arguments were relevant. At the same time the reforming popes turned to secular knighthood for help and all over Europe clerics began to teach that the profession of arms was worth-while when followed in support of the Church's cause. Particularly influential was a group, including Anselm of Lucca himself, which had gathered around Countess Mathilda of Tuscany, a great Italian magnate. One of them, John of Mantua, developed the theoretical grounds for papal control over the temporal sword wielded by laymen, using an argument that rested on the extraordinary fact that in the Garden of Gethsemane on the eve of the Crucifixion St Peter, the Prince of the Apostles whose vicar the pope was, had been wearing a sword. John pointed out that although Peter was rebuked by Christ when he drew his sword he was not ordered to cast it away but to return it to its scabbard. It was obvious that Peter, as a priest, could not perform a military action himself, but it was equally clear that he, and his heirs, had power to authorize violence. Historical precedents could be added to scriptural exegesis. For instance, the ninth-century popes Leo IV and John VIII had had to organize the defence of Rome and parts of Italy and in the middle of the eleventh century Pope Leo IX and Pope Alexander II had not only authorized wars in Italy and Spain but had also encouraged the invasions of England and Sicily. There had been, moreover, occasional papal declarations which could be treated as forms of authorization, and some of these were collected and published by Ivo of Chartres.

There was, therefore, some justification for Gregory VII's introduction in the 1070s and 1080s of the idea of a knighthood at his disposal, bound to him not strictly speaking as vassals under contract but by their acceptance of his position as head of the whole Church. These *fideles* – a feudal term denoting vassals – were absolved from their sins in return for their services. Imitating the practice of referring to the vassals of a bishop as *milites* of the patron saint of his cathedral church, Gregory called them *fideles* or *milites s. Petri*. The establishment of this scattered group of knights, in Germany, France and Italy, dedicated to war as knights of St Peter and called to that war by the pope as St Peter's vicar, was a step towards the crusades. But these knights fought St Peter's war and the significance of the development in 1095, when the *miles s. Petri* was superseded by the *miles Christi*, has been underestimated, partly because Gregory VII himself occasionally used the term 'soldiery of Christ' to refer to his supporters. Service to St Peter, which was anyway introduced tentatively and not entirely successfully, was in the ancient and continuing tradition of service to a bishop and in calling for it the pope was doing only on a larger scale – related to all of Christendom and not directly to a feudal contract – what any bishop might have done. Service to God or Christ was of quite a different order. Here again the roots of the idea lay in the writings of St Augustine.

For Augustine had envisaged war on God's command. On divine authority Abraham had been prepared to sacrifice Isaac, Moses had made war and Elijah had killed. These responses to God's orders had shown faithful submissiveness and obedience and they proved that God could directly command violence, not out of cruelty but in righteous retribution. It followed that when war was waged in obedience to him, who never required wrong, it had to be allowed to be righteous and a just war *par excellence*: it was not for men to judge what was good or bad to him. That God could enjoin war was proved by the Old Testament. It was true that the emphasis was different in the New, but, although Christ had preached forgiveness and meekness, he had, as St Luke related in his account of the Last Supper, also told the apostles to buy swords. Divine precepts, in fact, could change with the times, for different ages needed different remedies: it was one and the same God who ordered the prophets to make war and forbade the apostles to use violence. To dare to believe that God would not demand war of men or to dare to find fault in him for doing so showed an inability to comprehend divine providence. Augustine argued that God would physically help those whose wars he justified, as he had helped the Israelites to conquer the Amorite cities.

Some of these Augustinian texts were cited by Anselm of Lucca and to a lesser extent by Ivo of Chartres. And it is clear that when Pope Urban II preached the First Crusade he called out soldiers not in Peter's but in Christ's war, speaking as Christ's mouthpiece, on the grounds that the Eastern Christians, Christ's children, must be defended and that Jerusalem, Christ's own heritage, must be liberated. For the past 40 years there has been a tendency to play down the part Jerusalem played in Urban's plans for the crusade. Most historians have been persuaded that the pope's real aim was to bring relief to the Greek Church in the hope that this would lead to a happier relationship between Rome and Constantinople and that it was the public reaction to the use of Jerusalem as a devotional rather than a practical goal which, within months of his sermons at Clermont, turned its liberation into the primary aim of the expedition. But the evidence for this interpretation has been challenged recently and the interpretation is anyway unbelievable. Fraternal aid to the Greeks would hardly justify St Peter's substitution by Christ in the terminology used by the pope: indeed there would have been powerful reasons why St Peter should have been proposed as the patron of an expedition through which Rome brought aid to a fellow patriarchate which had, in Roman eyes, claimed a higher position in Christendom than was its due. On the other hand war for a place redolent with reminders of Christ's physical presence would fully justify it being called his own. It is hard now to conceive of the terms in which people thought of the potency of physical objects associated with past holiness. Rome was St Peter's city; there he had been bishop; there his body still lay under the *Confessio* in his church. He was still a present force and fighting for the bishop of Rome would naturally express itself in the idea of service to him. But what the Prince of the Apostles was for Rome was a pale reflection of what incarnate God was for Jerusalem, where he had suffered, had been buried and had risen again. Jerusalem was not only the city of the kings and prophets of Israel; it was also the place where God had redeemed mankind and in which his presence still lingered in the objects he had touched, the streets he had walked, the ground that had soaked up his blood, the sepulchre in which he had been buried. It had always been the focal point of his interventions in his created order and that rôle was reserved for it to the end of time, for it would play an important part in the events leading up to the Last Day, a sequence, it was suggested, that could not begin without its reoccupation by Christians (**3 iii**). Of importance to ordinary crusaders, moreover, seems to have been a literal interpretation of the concept of Jerusalem as the heritage of Christ. In an age in which the loyalties of European knights were focussed more than ever before on their estates nothing could have been more real to them than the idea that as Christ's children they were being called upon to win back for him his personal family property. The goal of Jerusalem could not be anything but central to the First Crusade; it was the catalyst that turned the knighthood of St Peter into the knighthood of Christ.

When churchmen called on knights to serve in the army of St Peter or the army of Christ they were speaking to a society in which there was, as there still is, a gulf between high theology and the views of the ordinary laity. Naturally, they would gear their message to their listeners, putting it to them in a comprehensible and attractive way. The ideals of eleventh-century western society were warlike, in so far as they are discernible in writings that were, even the *chansons de geste*, almost entirely clerical. Its heroes were fighting men whose attributes – strength, honour, bravery, skill at arms, loyalty – were typically martial. Of the heroes of the past none meant more than Charlemagne and the ghost of that great emperor, dead for nearly 300 years, stalked western Europe. He had conquered in Spain and Germany and where he had conquered he had converted. He had protected the Holy Places in Palestine; he was believed to have been a pilgrim, even a crusader, to Jerusalem. He was the ideal of Christian knighthood fighting the infidel and it is not surprising that at the time of the preaching of the First Crusade it was rumoured in Germany that he had risen from the dead. It is not generally realized that most of the leaders of the First Crusade could claim descent from him. Godfrey of Bouillon, his brother Baldwin and Robert of Flanders were particularly conscious of this and a contemporary historian of the crusade pointed out that when Baldwin became King of Jerusalem a descendant of Charlemagne sat on the throne of David. Men were, in fact, much concerned with ancestry and family and this was the period in which genealogies began to be composed for the higher nobility. Crusaders were called upon to deliver their brothers, the Eastern Christians, from bondage and persecution and to liberate their father's patrimony, the Holy Land, from those who had seized it and they were bound to look on these duties in the familiar terms of the endemic blood-feuding waged between families and over family properties that was a feature of the time. Most vernacular crusading poems, indeed, contained references to vengeance **(11)**.

Western society was largely feudalized and the laity tended to see everything to do with relationships – even those between God and man and husband and wife – in terms of the bonds linking lord and vassal, cemented by personal loyalty. The feudal relationship was private and contractual, with reciprocal obligations – the giving of protection and rewards on one side and the performance of services on the other – and senior churchmen were not happy with the application of feudal imagery to man's relationship with God, which was certainly not contractual, because it could imply that God or Christ as lord was obliged to reward a vassal who did his duty and was blameworthy if he failed him. But they could hardly avoid using it when trying to put across an appeal to fight for God in terms the laity would understand, and anyway the laity could not think of such service in any other way **(see especially 17, 20 ii, 26, 29)**. Men were also highly conscious of race: German, Goth, above all Frank (French). French national consciousness was strong and writers at the time of the First Crusade could seriously treat the French as the chosen people of God, whose election had been demonstrated by their Christian steadfastness, their special devotion to the Holy See and their preeminence in warfare **(3 ii, 4)**. God now called on this chosen people to undertake a special task, and there was a tendency (which French historians have never lost) to write about the First Crusade almost entirely in terms of the French, which led occasionally to a sour reaction on the part of writers

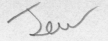

of other nationalities.

Lay society, it is clear, displayed a kind of Christianity that must have embarrassed senior theologians. This showed itself, it is important to stress, not in the cult of relics, although this was taken to lengths that did disturb some thinking contemporaries, nor in the searching of earth and sky for physical signs and portents of God's intentions – an approach to nature which was shared by the most sophisticated clergy and represented simply a different cosmology to ours – but in a xenophobic attitude to men of other faiths, expressed in fiction in the bloodthirsty scenes in the Song of Roland and in reality in the massacres of the Rhineland Jews early in the First Crusade and in the mass killings that punctuated the conquests in the East. A warlike society demanded an aggressive religion, and the conviction that it was praiseworthy to convert by force, which ran counter to the theological tradition that pagans, as opposed to heretics, could only be brought to the faith by reason, seems to have been very strongly held by laymen. Events in Spain and Germany, where border fighting, accompanied by the spread of Christianity, had been endemic, provided examples of missionary wars, and the romance of the Spanish Reconquest found expression in the *chansons*, many of which were associated with the legend of Charlemagne. But this same society, touched by the reform movement, desired salvation and was unsure how to achieve it; there must have been many participants in the First Crusade like Anselm of Ribemont, who had a local reputation as a pious layman. The Church had tried to reduce the level of violence and had voiced disapproval of the ideals of secular knighthood. It had been universally held, as we have seen, that the only sure way to salvation was to enter the religious life and turn one's back on the profession of arms: this was what Tancred, a South Italian Norman, saw as the only choice before him, and his relief at the discovery of another way, through the crusade, was described by his biographer. In this respect there was real significance in the moves the Church had begun to make in proposing the *militia s. Petri* and it is worth noting how many of the leaders of the First Crusade had had links with it. Robert of Normandy's father had received a *vexillum s. Petri* from Pope Alexander II, Robert of Flanders's father had been closely allied to Pope Gregory VII, Bohemond of Taranto's father had been a *miles s. Petri* and Raymond of St Gilles may have been a *fidelis s. Petri* himself; an exception, which is of interest since he became the first ruler of Jerusalem, was Godfrey of Bouillon, who had served the imperialist cause. But service to Christ even more clearly contributed to a man's salvation and to Guibert of Nogent, one of the most intelligent commentators on the First Crusade, God had instituted a holy war precisely in order to give knights and laymen a path to salvation that did not entail entering a monastery and could be taken following their normal profession **(4)**. There is strong evidence that this idea, often expressed in the contrast between the new knight fighting for Christ and the old quarrelsome reprobate, struck a real chord, the sound of which was still reverberating half a century later **(20 i, 21, 24)**.

A feudal, martial society, filled with pride in race, family and patrimony, fiercely intolerant of non-Christians and desiring salvation through works more in accordance with its secular *mores*, was obviously ready to respond to a message that could be interpreted in terms of feudal service, the election of a chosen people, family pride, the patrimony and the blood feud, the spreading of Christianity and personal salvation. The call to crusade was the right call for the time, but a problem was how to bridge the chasm that separated the ideals and aspirations of the higher clergy from those of the laity. Popes and preachers struggled to build that bridge for centuries, but they never entirely succeeded.

History

1095–1110

The sequence of events that led to the First Crusade began at Piacenza early in March 1095 with the appearance of a Byzantine embassy at a church council. The Greeks appealed to Pope Urban II for aid against the Turks, who had recently conquered most of Asia Minor and had almost reached the Bosphorus. Urban replied favourably and seems to have evolved a plan to send a comparatively small army to the East under the captaincy of Raymond of St Gilles, Count of Toulouse, and the spiritual leadership of Adhémar of Monteil, Bishop of Le Puy. About a month later he began a journey to France, where he was going to preside over a council at Clermont with the purpose of reforming the French Church. He reached Clermont probably on 15 or 16 November and on the 27th, at the end of the council, he preached the first of several sermons on the crusade to a crowd gathered outside the town **(3)**. He spent the next eight months promoting it in western and southern France and, as the news of a response probably far greater than he had expected began to come in, he addressed letters of encouragement to the faithful elsewhere **(2 i–ii)** and commissioned churchmen to preach the cross on his behalf.

There has been much speculation and no general agreement about what he said at Clermont, but it is likely that, preaching on the text from St Luke's Gospel (xiv, 27) 'Whosoever doth not carry his cross and come after me cannot be my disciple', he informed his audience that he was Christ's mouthpiece, summoning the faithful to Christ's own war; he justified this war in terms of the relief it would bring to the suffering Eastern Christians and the liberation of Jerusalem and the Holy Land, described in a traditional way as Christ's inheritance; he complimented the French on their abilities as warriors, but also rebuked them for brawling and spilling Christian blood; he compared the new knight, who loved Christ by bearing his cross and loved his neighbour by struggling to liberate him, with the old knight, who pursued his own ambitions and used violence on his fellow Christians; he referred to the indulgence for crusaders, in his eyes a limited remission of penance in consequence of the hardships that would be endured on the expedition; and he put forward the idea of armed pilgrimage to emphasize the goal of Jerusalem, to link it penitentially to the indulgence and to allow him to introduce for crusaders a vow, based on that made by pilgrims, which enabled the Church to exercise some control over them since as pilgrims they would be subject to Church courts. It is possible that the pope did not lay much stress on the fact that the crusade was a pilgrimage, for the terminology of pilgrimages occurs relatively infrequently in the earliest sources. The First Crusade certainly was a pilgrimage – the attraction of Jerusalem would have ensured that – and this contributed to its spirituality, but one cannot avoid the impression that in papal eyes it was a pilgrimage for the technical reason that the pope could make use of the vow and the privileges of pilgrims to subordinate the crusaders to the Church.

If Urban first planned to send a relatively small army from southern and western France, the response from the rest of France, the Low Countries, western Germany, Italy and Spain must have surprised him no less than it has generations of historians, who have been extraordinarily reluctant to face up to the implication that it was motivated by genuine piety. So repugnant has been the idea of Christians engaging in war as an expression of devotion that they have clung to the explanation of a general economic motivation. Certainly the pope and the bishops at the Council of Clermont envisaged men taking part 'to gain honour or money' **(1)** – and so did later preachers **(10, 13)** – but to suppose that this was a prime motivating force is to be blind to the absurdity of the picture of hordes of land-hungry men joining a 2,000-mile march when land was available nearer home, to disregard the motives of the great lords, to whom it would have been provident to stay at home, and to forget the fact that by 1100 there was a desperate shortage of manpower in the new Latin settlements in Palestine and Syria, presumably because most of the lesser knights had returned to the West. Some of the crusaders were doubtless swash-buckling adventurers, but the sources also reveal sorrow at parting from families, disorientation, worry about expense and a very natural fear of known and unknown dangers.

The pope had set 15 August 1096, the Feast of the Assumption, as the date of departure, but already during the previous late winter and spring parties of peasants and petty knights, moved by popular ideas that stemmed from the renewed religious fervour of the age and were perhaps heightened by poor living-conditions and recurrent disease, were marching through northern France and into the Rhineland under Peter the Hermit and Walter Sans-Avoir. They were followed by other bands, particularly one under a German count called Emicho of Leiningen, which were responsible for violent pogroms against the Jewish communities in Germany. Most of them were dispersed in Hungary, but Walter and Peter and their followers reached Constantinople in the middle of July and on 1 August respectively. On 6 August they crossed the Bosphorus and split into two groups, one of which was surprised, surrounded and captured by the Turks on 29 September. The other, deprived of the leadership of Peter the Hermit who had returned to Constantinople, was ambushed and wiped out near Civetot on 21 October. Only a few survivors of these disorderly companies haunted the fringes of the crusade, some of them, known as the Tafurs, later becoming, under their 'king', semi-mythical heroes of the European poor.

Meanwhile, better-organized forces were leaving the West. Hugh of Vermandois, the brother of the king of France, departed in the middle of August, as did Godfrey of Bouillon, duke of Lower Lorraine, and his brother Baldwin. In October Bohemond of Taranto, the eldest son of Robert Guiscard, left southern Italy with his nephew Tancred, and two armies, one under Count Raymond of Toulouse and Bishop Adhémar of Le Puy and the other under Duke Robert of Normandy, Count Robert of Flanders and Count Stephen of Blois, left France. Between November 1096 and May 1097 these leaders and their followers reached Constantinople. In April they began to be shipped across the straits to Asia Minor. On 6 May Godfrey of Bouillon's army advanced to Nicaea, where by 3 June he had been joined by the other crusaders. A Turkish relieving force was beaten off and on 19 June Nicaea surrendered to Byzantine troops accompanying the crusade. On the 26th the crusaders resumed their march and on 1 July won a great victory over the Turks at Dorylaeum. On about 10 September Baldwin and Tancred left the main body and, marching through Cilicia, reduced Tarsus, Adana and Mamistra. Tancred rejoined the crusade, but Baldwin struck out on his own and in the spring of 1098 became the first Latin ruler of an Asian state, with its capital at Edessa. Meanwhile on 21 October 1097 the main army had come up to the walls of Antioch in Syria. Antioch did not fall until 3 June 1098 and the Christians were then almost at once besieged by a large Muslim army. Heartened by reports of visions experienced by two men called Stephen of Valence and Peter Bartholomew and by the discovery on 15 June of what many of them believed was the relic of the Holy Lance, they sortied out on the 28th and spectacularly defeated the Muslims in a battle in which they came to believe that they had been helped by a heavenly host led by SS George, Demetrius and Mercury. The next few months were taken up with enlarging the area of Syria under their control and also with disputes among the leaders, particularly over the possession of Antioch. But on 13 January 1099 Raymond of Toulouse, responding to popular demands to press on to Jerusalem, led his own forces south. Robert of Normandy followed him and in March he was joined by Godfrey of Bouillon and Robert of Flanders. An attempt to take the town of 'Arqah, north of Tripoli, had to be abandoned, but the crusaders marched down the coast by way of Tripoli, Beirut, Sidon, Tyre, Caesarea and Arsuf, reaching Ramla, on the road to Jerusalem, on 3 June. Tancred took Bethlehem on the 6th, and by nightfall on the 7th the Christians were encamped before Jerusalem itself, which, amid scenes of carnage, fell to them on 15 July. On the 22nd Godfrey of Bouillon was elected ruler of the new kingdom and on 12 August, near Ascalon, the Christians defeated a large Egyptian army that had been sent against them. Their possession of Palestine was assured for the time being.

In contemporary and near-contemporary accounts the suffering and deprivation the crusaders, great as well as lesser, had to endure comes across clearly and at certain times, particularly during the traumatic period at Antioch, the crisis point in the crusade, conditions in the army must have been nearly unbearable. In spite of occasional barbarisms and the ambitions of the leaders, moreover, one gets the impression of a profound piety, to be seen not only in the willingness to undergo danger and hardship, but also in the large number of visions experienced in the army **(43, 48)**, in the devotion to certain saints and to relics and, above all, in a very typical preoccupation with ritual, which expressed itself in public demonstrations of penitence: indeed in its later stages the crusade resembled a massive, slow-moving liturgical solemnity, culminating in a great penitential procession round the walls of Jerusalem shortly before it fell **(44)**. The idea of Jerusalem, and especially the Holy Sepulchre, as a place imbued with the power of Christ and as a special Christian possession dominated the crusaders' minds and drew them on, inexorably and at times against the wishes of the leaders. And this extraordinary series of events, in which a comparatively small army thousands of miles from home defeated the hosts of Asia, could only be ascribed by them and their contemporaries to the power of God, who had intervened directly on behalf of his chosen instruments. This idea began to be stated shortly after the victory of Dorylaeum and it had reached a crescendo by the end of the crusade: over and over again one comes across expressions of wonder at God's omnipotence and the conviction that this act of force could only be in accordance with his will. The crusade became a miracle, which Robert of Rheims thought to be as clear a demonstration of God intervening in this world as were the Creation and the Incarnation, and one that was foretold in the ancient prophecies of scripture (see **4**).

But it is remarkable how quickly the association of Jerusalem with crusading and the idea of God's benevolent aid were modified. Jerusalem's central rôle had been undermined by Pope Urban II even before the news of its liberation had reached the West. Some time between 1096 and his death in 1099 the pope wrote to a group of Catalan nobles and their knights encouraging them to restore Tarragona in Spain, comparing their support for the Spanish Church to the efforts of the crusaders in Asia, granting them the indulgence and adding that if any of them had intended to go to Asia he ought rather to satisfy his devotion in Spain, because it was no virtue to liberate Christians in one place while they were exposed to tyranny in another (**2 iv**). In fact by May 1098 Urban was openly associating the two wars with one another and in 1099 he sent home the archbishop of Toledo who had wanted to join the crusade to the East. His injunctions were repeated by his successor, Paschal II, and in 1101 King Peter of Aragon, who had taken the cross for Jerusalem, fulfilled his vow in Spain. Already, therefore, the aim of crusading had widened from a specific goal to the needs of Christendom in general. And this was confirmed in 1105–8 in the planning and preaching of a crusade under Bohemond of Taranto which, although officially aimed for Jerusalem, was supposed to defeat the Byzantine emperor on the way and so foreshadowed the crusades against Christian powers of the thirteenth century.

The conviction, moreover, that a crusade would always succeed because it had the active support of God could not survive the crusade of 1101. Before Urban's death on 29 July 1099 new forces were being recruited, and enthusiasm was shown in Lombardy, in France, whence Pope Paschal sent legates and where some of the greatest magnates, Duke William IX of Aquitaine, Count William II of Nevers and Duke Odo of Burgundy, took the cross, and in Germany, where Duke Welf IV of Bavaria enlisted. It is possible that the total numbers involved were almost as great as on the First Crusade, but in August and September 1101 the armies were separately defeated by the Turks in Asia Minor. Some of the crusaders struggled through to northern Syria where they re-formed and captured Tortosa, but thereafter they proceeded to Jerusalem only as pilgrims to fulfil their vows. Their failure, so soon after the striking successes of the First Crusade, needed explanation. How could an omnipotent God allow his instruments to be defeated and his plans to be frustrated? An answer could be found in the Old Testament and in the writings of St Augustine and it had been expressed during the First Crusade in the fasts and penitential processions that were the participants' reactions to any setback. Failure was God's judgement on the unworthiness of his agents. In the inveighing of the chroniclers against the arrogance, cruelty and wantonness of the crusaders of 1101 one can see early expressions of what was to become the standard response of churchmen to failure.

1110–1187

The first impression one has of the years between 1110 and 1187 is of relative quiet compared with the euphoria surrounding the First Crusade and the incessant activity of the period from 1187 to 1274. There was only one major crusade to the East and it was followed by nearly 40 years during which the popes tried in vain to mount large-scale expeditions. They must have been worried by their failure to rouse the West, but it is clear that, with Latins actually in possession of the Holy Places, it was going to take a major disaster to move the faithful: one should remember how strong were the reactions to the loss of Edessa in 1144 and the catastrophe at the Horns of Hattin in 1187.

Appearances are deceptive, moreover: a good deal more was going on than is generally realized. Even in the East, leaving aside the defence of the Latin settlements by the settlers, there was much crusading activity. The Norwegian crusade under King Sigurd of 1107–10 and the Venetian crusade of 1122–4 set a pattern that was often to be followed by little companies raised by enthusiastic rulers and magnates, although it is often hard to decide whether these should be classed as pilgrimages under arms or as crusades; sometimes they seem to have been one, sometimes the other. For instance Count Thierry of Flanders, who took part in the Second Crusade, also visited the East in 1139, 1157 and 1164; his wife ended her days as a nun at Bethany; his son Philip led a crusade in 1177 and took part in the Third Crusade. There was, in fact, an almost uninterrupted stream of minor expeditions in the apparently fallow years from 1150 to 1187. The Christian advance in Spain, moreover, was given the status of a crusade by the popes in letters of 1108, 1114, 1116, 1118, 1123 **(12)**,

1147, 1148, 1153 and 1175. It was marked by the participation of non-Spaniards, by the establishment of religio-military confraternities and, from 1164, by the founding of Spanish Military Orders. The association of the German drive east of the Elbe with crusading, first proposed in 1108 **(13)**, was legitimized by Pope Eugenius III in 1147 and by Pope Alexander III in 1171/2. In the eastward expansion of the Germans, which had long been associated with missions, there was above all to be found the links between crusading and forcible conversion. So deeply rooted was the idea of a war of conversion among the German laity that one finds preachers and popes – St Bernard, Eugenius III and Innocent III **(14)** – sailing close to the wind in their efforts to meet the aspirations of their audiences. Historians have not been wide of the mark in describing the German campaigns as 'missionary crusades'.

The period was an important one for theoretical development. It opened with intense literary activity inspired by the success of the First Crusade. Attention has usually been given to the eye-witness accounts of Raymond of Aguilers, Fulcher of Chartres, Peter Tudebode and the anonymous author of the *Gesta Francorum* or to those written by Bartolf of Nangis, Ekkehard of Aura and Ralph of Caen, who visited the East soon after the crusade. But from the point of view of ideas, the most important narratives were those written by learned clergymen in the West like Robert of Rheims, Baldric of Bourgueil, Guibert of Nogent and Albert of Aachen, who never left their churches and monasteries but had the intellect and command of language to place crusading convincingly in a theological and scriptural context; some of these accounts were widely read. The next advance came in the works of two theorists. The Camaldolite monk Gratian, whose *Decretum* of *c.*1140 was the most authoritative and well-organized treatment of canon law to date, considered crusading only indirectly, but produced a brilliant justification, resting on a mass of authorities, of the Church's right to legitimize the use of force (see **9**). St Bernard, the Cistercian abbot of Clairvaux and the chief preacher of the Second Crusade, persuaded the pope to grant the status of a crusade to the German war against the Wends and in his letters, treaties and sermons provided his contemporaries with the most persuasive exposition yet of crusading **(17, 20, 24)**. Very little that he wrote was new – perhaps only his promotion of the crusade as a test of God – but no one before him had written on the subject in such coruscant language and no one was to equal him until Pope Innocent III. His treatment of the concept of the new knight, a theme in crusading literature since 1095, provided his audience with a powerful evocation of the ideal of the *miles Christi* **(20 i, 24)** and after the failure of the Second Crusade – a failure which must have struck like a thunderbolt those who had been brought up on accounts of God's miraculous interventions in the course of the First Crusade – his calm and dignified acceptance of providence and divine judgement **(7)** supplied a model that was to be followed for centuries.

The development of theory was paralleled by institutional growth. With the Second Crusade came the encyclicals *Quantum praedecessores* **(5)** and *Divina dispensatione*. These were not as novel as historians, with their eyes fixed on the eastern expeditions, have supposed – the encyclicals for the *Reconquista* had already contained the basic elements **(12)** – but they set the pattern for all future papal authorizations. Governmental financing was established when King Louis VII of France asked for a general aid; this was followed by the levying of taxes for the crusades in France and England in 1166, 1185 and 1188 **(33)**. And between 1165 and 1181 Pope Alexander III gave the crusade indulgence its mature form **(22)**. It was also during this period that the Military Orders were established. The Order of the Knights Templar was founded in 1118/19 and the Order of the Hospital of St John of Jerusalem began to transform itself into a Military Order in the 1140s. In a sense their growth contradicted the principles of crusading, which was something that laymen rather than religious were supposed to be especially well equipped to undertake. Indeed the brothers of the Military Orders were not technically crusaders: they were religious permanently committed to what was for a crusader of its essence a temporary pilgrimage after which he would return to ordinary secular life; and the Hospitaller profession made no reference at all to the defence of Christendom. But they were closely linked to the movement and the course of the history of the crusades can hardly be considered without them; in the late eighteenth century crusading survived vestigially in the activities of the Knights Hospitallers, who were still preying on Muslim shipping from their fortress on Malta.

The Second Crusade was especially St Bernard's enterprise. In the summer of 1145 the news of the fall of Edessa reached the West. On 1 December Pope Eugenius III issued the crusade encyclical *Quantum praedecessores*, but King Louis VII of France independently proposed to his Christmas court a French expedition to help the East: it may be that the issuing of *Quantum praedecessores* was Eugenius's response to news of Louis's plans, which do not seem to have involved papal authorization. The king's suggestion was not very well received by his subjects, a decision was put off until Easter and St Bernard was consulted. Bernard insisted that the matter be referred to the pope and on 1 March 1146 Eugenius reissued his encyclical **(5)**. On 31 March Louis and Bernard had an enthusiastic reception when they addressed an assembly of nobles. Bernard devoted his very considerable energies to recruitment **(20)**, travelling to northern France and Flanders and then into Germany, drawn partly by worry about the consequences of the rabid preaching of a Cistercian monk called Radulph, which led to anti-Jewish riots in the Rhineland. The German Emperor Conrad III and many of his magnates joined the crusade. Meanwhile the pope, who had been recruiting in Italy, had agreed to the request of the king of Castile for an extension of the crusade indulgence to those engaged in war against the Moors in Spain and he permitted crusaders from Genoa and southern France to join the Spaniards. In March 1147 a group of Saxon crusaders petitioned Bernard to allow a campaign against the Wends east of the Elbe to count as crusading. Bernard persuaded the pope to agree and Eugenius gave the Wendish expedition the status of a crusade in an encyclical of 11 April.

On 16 June 1147 men from Frisia, Flanders, Cologne, Normandy and Britain, who were journeying by sea **(42)**, arrived at Oporto in Portugal, and on 24 October they took Lisbon from the Moors. On the other side of Spain, Almeria was taken on 17 October, to be followed by the conquests of Tortosa, Fraga and Lerida. In north-eastern Germany one army left Artlenburg in mid July and another Magdeburg in early August; very little was achieved by either. In the middle of May Conrad of Germany and his forces began their journey overland to the East. They reached Constantinople by 10 September and pressed on into Asia Minor. Louis of France, who had also chosen an overland route, left in June and arrived at Constantinople on 4 October. He too crossed the Bosphorus, to learn that the German force had been defeated by the Turks and had retreated in disorder to Nicaea, where it was breaking up. The French, badly mauled by the Turks near Cadmus, forced their way across Asia Minor, but after Louis and some of his followers had taken ship at Adalia for Antioch, the troops he was forced to leave behind were almost entirely wiped out. In June 1148 Louis reached Jerusalem, whence in April Conrad had come with a new company, consisting of late arrivals and perhaps some of the Lisbon crusaders. On 24 June a gathering of crusaders and leading personalities in the kingdom of Jerusalem decided to launch an attack on Damascus. Their armies arrived before the city on 24 July but were forced to withdraw a few days later. An attack upon Ascalon never materialized. Conrad left Palestine soon afterwards, but Louis remained for some months before returning home on a Sicilian ship, which only just escaped capture by a Greek fleet. He was still enthusiastic about crusading and gained the support of the pope and St Bernard for a new expedition, but nothing came of the plans.

The campaign in the East had been a failure. But in the Second

Crusade the principle of papal headship had been firmly established; so had been the conviction that the crusade was a general war that could be fought on all the Christian frontiers: several writers referred to this at the time, none more strikingly than the Englishman Henry of Huntingdon who, seeing divine judgement in failure, compared God's rejection of the pride and sinfulness of the followers of the emperor and the king of France with the heavenly aid given to the poor (and English) crusaders in Portugal.

1187–1229

The crusading movement is often treated as an eleventh- and twelfth-century phenomenon that went into rapid decline in the thirteenth. But in fact no period can equal the activity of the 87 years from 1187 to 1274, in almost every one of which a crusade was being waged somewhere. For most of the twelfth century westerners had been complacent about the Holy Land, but events in 1187 changed that. On 4 July in the Battle of Hattin Saladin annihilated the largest army ever put into the field by the Latins and he was then able to storm through Palestine. Jerusalem fell to him on 2 October and by 1189 all that was left of the kingdom of Jerusalem was the port of Tyre. Although the Christians were later to reconquer much of Palestine, Jerusalem was only to be in their hands from 1229 to 1244. The loss of Jerusalem and the precarious nature of the Christian hold on the coast, in spite of comparatively peaceful relations with the Muslims from Saladin's death in 1193 until 1244, meant that the fate of the Holy City and the plight of the Holy Land remained goads to European consciences. This accounts for the number of crusades to the East. But the thirteenth century was also marked by crusading in Spain, along the shores of the Baltic, against heretics in western Europe and against political opponents of the papacy in Italy. This activity, of course, was an expression of the determination of the popes, then at the height of their power, to use crusades in every way they could. But since there could be no crusade without crusaders, who in canon law had as votaries to be volunteers, papal calls to arms would have meant nothing unless people had responded to them. Everything points to the commitment of the European laity. Families like the royal houses of France, England and Germany, or those of the counts of Flanders and Champagne, sent generation after generation on crusades. Enthusiasts abounded, like Duke Leopold VI of Styria and Austria **(18)**, a member of another family with a strong crusading tradition, who went on the Third Crusade; took the cross for the Fourth Crusade in 1198; again in 1208 after the birth of a son; again in 1212 when he apparently fought in both Spain and Languedoc; and again before he left Europe on the Fifth Crusade in 1217. And crusading was much more than an exercise for the nobility: it was a mass movement, manifesting itself in the large numbers of people of all classes who took the cross and in the eruptions from below, reminiscent of those in 1096 and 1146, that found expression in the so-called Children's Crusade of 1212 and in the Crusade of the Shepherds of 1251 **(32)**.

Taking into account the mortality rate among European rulers in the years 1187 to 1189 – the deaths of Pope Urban III and Pope Gregory VIII and of King Henry II of England and King William II of Sicily – and the political differences between England and France, the reaction in western Europe to the news of the disasters in the East was not as slow as contemporary critics maintained. On 29 October 1187, only eight days after his election, Pope Gregory VIII issued *Audita tremendi*, one of the most moving of all crusade encyclicals and the proclamation of the Third Crusade **(8)**. In January 1188 Archbishop Joscius of Tyre, sent to the West for aid, persuaded King Henry of England and King Philip of France to make peace and take the cross. In fact war broke out again in France and Henry died on 6 July 1189, but his son Richard had already vowed to crusade. On 4 July 1190 the kings of France and England set out from Vézelay, but large numbers of crusaders were already on their way: Sicilians, Danes and Flemings, some of the English, a French army under the count of Champagne and, most important of all, the Emperor Frederick I and his German forces. Frederick had taken the cross on 27 March 1188 and had left from Regensburg on 11 May 1189. Taking the overland route, he wintered at Adrianople and in March 1190 crossed into Asia Minor, but on 10 June he was drowned in the River Calycadnus near Silifke. The German army began to disintegrate and was in a bad state when it reached Antioch on 21 June.

The kings of France and England had decided to go by sea, after wintering in Sicily. Philip of France reached the camp before the port of Acre, which the crusaders were besieging, on 20 April 1191, but Richard of England had a very difficult voyage, by way of Rhodes and Cyprus, which he had taken by the end of May 1191, before joining Philip and the siege of Acre on 8 June. Acre fell to the Christians on 12 July. Philip left for the West on 2 August, but Richard remained in Palestine, negotiating with Saladin over the terms which had been agreed on the surrender of Acre; when the talks broke down he massacred the Muslim hostages. He then decided to march down the coast to Jaffa, which would be a practicable base for an assault on Jerusalem. The march, a magnificent demonstration of what could be accomplished by military leadership, began on 22 August. The Christian army, supplied from the sea, kept to the shore, marching in divisions, with the infantry acting as a protective screen for the cavalry and the baggage train. The crusaders were constantly harassed by Muslim skirmishers, but they kept their formation for about 60 miles, forcing Saladin just north of Arsuf to opt on 6 September for pitched battle and defeat.

Three days later the army reached Jaffa, which was refortified. Richard now concentrated his forces, while entering into negotiations with Saladin, and in late October he began a slow advance into the interior. He spent Christmas at Latrun, over half way from Jaffa to Jerusalem, but, realizing that with a strong Muslim army in the vicinity a siege of Jerusalem would be perilous, he withdrew in January 1192 and refortified Ascalon, on the coast road to Egypt. Discussions with Saladin continued, as did Richard's attempts to resolve a constitutional crisis in the kingdom of Jerusalem, the crown of which was being disputed by King Guy and Conrad of Montferrat, who was married to the heiress Isabella. On 16 April Richard, who had favoured Guy, a member of a family who were his vassals in France, was forced to accept that Conrad was better placed to rule; but on the 28th Conrad was murdered, perhaps with Richard's connivance, and Isabella was then married to Count Henry of Champagne, one of the leading crusaders and a supporter of Richard's. Guy was made lord of Cyprus.

In May Richard took the southern fortress of Darum by storm; and on 7 June his troops marched for Jerusalem, reaching Bait Nuba, only 13 miles from their goal, on the 11th. But they were in an exposed position; it was clear that they must retire and the French crusaders still in Palestine opposed the idea of an invasion of Egypt, which Richard favoured; on 26 July he returned to Acre. Saladin now decided to surprise Jaffa, which had been hastily fortified. On 30 July the garrison asked for terms of surrender, but Richard was already on his way by sea with a picked force of knights and crossbowmen. He landed and drove the Muslims out of the town and on 5 August a dispirited Muslim army could make no impression on his disciplined troops. He fell ill soon afterwards and the news from England and France was worrying. On 2 September his representatives signed a truce with Saladin and on 9 October he set sail for home. Forced by bad weather to change his route and travelling in disguise through Austria, he was recognized, arrested and imprisoned by Duke Leopold, a cousin of the murdered Conrad of Montferrat; he did not get back to his kingdom until the spring of 1194.

The Third Crusade had recaptured much of the coastline, but Jerusalem was still in Muslim hands. Within three years of Richard's departure the Emperor Henry VI had taken the cross, no doubt partly to fulfil his father's uncompleted vow. On Easter Day 1195 he summoned the empire to a crusade; in October the German princes began to commit themselves to the expedition and at Worms in December Henry and the papal legate sat for hours in the cathedral receiving vows. From March 1197 German crusaders were leaving by ship from South Italian ports. They occupied Sidon and Beirut, but the news of Henry's death on 28 September 1197 led to a stampede home as they returned to safeguard their interests in Germany.

With the election of Innocent III on 8 January 1198 there came to the papal throne the most important figure in the crusading movement after Urban II. It is no exaggeration to say that Innocent was obsessed by the crusades. Whether he wrote his magnificent crusade encyclicals himself or left the composition of them to draftsmen in the curia, they are theological documents of the first order, original not so much in their ideas as in the way these ideas were presented **(15, 26)**. Innocent stated unambiguously the papal rôle as authorizer on God's behalf; he refined the formulae for indulgences and systematized the practice of redemptions, the payments of sums of money in place of the fulfilment of the vows of those who were not fit to take part **(26, 28 ii)**; he was the first pope to tax the Church for the crusades **(34)**; he laid down elaborate rules for the organization of the preaching of the cross **(26, 28)**; he extended the use of crusades, employing them against heretics **(15)** and against a political opponent. Most important of all, no one presented the essential cause of crusading, the need to defend Christendom against all threats, external and internal, so cogently; no one expressed so movingly the notion of the power of an intervenient God **(6)**; no one spoke with such fire of the love of God and fellow men shown by crusaders or so powerfully on the relationship between crusader and cross **(18)**. His language was not always safe: he was an impetuous man and indiscretion led to his statement, quite extra-ordinary in terms of canon law, that a husband could take the cross without his wife's permission **(28 ii)**. And his fondness for using images drawn from the everyday world could be theologically dangerous. For instance, he liked to compare Christ to a secular king, to whom was owed the loyalty of a subject and the services of a vassal, and it is clear that these words of his made a great impression, even though they invoked a spectre which, as we have seen, had haunted churchmen since the eleventh century **(26, 29)**. Even more striking was his use of the language of the blood feud. We have already pointed out that it was easy in an age of vendettas to see the crusade as an act of revenge by Christ's family on those who had oppressed his children and had taken or threatened his patrimony or, in the case of the Baltic crusades in which Livonia was treated as the personal property of Our

Lady, his mother's patrimony. The concept of revenge had hardly appeared in the voluminous ecclesiastical writings on the First Crusade, but it was a theme in twelfth-century vernacular crusading poetry **(11)** and Innocent, obviously eager to arouse his audience, seized on it. It pervaded his appeals.

At the start of his pontificate the German crusaders were still in the East and it was not until August 1198 that he issued an encyclical summoning the faithful to a new crusade. It has often been noted that his appeal was directed not to kings but to their subjects, and it has been assumed that he did not want rulers to take part. But he was later to write passionate letters to the kings of France and England, not asking them to participate, it is true, but exhorting them to encourage recruitment in their kingdoms and demanding that they send fighters at their own expense. This does not suggest that he was steering clear of them, nor is there any convincing reason why he should have done so. Indeed, like all popes, he would have been far more worried by the possibility of a lack of response than by the prospect of the manipulation of a crusade by a king for political ends. It is more likely that in the early months of his pontificate he had been testing the reactions and that by August he knew that nothing on earth would induce the kings of France and England to go. And at first there was very little response to his call; it was not until November 1199 that the enthusiasm that would lead to the Fourth Crusade began to sweep France. The counts of Champagne, Blois and Flanders took the cross; envoys were sent to Venice to arrange for transport; and after the count of Champagne had died in May 1201, Boniface of Montferrat, a brother of Conrad and a member of a prominent North Italian family related to the German Staufen and the French Capetians and with close links with the East, was chosen to be leader of the crusade **(37)**.

In the summer of 1202 parties of crusaders began to arrive in Venice, but their number came to no more than about one-third of the estimate made in the agreement for transport. From the first, therefore, they found themselves heavily in debt to the Venetians and, in exchange for a postponement of payment, they were persuaded to help Venice regain the town of Zara on the Dalmatian coast, which was in Hungarian hands. Innocent had forbidden this attack on a Christian city, but he was ignored and on 24 November 1202 Zara was taken. Anxious to keep the crusade in being, the pope absolved the crusaders from the excommunication they had automatically incurred, but he now formally excommunicated the Doge of Venice and the Venetians.

What had happened so far was nothing to what now ensued. In 1201 the young Greek prince Alexios Angelos, whose father Isaac had been deposed from the emperorship by his uncle, had escaped to the West and had sought help from Philip of Swabia, the Staufen candidate for the throne of Germany, who was married to his sister. It is possible that at this stage Boniface of Montferrat had been drawn into discussions with Alexios and Philip and it is certain that before the crusade had left Venice Alexios had been in touch with it, proposing that on their way to the East the crusaders should help him recover his father's empire. Now, after the attack on Zara, formal proposals were made and were accepted by the majority, in spite of the bull of excommunication of the Venetians, which Boniface and his fellow-leaders refused to publish, explaining to the pope that they did not want the crusade to disintegrate. The fleet sailed early in April 1203 and on 24 June disembarked across the Bosphorus from Constantinople. It was not until now that Innocent wrote to forbid any attack upon the Greeks and to order the publication of his bull. His long silences have led some to suppose that he was involved in a conspiracy to divert the crusade: by November 1202 he had certainly heard of the discussions between Alexios and Philip of Swabia and of the proposal to attack Constantinople; by June 1203 he knew that some of the crusaders were planning to go further and occupy parts of Greece; and he did nothing until it was too late. But it is probable that this was because he was hesitant and uncertain rather than that he was involved in a plot that, on the face of it, would have benefited directly the Staufen cause in Germany, with which he was in conflict.

On 5 July 1203 the Latin fleet crossed the Bosphorus and on the 17th Constantinople was assaulted. The usurping emperor fled and Isaac was restored to the throne. On 1 August Alexios was crowned co-emperor. The agreement with him had specified that the Greek Church would submit to Rome; the Greeks would contribute 200,000 marks of silver to the crusade and would provision it for a year; Alexios would send an army of 10,000 Greeks and would maintain for life a garrison of 500 knights in the Holy Land; and he would join the expedition in person if requested to do so. He now began to pay the 200,000 marks and the crusaders could at last settle their debt to the Venetians, but he asked them to remain encamped before Constantinople until the following March to ensure his safety and to give him time to raise the rest of the cash; meanwhile he promised to pay for an additional year's service by the Venetian fleet. Relations between the Latins and the Greeks deteriorated rapidly. In late January and early February 1204 a *coup d'état* in Constantinople removed Alexios and his father. In March the crusaders and the Venetians decided to take the empire and reached agreement on the division of spoil and the constitution of the future Latin state. Priests in the army justified the attack in terms of the right to crusade against schismatics and accomplices to the murder of the emperors. On 13 April the crusaders took Constantinople, sacked it for three days and stripped it of its priceless collection of relics **(46)**. They occupied much of the rest of Greece and the Greek islands, parts of which were to be held by them until the eighteenth century.

The Fourth Crusade was a tragedy. The Latin settlement in Palestine and Syria was hardly helped at all and the Greeks and the Greek Church have never forgiven the Latin West for what was done in its name. The pope seems to have been genuinely horrified, although he did his best to exploit the *fait accompli* of the occupation of the second patriarchate in Christendom by the Latins and its submission to Rome. Whatever one thinks of the part he had played there can be no doubt that the crusade had demonstrated just how weak he was in practice. Yet nothing could dampen his ardour: in 1208 he started to promote a new crusade to the East, although it came to nothing; and then in 1213 came the planning of the Fifth Crusade, the most considered of his undertakings, launched by *Quia maior*, the greatest of his encyclicals **(26)**.

Innocent associated the new crusade with a general council of the Church, to be summoned to Rome in 1215, and to ecclesiastical reform in a way that was to be typical of papal policy until the early fourteenth century and must have been partly a result of the conviction that failure in crusading was a consequence of sin: it was believed that a crusade could not succeed except against the background of Christian renewal and that at the same time its success would demonstrate the reinvigoration of Christendom. Innocent also created an elaborate structure for preaching the cross **(26, 28–30)** and energetically promoted the crusade himself: his opening sermon at the Fourth Lateran Council dealt with it and he died on 16 July 1216 while preaching the cross in central Italy. At the council the date of departure was set for 1 June 1217 **(27)**. Small parties of crusaders were in fact leaving throughout 1217, but the first large army, made up of Germans and Hungarians under King Andrew of Hungary, who had taken the cross many years before, gathered at Split in the late summer. On reaching Acre it was agreed as a first step to reconnoitre the interior in force. Crossing the Jordan on 10 November the army raided Transjordan and then tried unsuccessfully to take Mt Thabor, which the Muslims had fortified; a final raid into the mountainous hinterland of Sidon met with disaster. Early in January 1218 the King of Hungary left, but now more crusaders were arriving, including the first ships of a fleet carrying men from the Low Countries and western Germany who had helped take Alcácer do Sal in Portugal on their way out. It had already been decided that once enough crusaders had arrived an attack would be made on the Egyptian port of Damietta. It had long been recognized that Egypt was the key to control of the Near East: in the 1160s Amalric of Jerusalem had tried to dominate it, during the Third Crusade its conquest had been discussed and an invasion had been planned during the preparations for the Fourth Crusade. On 27 May 1218 the vanguard of the army arrived at Damietta, to be reinforced by the end of October by new arrivals from the West, including Italians, French and English. After a long siege **(45, 47 i)** the city fell on 5 November 1219 and within three weeks the crusaders had taken the neighbouring town of Tinnis, but they were then inactive for 18 months, rejecting the offer from the Egyptians of Jerusalem and all previously held Christian territory in Syria and in Palestine west of the Jordan. In May 1221 a German army arrived and on 17 July the crusade began to march into the Egyptian interior, but it was trapped near Mansurah by a Muslim fleet that blocked the route back to Damietta. On 26 August it tried to retreat, but the Egyptians cut the dykes and flooded the delta. The Christians were forced to sue for peace, Damietta was surrendered and Egypt evacuated.

A later enterprise may be regarded as the final act of the crusade. The Emperor Frederick II had taken the cross at Aachen on 25 July 1215, when in the ancient capital of the Carolingian empire he had been re-crowned king of Germany and had supervised the translation of Charlemagne's relics; the association by him of these three acts was highly significant, given the power of the image of Charlemagne in crusading thought. There is no reason to suppose that he was not sincere: his mould of mind, his commitment to orthodoxy and to the persecution of heretics and his obvious devotion to relics suggests that he was more conventional in his religious beliefs than he appeared to be in the stories put about by his enemies. But, although he sent part of his crusading army to Damietta in 1221, he did not set out himself, probably because of the need to restore order in the kingdom of Sicily. On 25 July 1225 he pledged himself in the strictest terms to depart in just over two years and on 9 November he married the heiress to the kingdom of Jerusalem. In 1224 his crusade plans had envisaged an attack upon Egypt, but now a direct assault upon Jerusalem became his goal. A large body of crusaders from Germany, England and Italy gathered near Brindisi in southern Italy and were embarking by the middle of August 1227. The emperor intended to leave a few weeks later, but he fell ill and had to put off his departure. Pope Gregory IX excommunicated him, infuriated by his treatment of the Sicilian Church and perhaps already planning to invade his South Italian possessions, which he could not do if Frederick was a legitimate crusader whose property should be safe-guarded in his absence. The crusade began to disintegrate as soon as news of the emperor's illness reached it and most of the crusaders had returned home by the time Frederick, ignoring the excommunication, left for Palestine on 28 June 1228. He reached Acre with a small following on 7 September and, combining diplomacy with a show of force, wrung from the Egyptians the surrender of Jerusalem (although not the Temple area) and parts of Palestine, including Bethlehem and Nazareth. On 17 March 1229 he entered Jerusalem and on the 18th he went through the ceremony of an imperial crown-wearing in the church of the Holy Sepulchre. When he left for home on 1 May he, an excommunicate and not a true crusader, had succeeded where his more legitimate predecessors since 1187 had failed.

Innocent III had not only launched crusades to the East; he had also promoted them as energetically elsewhere. In the first two years of his pontificate he proclaimed crusades against Markward of Anweiler and into Baltic Livonia; in 1207 the Albigensian Crusade was authorized and in 1211 a crusade in Spain. The crusades in Livonia and Spain were, of course, by this time quite traditional. On 5 October 1199 Innocent authorized a crusade in defence of the young missionary Livonian Church under its warlike bishop Albert and, although it seems that he did not give this campaign exactly the same status as crusading in the East, it was treated as a true crusade by participants and contemporaries (see **14**). By 1215 Livonia, the area around the newly founded town of Riga, had been conquered and the crusade had turned north into Estonia, rule of which was shared by Germans and Danes. Further south, the conquest of Prussia by the Teutonic Knights began in 1230 and took the rest of the thirteenth century. Indeed relentless and almost continuous campaigning along the Baltic, authorized by papal encyclicals, lasted until the fifteenth century. In Spain, Innocent encouraged Alfonso VIII of Castile to go over to the offensive and the loss of the Military Order of Santiago's castle of Salvatierra in September 1211 rallied Christianity to the cause. With papal support, appeals for crusaders in France bore fruit and a French force, estimated by Alfonso at 2,000 knights, 10,000 other horse and 50,000 foot, joined the Spaniards in the summer of 1212. The Christian army left Toledo on 20 June and on 16 July, in one of the few crusading successes of a pontificate so dedicated to the movement, crushed the Muslims at Las Navas de Tolosa **(6)**. Although Innocent revoked the crusade indulgences for the Spanish crusade in 1213, on the grounds that the needs of the East were now greater **(26)**, the *Reconquista* was again associated with the crusading movement in 1217 and was closely linked to it until Granada, the last Muslim stronghold, fell in 1492.

Innocent also launched crusades against new enemies. In 1199 he proclaimed rather an ineffective crusade against Markward of Anweiler, an imperial lieutenant who was resisting his plans for Italy, because, he argued, Markward's activities were hindering the preparations for the Fourth Crusade. In 1207 he authorized what became known as the Albigensian Crusade against the heretical Cathars in Languedoc **(15)**. The ground for the preaching of crusades against heretics had already been laid by the wars of the Investiture Contest in the late eleventh century and by a decree of the Third Lateran Council in 1179, which came near to equating military action against heretics with crusades to the East, and the Albigensian Crusade had been foreshadowed by the arguments put forward in 1203–4 by those on the Fourth Crusade who were justifying attacking the Greeks because they were schismatics. Innocent and his successors regarded crusading against heretics as justified when local civil powers, traditional defenders of the Church against heresy (in 1207–8 Count Raymond VI of Toulouse and his suzerain the king of France), proved themselves to be unwilling or unable to perform their function; in that case Christendom as a whole could be called upon to cut out the canker. By the spring of 1209 a large force, drawn mostly from northern and central France, had gathered to attack the Midi; over the next 20 years it was to be followed by a succession of armies, containing soldiers from many parts of western Europe, especially from France and Germany. Béziers fell on 22 July 1209 and Carcassonne on 15 August, after which the leadership of the crusade was granted by the papal legates to Simon, lord of Montfort and earl of Leicester, an able and pious French nobleman who had participated in the Fourth Crusade but had refused to countenance the diversion to Constantinople. Simon gradually reduced the territories around Toulouse, which was encircled by the autumn of 1212. An attempt by the king of Aragon to intervene on the side of Count Raymond was defeated by Simon in the Battle of Muret on 12 September 1213. In 1214 Simon was in control of nearly all the lands of the county of Toulouse, but the planning of the Fifth Crusade and Innocent's revocation of indulgences for the war in Languedoc **(26)** deprived him of recruits and in 1216 the exiled count, assured of much local support, went on to the offensive. Beaucaire fell to Raymond at the end of August and Toulouse in September 1217. Simon was killed on 25 June 1218 and by 1222 practically all of the Languedoc was again in Raymond's hands. The count died in August, but his son, Raymond VII, was even more popular than he had been. It was not until 1226 that King Louis VIII of France was able to lead a crusade to the South. Avignon fell to him on 9 September and, although he died on 8 November, he left a lieutenant,

Humbert of Beaujeu, ravaging the area. Raymond was forced to sue for terms and the Albigensian Crusade ended with the Peace of Paris of 12 April 1229. Raymond was reconciled to the Church, but succession to his county was assured only to his daughter Joan, who was to marry one of the king's brothers: no other immediate heir was to inherit. In November, at a council held in Toulouse, provisions for dealing with the remnants of the heresy were carefully laid down in conformity with what had been the original cause of the crusade.

1229–1274

It is popularly supposed that in the thirteenth century the growing interest in missions, with their emphasis on peaceful persuasion, told against the crusades. This might have been the case if the popular idea of the crusade as a war of conversion had been shared by theologians and official propagandists, but, as we have seen, theologians had always held that the heathen should be converted by reason not by force. It is true that some writers, including Roger Bacon and perhaps William of Tripoli, maintained that the inflamed passions that were a by-product of crusading hindered missionary work **(25)**, but the aims of crusades and missions were so fundamentally different that they could not really conflict: crusades were theoretically defensive; missions were aggressive in that their goal was the expansion of Christianity through proselytism. Contemporaries were on the whole less likely to see any conflict than we are and St Francis accompanied the Fifth Crusade to Egypt and preached before the sultan in Cairo.

Many of the great intellects of the century wrote on, and developed, the theory of crusading. St Raymond of Peñafort stressed the need for papal authority and clarified the question of the commutation of crusade vows. Pope Innocent IV issued what was to be the most authoritative treatment of crusades as just wars. Hostiensis defended the use of crusades against heretics and political enemies of the papacy and introduced a revolutionary idea, which was not accepted, that Christendom had an intrinsic right to extend its sovereignty over all who did not recognize the rule of the Roman Church or Roman Empire. Humbert of Romans answered the critics of the movement **(25)** and St Thomas Aquinas considered crusade indulgences. It cannot be denied that the treatment of crusading by some of these writers was cursory and highly legalistic and it has been suggested that this reflected the repugnance that theologians must feel when they have to face up to the subject of Christian violence. But everything we know of the background against which these men wrote suggests that this was not the case. It was rather that crusading had become so commonplace that intellectual interest in it was on the wane. The cool and occasional utterances of the theologians and canon lawyers reveals simply a practical concern with something that` was an everyday reality.

An unsteady rhythm had already been introduced into crusading to the East, determined by the laws of the Jihad, for it was known that Muslims would never make a permanent peace with the outside world but would only enter into truces for limited periods. In 1192 a truce for three years was agreed between Richard I of England and Saladin, towards the end of which, in 1195, the Emperor Henry VI took the cross. In 1198 the kingdom of Jerusalem entered into another truce, which Innocent III does not seem to have recognized in his planning of the Fourth Crusade. But the pope certainly paid attention to a later armistice. In 1211 the kingdom of Jerusalem and Egypt agreed to a cessation of hostilities for six years. In 1213 the pope proclaimed the Fifth Crusade and by 1215 he was planning for it to depart on 1 June 1217, exactly six years after the treaty had been made **(27)**. Although Frederick II's original date of departure would not have conformed to the conditions of an eight-year truce agreed with Egypt in 1221, the papacy came to accept the 10-year truce he made with Egypt in 1229. In September 1234 Pope Gregory IX began to enlist support for a new crusade, to leave in 1239 when the truce expired, and he strictly forbade crusaders to sail from Europe before the time of the general passage.

By 1235 French lords were beginning to take the cross and the pope, who had grandiose plans to maintain an army in Palestine for 10 years, was thinking of ways of raising cash for them. In 1236–7, however, he seems to have tried to divert the crusade to Greece, to help the Latin empire of Constantinople against its Greek and Bulgarian enemies. This was not popular and he had to accept a situation in which two separate crusades were mounted. Little is known of the results of the expedition in aid of Constantinople. The crusaders bound for the East gathered at Lyons in July 1239, under the leadership of Count Thibault of Champagne, who was also king of Navarre, and Duke Hugh of Burgundy, and they left in August, most sailing from Marseilles. Thibault of Champagne reached Acre on 1 September. After two months spent in debate his army marched down to Ascalon to build a castle before reversing its steps and mounting an attack on Damascus. The war, in other words, was to be fought on two fronts, against both Egypt and Damascus. On 12 November the crusaders arrived at Jaffa, where news reached them of a strong Egyptian army near Gaza. A number of nobles, ignoring Thibault's advice and defying his leadership, rode on ahead, were surprised and cut to pieces. Thibault, who was advised against engaging the Egyptians, withdrew to Acre. He did not react to the capture of Jerusalem by the Muslim lord of Kerak, but in the spring of 1240 he led his forces on a fruitless expedition to Tripoli. Once back in Acre he made an agreement with the ruler of Damascus, who offered to restore to the Christians Jerusalem and much of Palestine in return for help against Egypt. There was opposition to this on the Christian side and Thibault, beguiled by a promise to free the prisoners taken at Gaza, next agreed to a treaty with Egypt. He had begun by waging an impossible war; he ended by making two impossible, because contradictory, truces. Without even waiting to see the agreement with Egypt carried out he departed in the middle of September, leaving the duke of Burgundy and the crusaders who remained with him building the fortress of Ascalon. On 8 October Richard earl of Cornwall, the brother of King Henry III of England, reached Acre with an English force. Marching down to Jaffa he entered into negotiations with Egypt and confirmed Thibault's agreement. Jerusalem, Galilee and a large part of Palestine, more of it than at any time since 1187, were returned to the Christians.

Much that had been gained was lost in 1244 when Jerusalem fell to the Khorezmians and a combined Latin-Damascene army was defeated by the Egyptians near Gaza. These disasters were the background to the taking of the cross by King Louis IX of France in December 1244, although a serious illness had put the idea into his mind. St Louis was to be the archetypal crusader. He came from a family with strong crusading traditions: four previous generations of his father's family had taken the cross and, although she was in fact opposed to his crusade, his mother, Blanche of Castile, was the daughter of the victor of Las Navas de Tolosa. He was strong, able, devout and virtuous and he was regarded by his contemporaries as a model of fair-mindedness. He was, like many laymen of the twelfth and thirteenth centuries, mesmerized by the crusading movement and from 1244 to his death in 1270 his attitudes were largely conditioned by its needs. Like his great-grandfather Louis VII he initiated his crusade, but unlike Louis VII he insisted from the first that papal authorization was necessary. This he got and preparations began early in 1245, when the pope gave Cardinal Odo of Châteauroux **(38)** the task of preaching the crusade in France; preachers were also sent to England, Germany and Scandinavia. Money was raised from the taxation of the Church and from French towns. The king arranged for shipping from Genoa and Marseilles and sent agents ahead to Cyprus to stock provisions. He sailed from the newly enlarged port of Aigues-Mortes on 25 August 1248 **(see 41)** and reached Cyprus on 17 September. By the following spring about 15,000 men had gathered in Cyprus and

Damietta in Egypt was again selected for attack. A landing was made on 5 June and the town, abandoned by its defenders, was entered on the next day. It had fallen much more quickly than plans had allowed for and conditions were not ideal for further campaigning: it was not until 20 November that an advance into the interior – a decision that had been hotly debated – began. A month later the Christians reached the main Egyptian positions at Mansurah. On 8 February their advance-guard managed to cross a branch of the Nile, but its leader, the king's brother Robert of Artois, went straight on to attack Mansurah, leading his forces into narrow streets where they were trapped and destroyed. The main Christian army followed Robert across the Nile and camped before the town, but it was now in an impossible situation. By early March the Egyptians were blocking the Nile with their own vessels and cutting off the supply of provisions and on 5 April the crusaders, weak and demoralized, were forced to retreat. Half-way back to Damietta they could go no further and surrendered. Louis had to promise to pay a ransom of 800,000 besants and to give up Damietta. He sailed to Acre, where he remained for almost four more years **(35)**, negotiating a truce with the Muslims and refortifying the strongpoints of the kingdom of Jerusalem.

He continued to dream of the Holy Land. When the Mamluk conquests of the 1260s and the perilous situation of the Latins in Palestine led to the proclamation of a new crusade, he told the pope of his intention to join and on 24 March 1267 he and his three sons took the cross. Although there is evidence that his decision was not very popular in France, there was some enthusiasm for the crusade in England **(36)** and in Aragon. But Louis was clearly its leader and summoned a council-of-war to Paris in August 1269. Money was again raised and contracts for shipping were again entered into with Genoa and Marseilles, but this time it was decided to make a pre-liminary attack upon Tunis in North Africa, perhaps, although it seems to be out of character, because Louis was persuaded to go there by his brother Charles of Anjou, who was now ruler of Sicily and would benefit from the conquest of Tunisia, perhaps because he mistakenly believed that Egypt was dependent on Tunisia for supplies. He sailed on 2 July 1270 with a relatively small force and landed in Tunisia on the 18th, but the Christian camp was struck by disease and he died on 25 August. Charles of Anjou made a treaty with Tunis and withdrew. Edward of England, the son of Henry III, who arrived just when negotiations with the Muslims were being completed, went on with a small army to Palestine, where he stayed until 1272.

Thus ended the last great crusade of the thirteenth century, but we should not read too much into that. It is clear that as early as the 1250s a new strategical approach to crusading to the East was emerging. Many if not most of the leaders of Latin Christendom were thinking more of permanently raising the strength of the garrison in Palestine and of sending out small expeditions, which could be put together more easily to succeed one another, than of great, laboriously organized armies that, it was believed, did little long-term good. It was in this period that one comes across individual knights, like Geoffrey of Sergines and Oliver of Termes, who won fame in the West for the way they spent almost all their lives in defence of the Holy Land. In fact quite a lot of thought seems to have been put into crusading, particularly under Pope Gregory X, who was an enthusiast. Four memoirs presented to him at the time of the Second Council of Lyons in 1274 survive. Their authors expressed concern about the way crusades had been organized in the past and an awareness of growing criticism of the movement **(25)**, but they also showed an acceptance of a wide range of crusading activities and, with one exception, a commitment to them. They foreshadowed the armchair strategists of the fourteenth century.

Besides the crusades to the East, the years from 1229 to 1274 witnessed a new crusade in 1230 against heretics, the Stedinger peasants, and an extension of crusading in a field onto which Innocent III had first ventured when he had preached his crusade against Markward of Anweiler. In 1240 Pope Gregory IX, at war with the Emperor Frederick II who was threatening Rome, authorized the preaching of the cross in Lombardy, Germany and Hungary **(16 i)**. In 1246 a new crusade was proclaimed against Frederick; and after his death in 1250 and that of his son Conrad in 1254 there began a series of crusades, first against the Staufen and the Aragonese to maintain papal claims to sovereignty in the Papal State and the kingdom of Sicily and later, from 1302 to 1343, against the Ghibelline revival in central and northern Italy. We can now appreciate how popular these campaigns were and how reasonable, from the point of view of the popes, were the arguments for them **(16 ii)**. But there can be no denying that, in contrast to the theatres of war in Spain and along the Baltic coast, there was at the heart of the crusading movement, in the papal curia itself, a conflict of interests. The popes had to weigh their concern, often profound, for the needs of the Latin settlements in the East and the recovery of Jerusalem against the threat posed to their position in Italy by the Ghibelline powers.

1274–1798

The Latins were driven from the Holy Land in 1291 and this of course led to a change in attitudes to crusading, the aim of which could no longer be to prop up an existing, if threatened, régime. A whole area had now to be reconquered and naturally the idea of the grand expedition came again to the fore. But 1291 is not nowadays regarded as the watershed in the movement it once was. The following century was rich in elaborate schemes for the recovery of the Holy Places, but this intellectual approach to strategy, characterized by the writing of memoirs and by the distinction made between great expeditions, *passagia generalia*, and minor ones, *passagia particularia*, had already emerged by 1274. Its development coincided with a decline in the popularity of crusading, which was no longer the force it once had been, but it would be wrong to believe that the movement was greatly decayed. In the late thirteenth century there was much activity and kings like Edward I of England were almost as committed to it as Louis IX of France had been. In the fourteenth century there were still explosions of popular fervour. Great expeditions to the East were planned in the fourteenth and fifteenth centuries and some set off. War went on in Spain and along the Baltic. In Italy crusades against the Ghibellines occupied the first half of the fourteenth century and during the Great Schism a crusade was preached against an anti-pope. Crusades were launched against the Hussite heretics between 1420 and 1431. In the sixteenth century popes and kings still dreamed of crusading; in the seventeenth there were perhaps still a few crusaders; in the eighteenth the Military Order of St John of Jerusalem carried on an increasingly ineffective war against the Turks until 1798, when it was driven from the island of Malta by Napoleon, who was on his way to Egypt on a campaign which was in no sense a crusade. The crusading movement, like the Inquisition, took a long time to die and it was the French Revolution and the conquests of Napoleon that delivered the *coup de grâce*.

Principles of Selection

We have tried to give a representative selection of sources – old favourites as well as little-known documents – to illustrate as many aspects of the crusades as possible and to show what it was in them that appealed to so many people of all classes and what it was like to take part in them. Unfortunately, we have been able to give very little sense of development: one document has often had to represent two centuries of thought or activity and our picture of experiences during the preparation and course of a crusade has had to be built up from material spanning 200 years and many different kinds of expedition. We have chosen sources that are available in print so that a reader can check our translations against the original Latin or Old French. We have italicized quotations from scripture, but we did not want to break the flow of argument by giving references; a reader who is interested can find most of the quotations identified in the original editions. We have used the Douai translation for all scriptural quotations, because it is the closest in ethos to the Latin Vulgate, but we have substituted the proper names familiar to most English readers from the Authorized Version: for instance Joshua for Josue and Elijah for Elias.

The terminal dates of our selection are 1095 and 1274. At first we wanted to show what crusading was like over a longer span of time and we were particularly keen to include some of the interesting projects of the early fourteenth century, but it soon became clear that what would be gained in introducing readers to the later crusades would not compensate for the loss of crucial documents of the twelfth and thirteenth centuries. It is usual to end the classic age of crusading in 1291, when the Latins were driven from the Holy Land, but we are persuaded by recent research that the significance of 1291 has been overstressed and that a real change in thinking had occurred some years earlier. And so 1274, the year of the Second Council of Lyons when in the aftermath of the last great thirteenth-century expedition many of the new ideas surfaced, seemed to be a good stopping-point.

We have interpreted the word 'crusade' fairly strictly. We have naturally included material on crusades in Spain, along the Baltic shore and within western Europe as well as on those to the East. But we have not chosen documents relating to the Military Orders, the brothers of which were not true crusaders, unless they have some bearing on the crusades themselves; and similarly we have not picked material for its relevance to the history of the Latin settlements in the East, which were not the 'crusading states' they are so often called, but were normal secular communities, even if they originated out of and were supported by crusades. We have also tried to adhere to the principle that every document or extract from a narrative account must illustrate what was peculiar to crusading. We have, therefore, translated only one description of armed combat. Of course fighting must have dominated the minds of the crusaders, but one description of a battle or siege is very much like another: the confusion and the physical effort involved were no different from usual because the combatants were on crusade and there did not seem to be much point in wasting space on them. For the same reason we have not included Greek, Arabic, Armenian or Syriac accounts, which help to piece together what actually happened, but for obvious reasons tell us little about what was going on in the minds of the crusaders. And we have reluctantly decided to illustrate criticism of crusading only with reference to the answers to it preachers might make. Ideally, some critical writings should have been selected, but it cannot be said strongly enough that fundamental critics, as opposed to those who wanted to improve the movement or were concerned about certain aspects of it, were rare and unrepresentative of the society in which they lived. There seemed to be no good reason for including them at the expense of the coverage given to crusading itself.

I   The Preaching of the First Crusade

We have chosen a conciliar decree, four of Pope Urban II's letters and four reports of his sermon at Clermont to illustrate Urban's intentions and the impression the preaching of the crusade and the success of the expedition made on public opinion. These sources reveal the establishment of a pattern of thought in which most of the later elements were already present in embryo: the desires of an intervenient and omnipotent God relayed to the faithful by the pope; the just cause engendered by the injuries done to Jerusalem, the Eastern Christians and, in the pope's letter to Spain, Christendom in general; the crusade as a pilgrimage; the moral duty of laymen to take part in this meritorious activity, in which they would express love of God and their neighbour; and the indulgence.

1 The Council of Clermont grants an indulgence to crusaders, 18–27 November 1095

The canons of the Council of Clermont have not survived in any official transcript, but in private collections of the decrees, containing the full texts of some and synopses of others, and in personal notes made by participants. From them it is possible to reconstruct the conciliar decisions. This decree granted a very restricted indulgence, merely an exemption from penance, but it will be noticed that it stated explicitly that the aim of the crusade was the liberation of the patriarchate of Jerusalem.

Source: R. Somerville, *The Councils of Urban II. 1. Decreta Claromontensia* (Annuarium Historiae Conciliorum. Supplementum 1. Amsterdam, 1972), p. 74

Whoever for devotion alone, not to gain honour or money, goes to Jerusalem to liberate the Church of God can substitute this journey for all penance.

2 Four letters on crusading from Pope Urban II

Three of Urban's surviving letters on the crusade, to Flanders, to his partisans in Bologna and to the monks of Vallombrosa, dealt with the expedition to Jerusalem. The fourth, to four counts and their knights in Catalonia, extended crusading to Spain.

i Urban to all the faithful in Flanders, December 1095

Source: H. Hagenmeyer, *Die Kreuzzugsbriefe aus den Jahren 1088–1100* (Innsbruck, 1901), pp. 136–7

We believe that you, brethren, learned long ago from many reports the deplorable news that the barbarians in their frenzy have invaded and ravaged the churches of God in the eastern regions. Worse still, they have seized the Holy City of Christ, embellished by his passion and resurrection, and – it is blasphemy to say it – they have sold her and her churches into abominable slavery. Thinking devoutly about this disaster and grieved by it, we visited Gaul and urged most fervently the lords and subjects of that land to liberate the eastern churches. At a council held in' Auvergne, as is widely known, we imposed on them the obligation to undertake such a military enterprise for the remission of all their sins and we appointed in our place as leader of this journey and labour our dearest son Adhémar, bishop of Le Puy. It follows that anyone who decides to go on this journey should obey his orders as though they were our own and should be entirely subject to his power to 'loose and bind' in any decisions that appear to concern this business. If God calls any men among you to take this vow, they should know that he will set out, with God's help, on the Feast of the Assumption of the Blessed Mary [15 August] and that they can join his company on that day.

ii Urban to his partisans in Bologna, 19 September 1096

Source: Hagenmeyer, *Die Kreuzzugsbriefe*, pp. 137–8

We offer thanks for your integrity, because, although living among schismatics and heretics, some of you have always stood firm in the Catholic faith, while others have had the truth revealed to them by the grace of God and have left the error of their ways and are now wise in the doctrines of the Catholic faith. And so we encourage you, most beloved in the Lord, to keep following bravely the path of truth and to try to bring what you have begun so well to an even better conclusion, because not he who begins, *but he that shall persevere unto the end, he shall be saved*. We commend especially to your affection our venerable brother and fellow bishop Bernard, whom divine providence through our agency has found fit to be bestowed on you as pastor. If you have any love for God, therefore, you should show it to his vicar, for Christ himself said of such a person that *he that heareth you heareth me*. We have heard that many of you have felt the longing to go to Jerusalem, which you should understand pleases us exceedingly. You should know, moreover, that if any men among you go there not because they desire earthly profit but only for the salvation of their souls and the liberation of the Church, we, acting as much on our own authority as on that of all the archbishops and bishops in Gaul, through the mercy of almighty God and the prayers of the Catholic Church, relieve them of all penance imposed for their sins, of which they have made genuine and full confession, because they have risked their belongings and lives for the love of God and their neighbour. But we do not allow either clerics or monks to go unless they have permission from their bishops and abbots. Bishops should also be careful not to allow their parishioners to go without the advice and foreknowledge of the clergy. You must also see to it that young married men do not rashly set out on such a long journey without the agreement of their wives. May almighty God strengthen you in fear and love of him and may he lead you, freed from all sins and errors, to understand how to love him above all things and show him true devotion.

iii Urban to the religious of the congregation of Vallombrosa, 7 October 1096

Source: W. Wiederhold, 'Papsturkunden in Florenz', *Nachrichten von der Gesellschaft der Wissenschaften zu Göttingen*, Phil.-hist. Kl. (Göttingen, 1901), pp. 313–14

We have heard that some of you want to set out with the knights who are making for Jerusalem with the good intention of liberating Christianity. This is the right kind of sacrifice, but it is planned by the wrong kind of person. For we were stimulating the minds of knights to go on this expedition, since they might be able to restrain the savagery of the Saracens by their arms and restore the Christians to their former freedom: we do not want those who have abandoned the world and have vowed themselves to spiritual warfare either to bear arms or to go on this journey; we go so far as to forbid them to do so. And we forbid religious – clerics or monks – to set out in this company without the permission of their bishops or abbots in accordance with the rule of the holy canons. The discretion of your religious profession must prevent you in this business from running the risk of either insulting the apostolic see or endangering your own souls. We have heard it said that your confrère, the abbot of the monastery of St Reparata, is considering leaving the order shared by your congregation in common. And so in this present letter we send him an order, and by that we mean we forbid him to dare to rule the same monastery any longer without the permission of your common abbot, whom you call your major abbot. And if he does not obey, he or anyone else who perhaps dares to leave your congregation should be cut off with the sword of apostolic excommunication.

Given at Cremona on the seventh day of October. We want you to read this letter to the assembled monks and lay brothers and to let the other monasteries know its contents.

iv Urban to the counts of Besalú, Empurias, Roussillon and Cerdaña and their knights, c. January 1096–29 July 1099

Source: P. Kehr, *Papsturkunden in Spanien. I Katalonien* (Berlin, 1926), pp. 287–8. For the date, see C. Erdmann, *The Origin of the Idea of Crusade* (Princeton, 1977), p. 317 note 37.

We beseech most carefully your lordships on behalf of the city or rather the church of Tarragona and we order you to make a vigorous effort to restore it in every possible way for the remission of sins. For you know what a great defence it would be for Christ's people and what a terrible blow it would be to the Saracens if, by the goodness of God, the position of that famous city were restored. If the knights of other provinces have decided with one mind to go to the aid of the Asian Church and to liberate their brothers from the tyranny of the Saracens, so ought you with one mind and with our encouragement to work with greater endurance to help a church so near you resist the invasions of the Saracens. No one must doubt that if he dies on this expedition for the love of God and his brothers his sins will surely be forgiven and he will gain a share of eternal life through the most compassionate mercy of our God. So if any of you has made up his mind to go to Asia, it is here instead that he should try to fulfil his vow, because it is no virtue to rescue Christians from the Saracens in one place, only to expose them to the tyranny and oppression of the Saracens in another. May almighty God arouse in your hearts a love of your brothers and reward your bravery with victory over the enemy.

3 Four reports of Pope Urban II's sermon at Clermont, 27 November 1095

All the reports of Urban's address at the end of the Council of Clermont were written after the success of the crusade, and the words put into the pope's mouth reflected these subsequent events. But at least three of the authors had been at the council and it has been argued recently that several had at their disposal notes made at the time. Four reports are translated here; two other important ones are those of William of Malmesbury (*De gestis regum Anglorum libri quinque,* ed. W.

Stubbs, II (London, 1889), pp. 393–8), a very theological account, and of the anonymous author of the 'Historia de via Hierosolymis' (*RHC Oc.*, III, pp. 169–70), who seems to have followed a conciliar text.

i The account of Fulcher of Chartres (written 1100–6)

Fulcher of Chartres was at the council and took part in the crusade, in which he served first Stephen of Blois and then, as chaplain, Baldwin of Boulogne. He went with Baldwin to Edessa, which may be the reason why he alone did not make Urban give in his sermon the Muslim occupation of Jerusalem as a cause for the crusade. In his *Historia* he revealed himself to be a reformer and a down-to-earth observer: he was one of only two writers who were openly sceptical about the authenticity of the relic of the Holy Lance. It has been suggested that he possessed a copy of the decrees of Clermont.

Source: Fulcher of Chartres, *Historia Hierosolymitana*, ed. H. Hagenmeyer (Heidelberg, 1913), pp. 132–8

Since, oh sons of God, you have promised God more strongly than usual to uphold faithfully peace-keeping at home and the preservation of the rights of the Church, it appears worth while for you in addition to turn the vigour of your goodness to a certain other matter, the concern of God and yourselves, now that you have been invigorated by the correction of the Lord. For it is necessary for you to run as quickly as you can to the aid of your brothers living on the eastern shore; you have often been told that they are in need of your help. For, as many of you have already been told, the Turks, a Persian race, have overrun them right up to the Mediterranean Sea, to that strait called the Arm of St George. Occupying more and more of the land of the Christians on the borders of Romania, they have conquered those who have already been overcome seven times by warlike invasion, slaughtering and capturing many, destroying churches and laying waste the kingdom of God. So, if you leave them alone much longer they will further grind under their heels the faithful of God.

On this matter I exhort you, heralds of Christ, with an earnest prayer – not I, but the Lord – so that by preaching frequently you may persuade everyone of no matter what class, be he knight or foot-soldier, rich or poor, to strive to bring aid to the Christian inhabitants in time by driving this infamous race from our territories. I appeal directly to those present; I order those absent; but Christ commands. All men going there who die untimely deaths, whether on the journey by land or by sea or while fighting the pagans, will immediately have their sins remitted. I am entitled to grant this to those about to go by the gift of God. Oh how shameful if a race so spurned and degenerate, the handmaid of devils, should conquer a race endowed with the faith of almighty God and resplendent with the name of Christ! Oh what a great disgrace will be imputed to you by the Lord himself if you do not help those who by the profession of their faith are rated, like you, as Christians! Let those who in the past have been accustomed to spread private war so vilely among the faithful (he said) advance against the infidels in a battle which ought to have been begun already and which ought to end in triumph. Let those who were formerly brigands now become soldiers of Christ; those who once waged war against their brothers and blood-relatives fight lawfully against barbarians; those who until now have been mercenaries for a few coins achieve eternal rewards. Let those who have been wearing themselves out to the detriment of both body and soul labour for a double honour. If they really continue to live in their former state they will be sad and poor, but if in the latter state happy and rich; in the former they will be the enemies of the Lord, in the latter they will be his friends. And those who are about to depart must not delay, but when winter is over and spring has come they must get eagerly under way with the Lord as their leader, after setting their affairs in order and collecting money for their expenses on the journey.

ii The account of Robert of Rheims (written before 1107)

A monk of Marmoutier-lez-Tours, Robert (also known as Robert the Monk) became Abbot of Saint-Rémi, but, after a dispute over his leadership, he retired to the Priory of Senuc, where he wrote one of the most popular contemporary histories of the First Crusade. He had been present at the Council of Clermont and the speech he put into Urban's mouth reflected the theme of his narrative: that an omnipotent God was working through his elect, the French, so that the crusade was, after the Creation and the Incarnation, the greatest demonstration of divine intervention in the affairs of this world and the fulfilment of the prophecies of scripture.

Source: Robert of Rheims, 'Historia Iherosolimitana', *RHC Oc.*, III, pp. 727–30

Race of the French, race living beyond the Alps, race chosen and beloved by God, as is radiantly shown by your many deeds, distinguished from all other nations as much by the situation of your lands and your Catholic faith as by the honour you show to Holy Church; to you we direct our address and to you we send our exhortation. We want you to know what grievous cause leads us to your territory, what need of yours and all the faithful brings us here. A grave report has come from the lands around Jerusalem and from the city of Constantinople – we have heard it very often already – that a people from the kingdom of the Persians, a foreign race, a race absolutely alien to God, a *generation*, that is, *that set not their heart aright: and whose spirit was not faithful to God*, has invaded the land of those Christians, has reduced the people with sword, rapine and flame and has carried off some as captives to its own land, has cut down others by pitiable murder and has either completely razed the churches of God to the ground or enslaved them to the practice of its own rites. These men have destroyed the altars polluted by their foul practices. They have circumcised the Christians, either spreading the blood from the circumcisions on the altars or pouring it into the baptismal fonts. And they cut open the navels of those whom they choose to torment with a loathsome death, tear out their most vital organs and tie them to a stake, drag them around and flog them, before killing them as they lie prone on the ground with all their entrails out. They tie some to posts and shoot at them with arrows; they order others to bare their necks and they attack them with drawn swords, trying to see whether they can cut off their heads with a single stroke. What shall I say of the appalling violation of women, of which it is more evil to speak than to keep silent? The kingdom of the Greeks has been so mutilated by them and made so subject to their practices that it cannot be crossed in two months. On whom, therefore, does the task lie of avenging this, of redeeming the situation, if not on you, upon whom above all nations God has bestowed outstanding glory in arms, magnitude of heart, litheness of body and the strength to humble anyone who resists you to their *hairy crown*?

May the stories of your ancestors move you and excite your souls to strength; the worth and greatness of King Charlemagne and of Louis his son and of others of your kings, who destroyed the kingdoms of the pagans and extended into them the boundaries of Holy Church. May you be especially moved by the Holy Sepulchre of Our Lord and Saviour, which is in the hands of unclean races, and by the Holy Places, which are now treated dishonourably and are polluted irreverently by their unclean practices. Oh most strong soldiers and the offspring of unvanquished parents, do not show yourselves to be weaker than your forbears but remember their strength! If the dear love of children, parents or wives holds you back, remember what the Lord says in the Gospel: *He that loveth father or mother more than me is not worthy of me. Everyone that hath left house or father or mother or wife or children or lands for my name's sake, shall receive an hundredfold and shall possess life everlasting.* Let no possession keep you back, no care for domestic affairs, for this land you inhabit is everywhere shut in by the sea, is surrounded by ranges of mountains and is overcrowded by your numbers; it does not overflow with copious wealth and scarcely furnishes food for its own farmers alone. This is why you devour and fight one another, make war and even kill one another as you exchange blows. Stop these hatreds among yourselves, silence the quarrels, still the wars and let all dissensions be settled. Take the road to the Holy Sepulchre, rescue that land from a dreadful race and rule over it yourselves, for that land *that*, as scripture says, *floweth with milk and honey* was given by God as a possession to the children of Israel.

Jerusalem is the navel of the world, a land fruitful above all others, like a second paradise of delights. The Redeemer of the human race made it famous by his birth, embellished it by his life, sanctified it by his passion, redeemed it by his death, left his seal upon it by his burial. This royal city, placed at the centre of the world, is now held captive by her enemies and is enslaved to pagan rites by a people which does not acknowledge God. So she asks and prays to be liberated and calls upon you unceasingly to come to her aid. It is, in fact, principally from you that she demands help, because, as we have already said, upon you before all other nations God has bestowed outstanding glory in arms. So take this road for the remission of your sins, assured of the unfading glory of the Kingdom of Heaven.

(When Pope Urban had with urbane delivery said these things and many more like them, everyone, moved by the same feeling, shouted in unison, 'God wills it! God wills it!' When the venerable Roman pontiff heard this he raised his eyes to heaven, gave thanks to God and, motioning with his hand for silence, said:) Dearest brethren, today there has been demonstrated to us what the Lord said in the gospel: *Where two or three* are *gathered together in my name, there am I in the midst of them*. You would not have spoken with a single voice if the Lord had not been present in your minds, because, although the exclamation came from many of you, the source of the voice was one; on account of this I say to you that God, who sowed this feeling in your hearts, has now called it forth. May that call be to you in military affairs a battle-cry summoning you to war, because it is brought from God. When the army draws up to attack the enemy this single shout will go up on God's behalf from all sides: 'God wills it! God wills it!' But we do not order or urge old men or the infirm or those least suited to arms to undertake this journey; nor should women go at all without their husbands or brothers or official permission: such people are more of a hindrance than a help, more of a burden than a benefit. The richer must help the less well-off and lead fighting men equipped at their own expense. Priests and clerics of any order whatever are forbidden to go without the permission of their bishops, because this journey would be of no profit to them without their licence. Lay people, moreover, ought not to go on pilgrimage except with the blessing of their priests. And everyone who has decided to make this holy pilgrimage and has made a promise to God and has vowed that he will pour himself out to him as a living, holy and pleasing sacrifice must bear the sign of the Lord's cross on his front or breast. Anyone who after fulfilling his vow wishes to return must put the sign on his back between his shoulder-blades. Such people, by these two actions, will carry out that command of the Lord, which he ordered in the gospel: *Whosoever doth not carry his cross and come after me is not worthy of me.*

iii The account of Guibert of Nogent (written before 1108)

Guibert was probably not present at the Council of Clermont, but he was in many ways the most distinguished of those who wrote about it. Born in 1053, he took the habit in the monastery of Flay. His reputation for learning led to his election as abbot of Nogent in 1104. Like Robert of Rheims, a theme of his history was the rôle of the French as the elect of God, but as a theologian only Baldric of Bourgueil stands comparison with him. An unusual feature of his report of Urban's sermon is its emphasis on eschatology and, linked to this, the central part that Jerusalem, as the focus of God's interventions in this world, played in the cause for crusading. Indeed he substituted a passage on the ill-treatment of pilgrims to the Holy City for the suffering of the eastern Christians that was presented as a cause by other writers.

Source: Guibert of Nogent, 'Historia quae dicitur Gesta Dei per Francos', *RHC Oc.*, IV, pp. 137–40

If some of the churches scattered throughout the world deserve more reverence than others on account of the people and places associated with them – I say on account of people, because the greater privileges are inherited by those places where apostles had their sees; on account of places, because the same dignity is awarded to royal towns such as the city of Constantinople as to kings – then we should give the greatest honour to the church of that city from which we have received the grace of redemption and the source of all Christianity. If what the Lord said remains true, that *salvation is of the Jews,* and if it is still true that the Lord of Hosts *left us seed* lest we should be *as Sodom* and become *like unto Gomorrah* – and our seed is Christ, in whom is salvation and the blessing of all nations – the land itself and the city in which Christ lived and suffered are known to be holy on the evidence of scripture. If, indeed, one reads in the sacred and prophetic writings that this land was the inheritance and the holy temple of God before the Lord walked and appeared there, how much more holy and worthy of reverence must we consider it became when the God of majesty was incarnate there, was nurtured, grew up and in his physical nature walked and travelled from place to place? And so as to be suitably brief about all the things that could be told at great length, what veneration do we consider to be fitting for the place where the blood of the Son of God, holier than heaven or earth, poured out and where his body, dead to the fearful elements, rested in the grave? If when Our Lord himself had recently been killed and the city was still in the hands of the Jews it was called holy by the evangelist when he said, *Many bodies of the saints that had slept arose and came into the Holy City and appeared to many*, and it was said by the prophet Isaiah, *his sepulchre shall be glorious*, no subsequent evil can remove that same holiness, since it has been imparted to the city by God himself, the sanctifier, by his own action. In the same way nothing can be taken from the glory of his Sepulchre.

You, dearest brothers, must take the greatest pains to try to ensure that the holiness of that city and the glory of his Sepulchre will be cleansed, for the gentiles by their presence continually sully them in so far as they can. And you will achieve this if you desire to approach the author of that sanctity and glory, if you love those things which are left on earth as traces of his footsteps and if you seek them with God going before you and with God fighting for you. If the Maccabees in days of old were renowned for their piety because they fought for the sacred rituals and the Temple, then you too, Christian soldiers, may justly defend the freedom of the fatherland by the exercise of arms. If you consider that you ought to take great pains to make a pilgrimage to the graves of the apostles [in Rome] or to the shrines of any other saints, what expense of spirit can you refuse in order to rescue, and make a pilgrimage to, the cross, the blood, the Sepulchre? Until now you have fought unjust wars: you have often savagely brandished your spears at each other in mutual carnage only out of greed and pride, for which you deserve eternal destruction and the certain ruin of damnation! Now we are proposing that you should fight wars which contain the glorious reward of martyrdom, in which you can gain the title of present and eternal glory. Just suppose that Christ had never died, nor was buried, nor had lived at any time in Jerusalem. If none of these things had in fact occurred you ought still to be moved to help the land and the city by this thought alone: that *the law* will come out *of Zion and the word of the Lord from Jerusalem*. If it is true that we derive the whole of our Christian teaching from the fountain of Jerusalem, the hearts of all Catholics should be moved by the streams which spread through the whole world to remember sagaciously the debt they owe to a spring so bounteous. If *unto the place from whence the rivers come they return, to flow again*, according to the word of Solomon, you ought to think it a glorious thing to cleanse again that place from which it was ordained that you should receive the cleansing power of baptism and the testament of faith.

And you must consider with the most full deliberation this: if, with God acting through you, the mother church of all churches herself with your co-operation flourishes anew in the furtherance of the Christian faith, does God wish some regions of the East to be restored to the faith against the approaching times of Antichrist? For it is clear that Antichrist will wage war not against Jews nor against gentiles, but, according to the etymology of his name, he will attack Christians. And if Antichrist finds no Christian there, just as today when it is thought that there is scarcely a single one in that place, there will be no one to resist him nor any whom he may rightly attack. According to Daniel, and to Jerome his interpreter, he will pitch his tents on the Mount of Olives and it is certain that, according to St Paul, he will sit in Jerusalem *in the Temple of God, as if he were God*, and, according to the same prophet Daniel, there is no doubt at all that he will kill three kings, those of Egypt, Africa and Ethiopia, before all others for their Christian faith. This cannot possibly come to pass unless Christianity will take the place of paganism. If, therefore, you stir yourselves to the exercise of holy battles, so that you may repay Jerusalem the debt you owe her for the grace which she has lent you – it is from her that you have received the first implantations of the knowledge of God – and so that through you the Catholic name, which will resist the perfidy of Antichrist and the Antichristians, may be spread, who cannot but infer that God, who surpasses the hope of all in the superabundance of his power, will burn up through your spark such thickets of paganism that he will spread the rudiments of this law throughout Egypt, Africa and Ethiopia, which are withdrawn from the communion of our belief? And will *the man of sin, the son of perdition* find any other rebels? See, the evangelist cries, *Jerusalem* must *be trodden down by the gentiles till the times of the nations be fulfilled. The times of the nations* can be understood in two ways. Either they have dominated the Christians at their pleasure and have pursued the wallowings of all their filthy ways according to their lusts, and in all these things nothing has stopped them; for those who get their own way in all things are said to have their time, as in this: *my time has not yet come: but your time is always ready*; from which it is usual to say to the lustful, 'You have your time now'. Or, on the other hand, *the times of the nations* means the fulfilment of the gentiles who will enter by stealth before Israel is saved. Dearest brethren, these times will perhaps only be fulfilled when through you, with God working with you, the powers of the

47

pagans will be thrust back. And the end of the world is already near, although the gentiles have not been converted to the Lord: according to the apostle Paul there must be a revolt from the faith. But first before the coming of Antichrist a renewal of the Christian empire in those regions is necessary according to the prophecies, either by means of you or by means of those whom God chooses, so that the head of all the evil ones, who will sit on the throne of the kingdom in that place, should discover some support of the faith against which he may fight. Consider that perhaps the almighty has provided you for this task, so that through you he may restore Jerusalem from so great an abuse. Think, I beseech you, of the hearts giving birth to such rejoicing when we see the Holy City revived by your assistance and the prophetic, nay rather divine, predictions fulfilled in our own times. May what the same Lord said to the Church stir your memory. *I will bring*, he said, *thy seed from the East and gather thee from the West*. God has led our seed from the East, because in two ways that eastern province gave us the early growth of the Church. But, because we think it can be done through you with God's help, he gathers the Church together from the West when he restores the ruins of Jerusalem by means of those who came last to the tenets of the faith: that is to say westerners.

If the sayings of scripture do not stir you, nor our warnings penetrate your minds, at least the great misery of those who wish to visit the Holy Places should excite you. Consider those who go on pilgrimage and travel across the Mediterranean. How many payments, how much violence are the richer subjected to, being forced to pay tolls for almost every mile they go and taxes; at which city gates, entrances of churches and temples they have to pay fees; how they have to journey from one place to the next, accused of having done something; how it is the habit of the governors of the gentiles to force them savagely with blows to pay for their release when they have refused to pay a bribe! What shall we say of those who, quite penniless, putting their faith in naked poverty, seem to have nothing to lose but their bodies and undertake this pilgrimage? Non-existent money is exacted from them by intolerable tortures, the hard skin on their heels being cut open and peeled back to investigate whether perhaps they have inserted something under it. The cruelty of these impious men goes even to the length that, thinking the wretches have eaten gold or silver, they either put scammony in their drink and force them to vomit or void their vitals, or – and this is unspeakable – they stretch asunder the coverings of all the intestines after ripping open their stomachs with a blade and reveal with horrible mutilation whatever nature keeps secret. Remember, I beseech you, the thousands who have perished horribly and take action for the Holy Places, from which the first principles of your religion have come to you. Believe assuredly that Christ, as standard-bearer and your inseparable guide, will go before you who are to be sent to his war.

iv The account of Baldric of Bourgueil (written *c*. 1108)

Baldric is the most underrated of the historians of the First Crusade. He was prior and abbot of Saint-Pierre-de-Bourgueil from 1089 to 1107 and he attended the Council of Clermont. In 1107 he was elected archbishop of Dol in Brittany. He was a prolific and elegant writer, but his history of the crusade is regarded nowadays as being of little worth. This is unjust: he made interesting use of his material, writing a very theological account. In his version of Urban's sermon he stressed the brotherhood of all Christians, eastern as well as western.

Source: Baldric of Bourgueil, 'Historia Jerosolimitana', *RHC Oc.*, IV, pp. 12–16

Most beloved brethren, we have heard and you are now hearing – we cannot recall it at all without profound sorrow – with how many disasters, how many harassments, what dreadful tribulations the Christians, our brothers, members of Christ's body, are scourged, oppressed and injured in Jerusalem and Antioch and other cities along the eastern coastline. Your blood-brothers, your comrades-in-arms, those born from the same womb as you, for you are sons of the same Christ and the same Church, are subject to foreign lords in their own heritages or are driven out of them or come begging here among us; or, which is more serious, they are in their own estates being sold into slavery, exiled and flogged. Christian blood, which has been redeemed by the blood of Christ, is spilled and Christian flesh, flesh of Christ's flesh, is delivered up to execrable abuses and appalling servitude. Throughout those towns there is everywhere mourning, everywhere grief, everywhere groaning – I sigh as I speak. The churches where once the divine mysteries were celebrated are, alas, being converted into stables for their cattle. Vile men occupy the holy cities; false, unclean Turks lord it over our brothers. Blessed Peter was the first bishop to hold Antioch. See now how the gentiles have established their false practices in that church and instead of cultivating, as above all they should, the Christian religion in the temple dedicated to God they have wickedly suppressed it. The estates set aside for the stipends of the saints and the patrimonies of the nobles made over for the upkeep of the poor are subjected to pagan tyranny and cruel overlords exploit them for their own purposes. The priesthood of God has been ground under their heels. In every place the sanctuary of God – what blasphemy! – has been profaned. If there are still any Christians left in hiding, unheard-of tortures are employed to discover where they are.

Until now we have as it were disguised the fact that we have been speaking of holy Jerusalem, brethren, because we have been ashamed and embarrassed to talk about her; for that very city in which, as you know, Christ himself suffered for us, since our sins demanded it, has been overwhelmed by the filth of the pagans and, I say it to our shame, led away from the service of God. This is the worst of reproaches against us, even though we have deserved all this. To what use now is put the church of Blessed Mary, where her own body was buried in the valley of Josaphat? What of the Temple of Solomon, not to mention the fact that it is the Lord's, in which the barbaric races worship their idols, which they have placed there against the law and against religion? We will not recall the Lord's Sepulchre, because some of you have seen with your own eyes to what abomination it has been handed over. And the Turks have violently seized the offerings which you have so often taken there as alms; there they overstep all bounds in their many and countless taunting insults to our faith. Yet in that place – I am only saying what everyone knows – God was laid to rest; there he died for us; there he was buried. How precious is that place of the Lord's burial, how desirable, a place beyond compare! Indeed God does not let a year go by without performing a miracle there: when the lamps in the Sepulchre and in the church around it have been put out at Passiontide, they are relighted by divine command. Whose stony heart could remain unmoved, brethren, by so great a miracle? Believe me, he is a bestial man with a senseless head whose heart is not shaken into faith by such direct divine power. And yet the gentiles see these things together with the Christians and they do not change their ways; certainly they are terrified, but they are not converted to the faith, which is not surprising because their minds remain unenlightened. You who are present, you who have returned, you, who have sacrificed your fortunes and your blood there for God's sake, know better with how many injuries they have afflicted you. We will have spoken, dearest brothers, about these things in order to have you yourselves as witnesses to what we have said. We could recall many other individual instances of the sufferings of our brothers and the depopulation of the churches of God, but we are overcome by tears and groans, sighs and sobs. We beseech you brothers, oh we beseech you, and we groan, weeping from the heart with the psalmist. We are unhappy. We are unfortunate. It is with regard to us that the following prophecy has been fulfilled. *Oh God the heathens are come into thy inheritance: They have defiled thy holy temple: They have made Jerusalem as a place to keep fruit. They have given the dead bodies of thy servants to be meat for the fowls of* the air: *the flesh of thy saints for the beasts of the earth. They have poured out their blood as water, round about Jerusalem: and there was none to bury them.* Alas for us, brothers, *we* who now *are become a reproach to our neighbours: a scorn and derision to them that are round about us* ought to sympathize and suffer with our brethren, at least with tears! We who have become *the reproach of men* and the least among men ought to mourn the most appalling devastation of that most Holy Land. We have deservedly called that land holy in which there is not one footstep which was not embellished or hallowed by the body or shadow of the Saviour or by the glorious presence of the holy Mother of God or the most beloved company of apostles or the delectable blood spilt by the martyrs. Oh Stephen, first of all the martyrs, how blessed are the stones which won you a martyr's crown! Oh John the Baptist, how blissful are the streams of the River Jordan which you used to baptize the Saviour! The children of Israel, who were led out of Egypt and prefigured you after crossing the Red Sea, appropriated by force, with Jesus as their leader, this land for themselves; they ejected the Jebusites and other communities and they lived in the earthly Jerusalem, the type of the heavenly Jerusalem.

What are we saying, brothers? Listen and understand. You have strapped on the belt of knighthood and strut around with pride in your eye. You butcher your brothers and create factions among yourselves. This, which scatters the sheepfold of the Redeemer, is not the knighthood of Christ. The Holy Church keeps for herself an army to come to the aid of her people, but you pervert it to knavery. To speak the truth, the preachers of which it is our duty to be, you are not following the path that leads you to life. You oppressors of orphans, you robbers of widows, you homicides, you blasphemers, you plunderers of others' rights; you hope for the rewards of brigands for the shedding of Christian blood and just as vultures nose corpses you watch and follow wars from afar. Certainly this is the worst course to follow because it is utterly removed from God. And if you want to take counsel for your souls you must either cast off as quickly as possible the belt of this sort of knighthood or go forward boldly as knights of Christ, hurrying swiftly to defend the eastern Church. It is from her that all the delights of your salvation have come. She has distilled the words of divine milk on your tongues, for she has given you to drink the sacrosanct dogmas of the evangelists. We say these things, brethren, so that you may restrain your murdering hands from slaughtering your brothers, go to fight nations abroad for the household servants of the faith and, following Jesus Christ your leader, you the Christian force, a force most invincible, better than the ancient tribe of Jacobites themselves, wage war for your own rights over Jerusalem and attack and throw out the Turks, more unholy than the Jebusites, who are there. It ought to be a beautiful ideal for you to die for Christ in that city where Christ died for you, but if it should happen that you should die here, you may be sure that it will be as if you had died on the way, provided, that is, Christ finds you in his company of knights: God distributes his own penny, at the first and the eleventh hour. It ought to be horrifying, brothers, horrifying for you to lay grasping hands on Christians: it is a lesser evil to brandish the sword against Saracens; in particular cases it is good, because it is love to lay down one's life for one's brothers. Do not worry about the coming journey: remember that nothing is impossible for those who fear God, nor for those who truly love him. You will get the enemies' possessions, because you will despoil their treasuries and either return victorious to your own homes or gain eternal fame, purpled with your own blood. You ought to fight for such an emperor, who is all-powerful and who lacks none of the rewards with which to repay you. It is a short journey and the task is slight that will, however, reward you with a *never fading crown*. And now we speak with the authority of the prophet. *Gird thy sword*, each man of you, *upon thy thigh, Oh thou most mighty*. Gird yourselves, I say, and act like mighty sons, because it is better for you to die in battle than to tolerate the abuse of your race and your Holy Places. Do not let the seductive lures of your women and possessions persuade you not to go; do not let the toil you will have to undergo deter you with the result that you remain behind. (And turning to the bishops), You (he said) brothers and fellow bishops, you fellow priests and fellow heirs of Christ, proclaim the message in the churches committed to your care and give your whole voice to preaching manfully the journey to Jerusalem. Confident in Christ, grant those who have confessed the ignominy of their sins a speedy recompense. And you who are preparing to go have us to pray for you, while we have you to fight for the people of God. Our duty is to pray. Yours must be to fight against the Amalekites. We will hold out tireless hands like Moses, praying to heaven; you must draw and brandish your swords, you fearless warriors against Amalek.

(When those present had heard those excellent words and others of the same kind from the lord pope, the eyes of some filled with tears, some were frightened and others argued about this matter. But among all at the council – and we all saw him – the bishop of Le Puy, a man of great repute and the highest nobility, went up to the lord pope with a smiling face and on bended knee begged and beseeched his permission and blessing to make the journey. He also gained from the pope the mandate that everyone should obey him and that he himself, in respect of his office, should have the leadership of the army in all things, especially since he was universally recognized as a leader of great physical energy and particular industry. After he had been pronounced to be a worthy chief of the army of God the great host of nobles gave its assent; and at once all pledged themselves to the sign of the holy cross by attaching it to their clothes, for the pope had ordered them to do this. And those who were going had decided to make this gesture, for the pope had said in his sermon that the Lord had said to his followers: *If anyone doth not carry his cross and come after me, he cannot be my disciple*.) Therefore (he said) you ought to attach a cross to your clothes, so that you may go forward the more protected by this and also serve as an example and encouragement to those who see you.

II The Attraction of Crusading

The appeal of crusading to contemporaries is exemplified by the sources that follow. Legitimate authority was believed to be conferred by God, on whose behalf a pope proclaimed a crusade. God intervened physically on the side of his crusaders, who were being tested by him. Victory was ascribed to the working of his power, and disaster to his judgement on his unworthy instruments. The just cause was either the recovery or preservation in Christian hands of Jerusalem and the Holy Land, itself regarded as a relic and also as Christ's patrimony which must be defended in the same way as the domains of the crusaders' temporal lords, or the defence of Christendom in general from enemies without and within. Other ideas, not often officially propounded but moving many people, were sometimes associated with the cause for war: the belief that a war of conversion was just and the deep-seated conviction that the crusade was a legitimate act of revenge on behalf of God and his suffering children. The right intention of those taking part was stressed: the crusade was portrayed as an expression of love for God and one's neighbour; participation in it was a moral duty and the crusaders, whose lands and families were protected in their absence, were rewarded not only with the indulgence, but also with martyrdom if they were killed.

A The Authority of God

4 Guibert of Nogent considers the First Crusade as an expression of God's will (written before 1108)

No idea in crusading literature was more consistently expressed than this. To illustrate it we have chosen a powerful passage in Guibert of Nogent's history of the First Crusade, in which the expedition was described as being fought by a chosen people under God's direct inspiration and was also seen as something instituted by God to provide the laity with a means of salvation through works.

Source: Guibert of Nogent, 'Historia' pp. 123–5

If we consider the battles of the gentiles and think of the great military enterprises in which kingdoms have been invaded, we will think of no army and absolutely no exploit comparable to ours. We have heard that God was glorified in the Jewish people, but we acknowledge that there is reliable proof that Jesus Christ lives and thrives today among our contemporaries just as he did yesterday among men of old. Kings, dukes, Roman dictators and consuls stirred up multitudes with the intention of fighting anywhere and from those positions of command they gathered together numerous armies made up of all kinds of races. But they came together driven by the fears of men. What shall I say of those who without a lord, without a prince, with only God to move them, have ventured not only beyond the frontiers of their native provinces, but even outside the kingdoms in which they lived, indeed also further than a host of nations and tongues that lie between, and have led their companies from their castles on the far-flung shores of Britain right to the centre of the world? We are speaking of the recent and incomparable victory of the expedition to Jerusalem. Those of us who have not grown foolish glory so much in it that we rejoice that our times are ennobled with a title that no former ones have deserved. What has driven our knights thither is not ambition for fame, for money, for extending the boundaries of their lands: almost all who take up or have taken up arms against anyone strive or have striven for these advantages. About them this verse could aptly be quoted:

> *Countrymen, why this madness and uncontrolled savagery*
> *To show blood of your own people to hated nations?*

and

> *They were bent on wars which they would never win.*
> (Lucan, Pharsal. 1; 8, 9, 12)

If they were to take up the cause of safeguarding liberty and defending the commonwealth, they might at least be able to put forward an honest excuse. When, moreover, an invasion of barbarians or of gentiles is feared no soldier ought to absent himself from the discipline of arms. Even if these conditions do not exist, wars traditionally have been fought absolutely legitimately only for the protection of Holy Church. But because nobody has had this right intention and the lust for possessions has pervaded the hearts of all, God has instituted in our time holy wars, so that the order of knights and the crowd running in their wake, who following the example of the ancient pagans have been engaged in slaughtering one another, might find a new way of gaining salvation. And so they are not forced to abandon secular affairs completely by choosing the monastic life or any religious profession, as used to be the custom, but can attain in some measure God's grace while pursuing their own careers, with the liberty and in the dress to which they are accustomed.

And so we see nations moved by the inspiration of God, putting their minds in readiness and steeling themselves for the possibility of all sorts of demands on body and mind, seeking exile with great eagerness to overthrow the enemies of the Christian name. And we have seen the Latin world surpassing its fame and hurrying with more alacrity than we would ever see anyone rushing to banquets or feast-days. The highest offices of government, the lordships of castles or cities were despised; the most beautiful wives became as loathsome as something putrid; the lure of every jewel, welcome once to both the sexes as a security, was spurned. These men were driven by the sudden determination of totally changed minds to do what no mortal had ever been able to urge by command or achieve by persuasion. There was no need for any churchman to exhort people from the pulpit to go and fight when both at home and abroad each man advertised to his neighbour, no less by his advice than by his example, the vow to go on the journey. All were on fire with eagerness; those who were not supported by great wealth considered that they were as able to make the journey as those who could raise a large sum for travel expenses by selling possessions or the contents of great treasure chests. This obviously fulfils the prophecy of Solomon: *The locust which hath no king, yet they all go out by their bands.* This locust had made no move to do any good all the time it had slept in a frozen state of long iniquity, but when the warmth of the sun of justice shone forth it sprang up at once on a flight of two-fold transmigration when it left its father's house and its family and changed its behaviour by assuming a holy intention. The locust itself did not have a king: for each faithful soul had no leadership but that of God alone, while he saw himself as God's companion-at-arms and did not doubt that God went before him, by whose will and inspiration he had started out and with whom he would rejoice as his consolation when he was in difficulties. But what can this universal response be except an expression of that plain goodness which moves the hearts of the most numerous peoples to seek one and the same thing? The instructions of the apostolic see on this matter reached only the French, as though intended particularly for them, but what race living according to Christian law did not at once supply forces? And while they thought they owed the same faith to God as did the French, they tried and sought to close the gap between them and the French as far as their resources allowed. You might see formations of Scots, who usually fight each other but not abroad, wearing leggings and hairy cloaks, their sporrans hanging from their shoulders, rolling down from their marshy borders; and those about whom we jested supplied us with copious arms to give us the aid of their faith and devotion. As God is my witness, I have heard of men of I know not what barbaric race driven to our seaport, whose tongue was until that time unknown, so that, since they could not talk to us, they made the sign of the cross by putting one finger over the other: not knowing how to tell us by word of mouth they showed us by these signs that they had set out for the sake of their faith.

5 Pope Eugenius III, writing to King Louis VII of France and his subjects, proclaims the Second Crusade on God's behalf (*Quantum praedecessores*), 1 March 1146

The pope spoke for God when he launched a crusade. The form in which he spoke was finally established by this letter, which was more elaborate than those issued before. This is the second version of it, published after St Bernard had appealed to Eugenius on behalf of the king of France. It is divided into three sections: a narrative in which the reasons for summoning a crusade were given; an exhortation to the faithful to take the cross; and a description of the privileges the crusaders would enjoy.

Source: P. Rassow, 'Der Text der Kreuzzugsbulle Eugens III', *Neues Archiv* XLV (1924), pp. 302–5

We have learned from what men of old have said and we have found written in their histories how greatly our predecessors the Roman pontiffs have worked for the liberation of the eastern Church. Indeed our predecessor of happy memory, Pope Urban, sounding forth like a heavenly trumpet, took care to induce sons of the Holy Roman Church from several parts of the world to free it. In answer to his call men from beyond the Alps, especially the most strong and vigorous warriors of the kingdom of the French, and also those from Italy, fired with the ardour of love, assembled and, once a great army had been collected together, not without much shedding of their own blood but attended by divine aid, freed from the filth of the pagans that city in which it was Our Saviour's will to suffer for us and where he left us his glorious Sepulchre as a memorial of his passion, together with many other places of which, to avoid being lengthy, we have refrained from reminding you. By the grace of God and the zeal of your fathers, who strove to defend them over the years and to spread the Christian name among the peoples in the area, these places have been held by Christians until now and other cities have courageously been taken from the infidels. But now, because our sins and those of its people demanded it, there has occurred what we cannot make known without great sadness and lamentation. The city of Edessa, in our tongue known as Rohais, which also, it is said, alone under Christian rule had respect for the power of God at that time when all the land in the East was held by the pagans, has been taken by the enemies of the cross of Christ, who have also occupied many Christian castles. And the archbishop of that city and his clerics and many other Christians have been killed there, while the relics of the saints have been trampled under the infidels' feet and dispersed. We recognize how great the danger is that threatens the Church of God and all Christianity because of this and we do not believe that it is hidden from your understanding. It will be seen as a great token of nobility and uprightness if those things acquired by the efforts of your fathers are vigorously defended by you, their good sons. But if, God forbid, it comes to pass differently, then the bravery of the fathers will have proved to be diminished in the sons.

And so in the Lord we impress upon, ask and order all of you, and we enjoin it for the remission of sins, that those who are on God's side, and especially the more powerful and the nobles, should vigorously gird themselves to oppose the multitude of the infidels who are now rejoicing in the victory they have gained over us, to defend in this way the eastern Church, which was freed from their tyranny, as we have said before, by so much spilling of your fathers' blood, and to strive to deliver from their hands the many thousands of our captive brothers, so that the dignity of the name of Christ may be enhanced in our time and your reputation for strength, which is praised throughout the world, may be kept unimpaired and unsullied. And let the good Mattathias be an example to you. He did not hesitate for a moment to expose himself with his sons and relatives to death and to leave all he had in the world to preserve his ancestral laws; and at length with the help of divine aid and with much labour he and his offspring triumphed powerfully over their enemies.

We, providing with a father's concern for your peace of mind and the abandonment of the eastern Church, by the authority given us by God concede and confirm to those who, inspired by devotion, decide to take up and complete so holy and very necessary a work and labour that remission of sins which our aforesaid predecessor Pope Urban instituted. And we decree that their wives and children, goods and possessions should remain under the protection of Holy Church: under our protection and that of the archbishops, bishops and other prelates of the Church of God. And by apostolic authority we forbid any legal suit to be brought thereafter concerning all the possessions they hold peacefully when they take the cross until there is absolutely certain knowledge of their return or death. Since, moreover, those who fight for the Lord ought not to care for precious clothes or elegant appearance or dogs or hawks or other things that are signs of lasciviousness, we, in the Lord, impress upon your understanding that those who decide to begin so holy a work ought to pay no attention to multi-coloured clothes or minivers or gilded or silvered arms, but should with all their strength employ care and diligence in taking such arms, horses and the rest with which they may the more ardently overcome the infidels. All those who are encumbered with debts and undertake so holy a journey with pure hearts need not pay usury on past loans; and if they or others on their behalf are bound by oath or faith to usurious contracts we absolve them from them by apostolic authority. And they may raise money on their lands or other possessions, having informed relatives or the lords to whose fiefs they belong, and they may freely pledge them to churches or churchmen or others of the faithful without any counterclaim, for otherwise they will not want or have the means to go. By the authority of omnipotent God and that of Blessed Peter the Prince of the Apostles conceded to us by God, we grant remission of and absolution from sins, as instituted by our aforesaid predecessor, in such a way that whosoever devoutly begins and completes so holy a journey or dies on it will obtain absolution from all his sins of which he has made confession with a contrite and humble heart; and he will receive the fruit of everlasting recompense from the rewarder of all good people.

6 Pope Innocent III, writing to King Alfonso VIII of Castile, ascribes victory to the invincible power of God, 26 October 1212

In this letter, thanking Alfonso of Castile for news of the victory over the Moors at Las Navas de Tolosa, Innocent marvellously evokes, with imagery drawn from the Old Testament, particularly the prophecies of Isaiah, the omnipotence of God that had been demonstrated in what was one of the few crusading successes of his pontificate.

Source: Innocent III, 'Opera Omnia', *PL* CCXVI, cols. 703–4

God, the protector of those who hope in him, without whom nothing is strong, nothing firm, multiplying his mercy on you and the Christian people and pouring out his anger on races that do not acknowledge the Lord and against kingdoms that do not invoke his most holy name, according to what had been foretold long ago by the Holy Spirit, has made a laughing stock of the races which rashly murmured against him and a mockery of peoples thinking empty thoughts by humbling the arrogance of the strong and causing the pride of the infidels to be laid low. They, *trusting in horses because they*

were *many and in horsemen because they* were *very strong*, had no trust in
the Holy One of Israel and scorned to call upon *the Lord*. Nay rather they
dared to put God, living and true, to the test, haughtily raising their
voices against him and lifting up their eyes. But blessed be God, who
put *a ring in* their noses and *a bit between* their *lips*, giving to them
according to their works and rewarding them according to the
wickedness of their intentions, so that Moab might know that his
anger and pride are greater than fortitude and strength and that all who
love his name may hope in the Lord, seeing that he does not abandon
those who hope in his mercy, but is near to all who call on him in truth,
giving fortitude to the fallen and multiplying their strength; so that
they should yet not doubt the truth of what they read, that those who
hope in the Lord will have *strength: they shall run and not be weary; they
shall walk and not faint*, because the Lord will give strength to his
people.

But we exult in the Lord our helper, having learned more fully in
letters from your serenity that he *who teacheth the hands* of his people *to
fight and* their *fingers to war*, renewing the miracles of the Old
Testament, has saved his humble people in so great and horrible a
battle and has humbled the eyes of the proud. And rejoicing in the
abundance of the grace that he has given we have made merry with
exceeding great joy. Calling together, therefore, the clergy and all the
people of the city [of Rome], we performed with them acts of thanksgiving, as many as we could although not as many as we ought, to him
who alone worked the great marvels, causing those same letters from
your highness to be read in the presence of the whole multitude. We
ourselves spoke in explanation of them. We would like others rather
than ourselves to inform your royal excellency how many eulogies we
proclaimed of your magnificence in this affair, after we had called to
mind the mighty works of divine power. As for the rest, most beloved
son, we want you to understand, beseeching and exhorting you in the
Lord, that you should reverently ascribe the victory given to you and
the Christian people to the Lord of Hosts, by humbly confessing, with
your mouth as well as in your heart, that it was not your highness's
hands but the Lord who has done all these things, according to what is
laid down in divine law. Do not say *in thy heart, my own might and* the
power *of my own hand* have achieved this great deed for me, but be
mindful of the Lord your God, because he himself gave you the faculty
of fortitude and strength. For that victory took place without doubt not
by human but by divine agency; and the sword of God, not of man –
we ought really to say of a man of God – destroyed the enemies of the
Lord's cross. For who gave them up to destruction and plunder, so
that *one* put *a thousand* to flight and *two ten thousand*, unless it was God

who subdued them and handed them over, pouring out his indignation on them because they had sinned against him and had not wanted to walk in his paths? So do not walk proudly because those who work wickedness have fallen there, but give glory and honour to the Lord, saying humbly with the prophet *the zeal of the Lord of Hosts* has done *this*. And while others exult in chariots and horses you ought to rejoice and glory in the name of the Lord your God and, considering it a punishment imposed by the Lord on unholy men, *wash* your *hands in the blood of* sinners.

As for us, know for certain that we have always loved your person with a pure heart and a good conscience and unfeigned faith and that we grow equally in your love, proposing to be present in all your serenity's affairs, as much as we can with God and with honesty. So strive always to do those things that will merit papal approval and through which you will be able to exchange the transitory and passing glory of an earthly kingdom for the everlasting blessedness of the eternal kingdom which will never fail. We hope that we are speaking prophetically about this matter and are referring accurately to what will certainly come to pass.

7 St Bernard explains why failure must be accepted as a judgement of God, 1148–9

A problem faced by all believers in sacred violence was how to explain failure, since it was hard to accept that an intervenient and all-powerful God would ever allow a war fought on his command and in furtherance of his intentions to end in defeat. The answer, provided by the Israelites in the Old Testament and repeated by St Augustine, that failure was God's judgement on the unworthy executors of his will was constantly given by apologists for the crusades. Nowhere was it more profoundly expressed than in Bernard of Clairvaux's 'De consideratione', a treatise written for Pope Eugenius III after the failure of the Second Crusade, which St Bernard had enthusiastically preached. He showed here a saintly resignation to God's will which should be compared to the optimism of the letters he wrote before the crusade departed **(20 i, ii)**.

Source: Bernard of Clairvaux, 'De consideratione', *Sancti Bernardi Opera*, ed. J. Leclercq *et al.* (Rome, 1963) III, pp. 410–13

Best of men, Pope Eugenius, I am mindful of the promise I made to you some time ago and I wish to keep it, even though belatedly. I would be ashamed of the delay if I felt I were guilty of negligence or contempt. It is not so; but we have fallen, as you yourself know, into difficult times which seem to point to an end almost to existence itself, not to mention enterprise, since the Lord, apparently provoked by our sins, has seemed to some extent to have judged the world before time, rightly, of course, but forgetful of his mercy. He has not spared his people, not even his own name. Surely they are saying among the nations, *Where is their God?* No wonder. The sons of the Church and those who are counted as Christians have been overthrown in the desert, slain by the sword or consumed by hunger; strife *has been poured forth upon their princes* and the Lord *has made them wander where there is no passing and out of the way;* grief and unhappiness are in their ways; fear and sorrow and confusion are *in the inner chambers of their kings.* How confused are the feet of those who preach peace, of those who bring glad tidings of good things! We have said 'Peace' and there is no peace; we have promised good things and you see there is disorder, so that it looks as though we have gone into this business rashly without stopping to think. On the contrary, we have hastened into it with clear minds, not like people going into something uncertain, but at your command, to be more accurate on the orders of God commanding through you. So why has God taken no notice of our fasting? Why has he ignored us when we humbled our souls? For in *all this his anger is not turned away, but his hand is stretched out still.* Why does he still listen so patiently all the while to sacrilegious voices and the blaspheming Egyptians, only to bring *them out craftily* to kill them in the desert? And again, who does not know that *the judgements of the Lord are true?* But this judgement is so profound that it seems to me that he is deservedly called blessed who is not shocked by it.

But how, on the other hand, can human beings be so rash as to dare to pass judgement on something that they are not in the least able to understand? It might perhaps be a comfort to us to bear in mind the heavenly judgements that were made of old. For someone once said this: *I remembered, oh Lord, thy judgements of old: and I was comforted.* I am saying something which everyone used to know, but now is known to no one. It is true that the hearts of mortal men are made in this way: we forget when we need it what we know when we do not need it. When Moses was about to lead the people out of the land of Egypt he promised them a better land, for on what other grounds would the people have followed him, since they had known only one land? It was he who led them out; but when he had led them to the land which he had promised it was not he who brought them into it. This sad and unexpected outcome cannot be imputed to their leader's rashness. He did everything on the Lord's command, with the Lord helping and confirming the work and with signs that he was complying with God's will. 'But that people', you will say, 'was stiff-necked, always acting obstinately against the Lord and Moses his servant.' Well and good: they were unbelieving and rebellious. But what of our contemporaries? Ask them! What need is there to tell me what they themselves acknowledge? I have one thing to say to them. What ground could the Israelites gain when they were always turning back in their tracks? When, at every step along the way, did they not want to return to Egypt? And so, if the Israelites fell and perished on account of their iniquity, are we surprised when our contemporaries, who make the same mistakes, suffer the same fate? But was the fate of the Israelites contrary to the promises of God? No, and neither is the fate of our contemporaries, because the promises of God never prejudice the justice of God. And I have something else to say.

The tribe of Benjamin sinned. The other tribes girded themselves for revenge, not without God's approval. Next, God himself appointed a leader of the men going to fight. And so they fought, relying on a stronger force and a more just cause, and, what was more important to them, with divine favour. But how terrible God is in his counsels concerning the sons of men! The avengers of the crime turned and fled from the criminals and the greater number of men from the lesser. But they ran back to the Lord and the Lord said to them, *Go up!* They went up again, and again they were overthrown and confounded. And so, with God favouring their first attempt and actually ordering the second, those just men went out to fight a just battle and they were defeated. But the weaker they were in battle the stronger was their faith. What do you think our contemporaries would do to me, if with my encouragement they were to attack once more, and once more they were to be beaten? What would they do if they were to hear me advising them a third time to take the road again, to undertake the task again, over which they had already been disappointed the first and second time? And yet the Israelites, not reflecting on their first and second rebuffs, prepared themselves a third time and conquered. But perhaps our contemporaries say, 'How can we know that what you say is truly inspired by the Lord? What proof can you give us to make us believe in you?' I have no answer to their questions; they must spare my embarrassment. You must answer for me and for you yourself according to what you have heard and seen or of course in the way that God inspires you.

8 In the face of disaster Pope Gregory VIII summons Christians to repentance and describes the crusade as a test imposed by God (*Audita tremendi*), October–November 1187

On 4 July 1187 Saladin destroyed the army of the kingdom of Jerusalem in the battle of Hattin. The news of this disaster was too much for the old pope, Urban III, who died on 20 October. His successor Gregory VIII, elected on the 21st, at once sent out this encyclical, proclaiming what was to be known as the Third Crusade. In it he wrote of God's desire that the Holy Land, sanctified by his presence, should be recovered. He combined this with a forceful call to repentance and conversion and he followed St Bernard and Pope Alexander III in explaining the need to crusade as God's test for his people **(19 ii, 20 i, ii)**. Gregory's letter survives in three versions, two of which are dated respectively 29 October and 3 November; the third, which is translated here, was sent to Germany at about the same time.

Source: 'Historia de expeditione Friderici imperatoris', ed. A. Chroust, *Monumenta Germaniae historica. Scriptores rerum Germanicarum*, nova series (Berlin, 1928) v, pp. 6–10

On hearing with what severe and terrible judgement the land of Jerusalem has been smitten by the divine hand, we and our brothers have been confounded by such great horror and affected by such great sorrow that we could not easily decide what to do or say; over this situation the psalmist laments and says, *Oh God, the heathens are come into thy inheritance.* Taking advantage of the dissension which the malice of men at the suggestion of the devil has recently roused in the land of the Lord, Saladin came upon those regions with a host of armed men. There advanced against him the king, the bishops, the Templars, the Hospitallers and the barons with the knights and the people of the land and the relic of the Lord's cross, which used to afford a sure safeguard and desired defence against the invasion of the pagans through remembrance and faith in the passion of Christ, who hung on it and redeemed the human race on it. They were attacked and, when our side had been overpowered, the Lord's cross was taken, the bishops were slain, the king was captured and almost everyone else was either killed by the sword or seized by hostile hands, so that very few were said to have escaped in flight. The bishops, moreover, and the Templars and the Hospitallers were beheaded in Saladin's sight. We do not think that we ought to describe the events in letters until somebody comes to us from those parts who can explain more fully what really happened: how, once the army had been overcome, the infidels invaded and ravaged everything so that it is said that there are very few places left which have not fallen into their hands. But, although we have to say with the prophet *Who will give water to my head and a fountain of tears to my eyes, and I will weep day and night for the slain of my people,* we ought not to be so downhearted that we fall into want of faith and believe that God, angered by his people in such a way as to allow himself to become infuriated by the manifold actions of a host of common sinners, will not through his mercy be quickly placated by penance, that he will not console us and that after weeping and tears he will not bring rejoicing. For anyone of sane mind who does not weep at such a cause for weeping, if not in body at least in his heart, would seem to have forgotten not only his Christian faith, which teaches that one ought to mourn with all those who mourn, but even his very humanity, since every sensible man can surmise the details which we have left out, from the very magnitude of the peril, with those savage barbarians thirsting after Christian blood and using all their force to profane the Holy Places and banish the worship of God from the land. First the prophets and then the apostles and their followers laboured with all their zeal so that the worship of God might be established in that land and flow out from it to all the regions of the world. Moreover – this is the greatest and most unutterable fact – God, through whom all things were made, desiring to be made flesh, wished in his ineffable wisdom and incomprehensible mercy to bring about our salvation there through the infirmity of the flesh, which is to say hunger, thirst, the cross and death, and through his resurrection, according to the saying, he *hath wrought salvation in the midst of the earth*; he deigned to work this through himself, which the tongue cannot speak of nor the heart of man contemplate. The Holy Land has now endured what we read that it suffered under men of old. What a great cause for mourning this ought to be for us and the whole Christian people!

We ought not to believe, however, that these things have happened through the injustice of a violent judge, but rather through the iniquity of a delinquent people, since we read that when the people turned to the Lord *one* pursued *after a thousand, and two* chased *ten thousand* and when the people itself was at peace the army of Sennacherib was consumed by an angelic hand. But on the other hand that *land* devoured *its inhabitants*, nor could it remain in a quiet state for long, nor could it keep in check transgressors against the divine law. And these instances served as lessons and examples to those who were making their way to the heavenly Jerusalem and those who may not reach it except by the exercise of good works and through many temptations. But these things could first have been feared when Edessa and other land passed into the power of the pagans and it would have been prudent if the people who were left had returned to penance and pleased the Lord by turning to him whom they had offended by transgression. For his anger does not come suddenly, but he puts off revenge and gives men time to do penance; in the end truly he, who does not fail to give judgement in his mercy, exacts his punishment to penalize transgressors and to warn those who are to be saved. Faced by such great distress concerning that land, moreover, we ought to consider not only the sins of its inhabitants but also our own and those of the whole Christian people, and we ought also to fear lest what is left of that land will be lost and the power of the infidels rage in other regions, since we hear from all parts of the world about quarrels between kings and princes, cities against cities, and about scandals. We can weep with the prophet and say, *There is no truth and there is no knowledge of God in the land. Theft and lying and killing and adultery have overflowed: and blood hath touched blood.* It is, therefore, incumbent upon all of us to consider and to choose to amend our sins by voluntary chastisement and to turn to the Lord our God with penance and works of piety; and we should first amend in ourselves what we have done wrong and then turn our attention to the treachery and malice of the enemy. And let us in no way hesitate to do for God what the infidels do not fear to attempt against the Lord.

And so consider, my sons, how you came into this world and how you are going to leave it, how all things are passing and how too your life is transitory, and accept with an act of thanksgiving the opportunity for repentance and doing good, as much as it pertains to you, and give yourselves not to destruction but to the service of him from whom you have received both your existence and all the things you have; because you cannot exist of yourselves or possess anything by yourselves, you who cannot create one single gnat upon the earth. We are not saying, 'Forgo what you possess', but, 'Send it ahead into the heavenly barn and deposit it in his house *where neither the rust or moth doth consume, and where thieves do not break through nor steal'*, labouring for the recovery of that land in which for our salvation truth arose from the earth and did not despise to suffer for us the gibbet of the cross. And do not make your way there for money or for worldly glory, but according to the will of God who taught by his own action that one ought to lay down one's life for one's brothers; and commend to his care your riches, which whether you like it or not you will leave in the end to heirs you will not know. It is nothing new for this land to be struck by divine judgement, nor is it unusual for it, once whipped and chastised, to seek mercy. The Lord, indeed, could save it by his will alone, but it is not for us to ask him why he has acted thus. For perhaps the Lord has wished to find out and bring to the notice of others whether there is anyone who has knowledge of him or is seeking after him and might joyfully embrace the chance of penitence offered to him and, in laying down his life for his brothers, may be killed in a brief moment and gain eternal life. Hear how the Maccabees, on fire with zeal for the divine law, exposed themselves to every danger to liberate their brothers and taught that not only riches but also persons ought to be laid down for the salvation of their brethren, encouraging each other and saying, *Gird yourselves and be valiant men, for it is better for us to die in battle than to see the evils of our nation and of the holies*. And may you, led to the light of truth through the incarnation of Our Lord Jesus Christ and instructed by the examples of many saints, perform without any fear what the Maccabees, set only under the law [of Moses], did; and do not fear to surrender earthly and few things that will last a short time in exchange for those good things which have been promised and reserved for you, *that eye hath not seen, nor ear heard: neither* have they *entered into the heart of man*; about which St Paul says *that the sufferings of this time* are *not worthy to be compared with the glory to come that shall be revealed in us*.

But to those who with contrite hearts and humbled spirits undertake the labour of this journey and die in penitence for their sins and with right faith we promise full indulgence of their faults and eternal life; whether surviving or dying they shall know that, through the mercy of almighty God and the authority of the apostles Peter and Paul, and our authority, they will have relaxation of the reparation imposed for all their sins, of which they have made proper confession. And their goods and families shall stand under the protection of the Holy Roman Church and also of the archbishops and bishops and other prelates of the Church of God from the time when they take the cross. And no legal suit will be brought concerning those things they hold peacefully up to the time of their taking the cross until there is absolutely certain knowledge of their return or death; their goods are to remain in the meantime undiminished and unmolested. Also they are not to be forced to pay usurious interest if they are bound to anyone, but let them remain absolved from it and unmolested. Nor are they to go in rich clothes and with dogs or birds or other things which might seem to serve rather for delight and luxury than for necessary use; but they should go with modest provision and dress, in which they may appear rather to do penance than to affect empty pomp.

B The Just Cause

9 James of Vitry justifies the use of violence against infidels and heretics, *c*. 1216–25

In this extract from a sermon preached to one of the Military Orders, probably while he was bishop of Acre in Palestine, James of Vitry provided the standard justification of violence, based on St Augustine's arguments as transmitted by Gratian.

Source: James of Vitry, 'Sermones vulgares', ed. J. B. Pitra, *Analecta novissima* (Paris, 1888) II, pp. 419–20

So when people falsely assert that you are not allowed for any reason whatever to take up the physical sword or fight bodily against the Church's enemies, it is the devil trying to attack the fabric of your Order and by means of these people to destroy it utterly. They misuse the authorities of scripture and bring in worthless interpretations. For instance they quote the passages in which St Paul says, *Revenge not yourselves, my dearly beloved; but give place unto wrath*; and in the gospel of Matthew, Whoever takes *the sword shall perish with the sword*; and Luke, *To him that striketh thee on one cheek, offer also the other*; and when the Lord said to the servants who wanted to gather the cockle, *Suffer both to grow until the harvest, and* then *I will say to the reapers: gather up the cockle, and bind* it *into bundles to burn*. And they put forward many arguments like these to seduce the simple-minded and unwary.

The precepts of forbearance should be observed not so much in a false show of action as in circumspectness of heart: you should keep forbearance together with benevolence in the secret places of your soul. That is why the Lord, when struck on the cheek, was not seen to offer the other, but patiently bore it and exposed his whole body to death. When St Paul was struck on the cheek in the same way he said to the high priest, *God shall strike thee, thou whited wall*. And so according to Augustine those precepts of forbearance should always be kept by a wary heart; this same benevolence ought always to fill the will, so that one does not repay evil with evil. For external wars are not fought without benevolence; indeed there are many wars which it is our duty to fight against enemies, who need to be bent with a benign harshness, because if you take away the licence to sin from a man you give him the reward of serving God.

If we were not resisting the Church's enemies, the Saracens and heretics would have destroyed the whole Church. For this reason the poisonous limbs must be cut off and the decayed flesh must be cut out, so that the sound part is not corrupted; and the mad must be bound and the wicked destroyed so that the good may be left unharmed. On this subject John says to the soldiers in the gospel, *Be content with your pay*. According to St Augustine, the reason that he did not forbid these men to fight when he told them that their own pay ought to be enough was because they did not carry the sword without cause.

Soldiering seems to have been instituted to repel violence, repulse injury and proceed with justice against wrongdoers. On this matter Augustine wrote, 'Do not think that anyone who serves in warlike arms cannot please God; among these was holy David, among these was that centurion who said in the gospel of Luke, *Lord I am not worthy that thou shouldest enter under my roof; I have under me soldiers*. The Lord pointed to him as a witness, because he had not found such great faith in Israel. So when you are armed for battle, first remember this, that your strength, your physical strength itself, is the gift of God.' And a little further on Augustine says, 'But war ought not to stem from the will but from necessity and be fought so that God may relieve you from necessity and keep you in peace.'

We do not seek peace so that we may wage war, but we wage war so that we may attain peace. Christ taught that tribute should be paid to Caesar because on account of wars it is necessary to pay soldiers: salaries are given to fighting men because it is necessary to make certain provision, that they do not become thieves and go plundering to try to find the cost of their upkeep. Wars should not be fought from greed or cruelty, but from the desire for peace, to refrain the wicked and uphold the good. On this subject, St Paul in the Acts of the Apostles appealed to the secular arm for help against the people who had plotted his death and a tribune accompanied by armed soldiers escorted him in peace. Ambrose said on this matter that 'physical strength which safeguards the fatherland in war from barbarians or defends the weak at home or companions from brigands is absolutely just'. But a man who is capable of opposing and confounding the wicked and fails to do so is doing nothing less than condoning their ungodliness; and if anyone fails to oppose open villainy he risks being suspected of being in secret alliance with it.

It is clear that your Order was founded with good reason and it is obvious how necessary it is to the Church of God, especially in these days when man's life on earth is taken up not only with knighthood but also with knavery. And when you would be useful to others begin with yourselves, so that you will not be like the elm tree which supports the fruit-bearing vine while remaining sterile itself or like the ass which carries the wine but does not taste it: 'so you do not pull ploughs for yourselves, oxen'. So always be prepared to shed your blood for Christ, that is to say to lay down your lives for God with desire and the sword, following the example of a certain soldier of Christ who on seeing a host of Saracens began to say to his horse with great confidence and rejoicing in his heart, 'Oh Morel, my good companion, I have done many a good day's work mounted and riding on you, but this day's work will be better than all the others, because today you will take me to eternal life.' And then, after killing many Saracens, he himself died, crowned in war by blessed martyrdom.

10 Abbot Martin of Pairis preaches the crusade to the Holy Land, *c.* September 1201 (written August 1207–June 1208)

Martin of Pairis, who helped to preach the Fourth Crusade and was present on part of it, recounted his experiences to the monk and historian Gunther. In his report of this sermon, preached in Basel cathedral, Gunther made the abbot touch on many of the themes that attracted men to the crusades to the East: the idea of the Holy Land as a relic and as the inheritance of Christ, unjustly seized by the infidels who had expelled the Lord from his patrimony; the achievements of past crusaders; the loss of the relic of the True Cross in the battle of Hattin; and the spiritual and temporal benefits of crusading.

Source: Gunther of Pairis, 'Historia Constantinopolitana', *Exuviae sacrae Constantinopolitanae*, ed. P. Riant (Geneva, 1877) I, pp. 62–4

Listen to my words, my lords and brothers, listen to my words; not my words, in fact, but Christ's. Christ himself is the author of the words; I am the frail instrument. Christ speaks to you today in his own words through my mouth and complains to you about the injuries that have been done to him. Christ has been driven out of his holy place, his seat of power; he has been thrown out of that city which he consecrated to himself with his own blood. Oh what an affliction! The place where it was promised of old by the holy prophets that the Son of God would come in the flesh, where he was then born and wanted to be presented as an infant in the Temple, where he preached in person and taught and often showed his power and miracles, where he instituted the sacrament of the most holy body and blood while at supper with his disciples, where he suffered and died and was buried, where he rose again after three days and ascended into heaven in the sight of his own disciples and on the tenth day poured out the Holy Spirit on them in tongues of fire; today that place is ruled by the savagery of an ungodly nation. Oh what misery! Oh what cause for lamentation! Oh what a dreadful calamity! The Holy Land which Christ trod with his own footsteps, in which he cured the sick, gave sight to the blind, cleansed the lepers, raised the dead; that same land, I say, is given over into the hands of wicked men. The churches have been destroyed, the sanctuary has been defiled, the throne of the kingdom and its authority have been handed over to the gentiles. That sacred and venerable wood of the cross, steeped in the blood of Christ, has been so concealed and hidden by those people to whom the message of the cross is foolishness that no Christian can discover what has been done to it or where to look for it. Nearly all of our people who used to live along that frontier of Christendom have been killed by the enemy's sword or have had to submit already to a long captivity. The few who were able to escape from that disaster fled to Acre or to other safer places and there they suffer frequent attacks from the barbarians. This is Christ's urgent need which forces him to beseech you today by means of my voice. And so, strong warriors, run to Christ's aid today, enlist in the knighthood of Christ, hasten to band yourselves together in companies sure of success. It is to you today that I commit Christ's cause, it is into your hands that I give over, so to speak, Christ himself, so that you may strive to restore him to his inheritance from which he has been cruelly expelled.

So that you do not allow yourselves to be frightened by the atrocities which have recently been inflicted on our peoples by the frenzy of the gentiles, I want you to recall earlier events. Remember the time when that famous expedition was made under the noble duke Godfrey and other princes of the French and Germans; when that faithless people, just as they have now, had either killed or captured all the Christians and for 40 years had occupied the Holy Land and had held the Holy City of Jerusalem and Tyre and Sidon and Antioch itself and other fortified towns, in fact the whole land up to Constantinople, securely and without fear. But it was God's will that all of this should be recovered very quickly by the Christian army, as though in passing. Nicaea, Iconium, Antioch, Tripoli and other cities were taken; furthermore the very throne of the kingdom of Jerusalem was restored to our people. And now, in spite of the fact that the infidel race has wrested by force that excellent throne and most of the land, Acre is ours, Antioch is ours and we still hold certain other fortified and strong cities which are defended by illustrious warriors, thanks to divine favour and our own strength. Even that famous throne of Jerusalem could, along with all the other places, be brought under our dominion.

But if you are asking what you can hope for as a sure reward for so great a work, I can promise you most certainly that anyone who takes the sign of the cross and makes a good confession will be absolved entirely from all his sins and wherever, whenever and in whatever circumstances he leaves this present existence he will gain eternal life. I will pass over the fact that the land for which you are making is richer by far than this one and more fertile; and it could easily come to pass that many of you will find a more prosperous way of life there, even in temporal things, than the one you have known here. See now, brethren, what assurance there is in this pilgrimage, which holds out both a sure promise of the kingdom of heaven and a greater hope of temporal prosperity. I pledge myself to be a companion on this journey and labour and I desire to share good times and bad with you as far as it shall please God. So now, brothers, take the triumphal sign of the cross with glad minds, so that, in faithfully prosecuting the cause of the Crucified One, you may have the strength to receive great and everlasting rewards in return for a modicum of service that is short.

11 Graindor of Douai, reworking *La Chanson d'Antioche*, tells of Christ's prophecy that he will be avenged, *c*. 1180

Vengeance was a powerful theme in vernacular crusading literature. The European knights saw in Christ their own fathers, in his patrimony their family estates and in other Christians their own brothers and it seems that to them the crusades were analogous to their own private vendettas. It is evidence for the strength of this feeling that one finds Pope Innocent III exploiting it in his propaganda, referring to crusaders being summoned 'as sons to take vengeance on injury to their father and as brothers to avenge the destruction of their brothers.' This scene in *La Chanson d'Antioche*, added by Graindor to the original poem, is startling, but it is also typical of the ideas to be found in vernacular poetry.

Source: La Chanson d'Antioche, ed. S. Duparc-Quioc (Paris, 1976) I, pp. 25–8

> Sirs, for the love of God, keep quiet in order to listen to me,
> So that when you leave this world you will be the better for it.
> When first God was tortured by the Jews
> And was wounded and pierced by the nails and lance,
> On his right was hung a robber.
> Dismas had he for name when he was baptized.
> He had great faith in God and was blessed because of it!
> When he saw Jesus so tormented,
> Although he was a man condemned to death, he began to say,
> 'King, son of the Virgin, your pity is very great,
> So save me and yourself when you are in heaven.
> It would be most just, moreover, if you should be avenged
> On these treacherous Jews by whom you are so tormented.'
>
> When Our Lord heard him he turned towards him:
> 'Friend', said he, 'the people are not yet born
> Who will come to avenge me with their steel lances.
> So they will come to kill the faithless pagans
> Who have always refused my commandments.
> Holy Christianity will be honoured by them
> And my land conquered and my country freed.
> A thousand years from today they will be baptized and raised
> And will cause the Holy Sepulchre to be regained and adored.
> And they will serve me as though they were my offspring;
> They will all be my sons, I promise them that.
> In heavenly paradise shall their heritage be.
> This day you will be crowned with me.'

On the other side, on the left, hung a robber.
He had been baptized with the name of Gestas.
He was the companion of the one who believed in Jesus,
Whom he saw in anguish from so great a suffering
From the nails and the lance and the bitter drink,
Which the criminal traitors had given him.
Through rank disbelief he spoke up:
'You are wrong', he said, 'who can hide it from you, my friend?
You think that he can help you in this need.
He cannot save his own body, so how can he rescue yours?
He says that help will come a thousand years from now.
When the day comes of which he speaks
You and all the others who await this gift
Will be confounded and will certainly not be redeemed.
It is mad to hope for what he is promising us.'

Next spoke the robber who believed truly:
'Alas! What have you said about almighty God!
I and you deserve to hang and remain in torment:
We have always stolen and behaved badly.
Not so the Lord of the world, who sees all and allows it to happen.

Anyone who believes in him is in no doubt at all
That the sinner feels the poison of hell.'
'Friend,' said Our Lord, 'know certainly
That from over the sea will come a new race
Which will take revenge on the death of its father.
Thenceforward there will be pagans only in the Far East.
The French will deliver all that land
And if anyone is captured and killed on that expedition
His soul will go from his body to our salvation.
And your soul will see salvation there today by my command,
Together with all those who believe like you.'

12 Pope Calixtus II, writing to all the faithful, proclaims a crusade in Spain, 2 April 1123

This encyclical was issued in support of a Catalan advance south, almost certainly at the time of the First Lateran Council, at which crusading to the East and in Spain was discussed: the tenth canon of the council ordered in much the same terms as this letter the enforcement of the vows of those who had taken the cross 'for the journey either to Jerusalem or to Spain'. Containing the elements of a true appeal to crusade, it is evidence – if evidence were needed – of the fact that in the eyes of the popes crusades could be fought in Spain, and the series of papal letters to which it belongs should long ago have been studied as precursors of *Quantum praedecessores* **(5)**, which is usually considered to have been the first crusade encyclical.

Source: Calixtus II, *Bullaire*, ed. U. Robert (Paris, 1891) II, pp. 266–7

The concern inherent in the pastoral office committed to us by God demands that we should look after and feed the flock of the Lord with all vigilance and foresight. Once you know that the Spanish Church is being continually worn down by such a succession of disasters and by so many deaths of the sons of God as a result of the oppression of the pagans, we believe that not one of you will lie low. It is on account of these things that we are appealing to your affection as though God, on whose behalf we act, were exhorting you through us; and we urge you with every prayer we can, as our dearest sons, to make absolutely no refusal to do your utmost to defend your brothers and to liberate the churches. With apostolic authority and the power divinely bestowed on us we graciously grant to all those fighting firmly on this expedition the same remission of sins that we conceded to the defenders of the eastern Church. But if those who have put the sign of the cross on their clothes for this purpose have not made an effort to fulfil their vows between this Easter and the next, we banish them thereafter from the bosom of Holy Church until they make satisfaction. Because in fact we cannot visit your army ourselves, as we would have liked, we have made it our business to send to it from our side our most beloved brother Oleguer, archbishop of Tarragona, making him our representative especially for this affair, so that on his advice and following his decisions the things that need correction will be corrected and the things that ought to be confirmed will, with God's help, be confirmed. Any sort of problem that arises in this army will be solved by this experienced man. And so we entrust him most carefully to your affection, beseeching you that he may find in you that love which compels us to send him to you. May almighty God, by the merits of the blessed apostles Peter and Paul, preserve us in his mercy and allow us to achieve a glorious victory over the enemies of Christians and a happy outcome.

13 An appeal to all Christians for aid against the Wends, 1108
This extraordinary letter, written by a Flemish clerk in the circle of the archbishop of Magdeburg, which purported to be an appeal from the archbishop and the bishops and chief laymen of his province and was addressed especially to the provinces of Mainz and Cologne, the county of Flanders and the duchy of Lorraine, was not a true crusading

document. The significant reference to the king of Germany as *auctor* of the war against the heathen is evidence that it was not: in fact the first crusade in north-eastern Germany was not to be preached until 1147. But it shows how soon the ideas expressed during the First Crusade were assimilated into the German war against the northern heathen.

Source: W. Wattenbach, 'Handschriftliches', *Neues Archiv* (1882) VII, pp. 624–6

We have been weighed down for a very long time by the many kinds of oppressions and disasters which we have suffered at the hands of the pagans; we sigh longingly for mercy from you, begging you to alleviate with us the ruin of your mother the Church. The most cruel gentiles, men without mercy and in their inhumanity glorying in malice, have arisen against us and have prevailed. They have profaned the churches of Christ with idolatry; they have torn down the altars and have not shrunk from perpetrating against us things that the human mind shuns to hear. They invade our region very frequently and, sparing no one, they lay waste, kill, overthrow and afflict with carefully chosen torments. They behead some and offer the heads to their demons. Some they disembowel, then bind their dismembered hands and feet and, reviling our Christ, they ask concerning them, 'Where is their God?' They allow some to endure the gibbet and to drag out a life that is more wretched than any death, employing greater tortures, since while they are still alive they see themselves put to death by means of gradual dismemberment; finally the pagans cut their stomachs open and lamentably disembowel them. They skin many while they are still living and, after scalping them, they disguise themselves with their scalps and burst into Christian territories; passing themselves off as Christians they drive away with impunity what they have stolen. On as many days they declare to be devoted to carousing their pagan priests cry out, 'Our Pripegala wants heads; it is our duty to make this kind of sacrifice!' The god whom they call Pripegala is Priapus and shameless Baalpeor. Then, after beheading the Christians before the altar where they practise profanity, they hold cups filled with human blood and, howling with terrible voices, shout out, 'Let us hold a day of rejoicing. Christ is conquered. The most victorious Pripegala has conquered.' We are enduring afflictions of this sort without respite, or we fear them, seeing that their constant advance and their good prosperity in all things cause us to lament.

And so, dearest brothers in all of Saxony, France, Lorraine and Flanders, bishops, clerks and monks follow the good example of the inhabitants of Gaul and emulate them in this also. *Proclaim ye this* in the churches, *sanctify a fast, call a solemn assembly, gather together the people*, announce the matter and make all the people in all parts of your dioceses and parishes listen to it. *Prepare* holy *war, rouse up the strong*. Arise, princes, take up your shields against the enemies of Christ. Gird yourselves, powerful sons, and come, *all the men of war. Let the weak say; I am strong*, because *the Lord is the strength of his people, and the protector of salvation of his anointed*. Sally forth and come, all lovers of Christ and the Church, and prepare yourselves just as did the men of Gaul for the liberation of Jerusalem. The cruelty of the Gentiles has made a servant girl of our Jerusalem, which has been free since her origins. Her walls have fallen because of our sins, but these ruins are now in your hands: let all the precious stones of her wall, and the towers of our Jerusalem, be built with jewels. Let her own squares be covered with *pure gold* and let a song of joy be sung in her to replace the terrible sound of the gentiles in the sight of Pripegala. And instead of sacrifice involving the spilling of Christian blood, let *the poor eat* flesh and blood *and be filled*, so that you may *praise the Lord that seek him*; and let your *hearts live for ever and ever*, so that 'alleluia, alleluia' will be your constant song.

The king of the Danes with his people and other princes round about offer faithful hands to this war. And our king himself, the authority who has declared this war, will bring most speedy assistance with all the followers he can muster. On Saturday in Rogation Week we will gather at Merseburg and wherever we have suitable places in eastern Saxony. Most holy fathers, monks, hermits and recluses, you have *chosen the best part* with Mary, but because now the times demand it you must arise with Martha from the peace of contemplation because, now that your brothers have been greatly troubled with Martha, Mary is absolutely needed. We speak to you; rather Christ speaks to you through us. *Arise, make haste, my love, my dove, and come*. The flowers of good works have appeared in the lands of our princes. The time of reckoning for idolatry approaches. *The voice of the turtle-dove is heard*, because our chaste mother the Church is lamenting over the filthy practices of idolatry. *No man lighteth a candle and putteth it under a bushel: but upon a candlestick, that they that come in may see the light. Let your light shine before men that they may see your good works*. And so arise, bride of Christ, and come; let your voice resound in the ears of the faithful of Christ, so that all may hasten to Christ's war and come to help the soldiers of Christ. These gentiles are most wicked, but their land is the best, rich in meat, honey, corn and birds; and if it were well cultivated none could be compared to it for the wealth of its produce. So say those who know it. And so, most renowned Saxons, French, Lorrainers and Flemings and conquerors of the world, this is an occasion for you to save your souls and, if you wish it, acquire the best land in which to live. May he who with the strength of his arm led the men of Gaul on their march from the far West in triumph against his enemies in the farthest East give you the will and power to conquer those most inhuman gentiles who are near by and to prosper well in all things.

14 Pope Innocent III encourages King Waldemar II of Denmark to take part in the Baltic Crusade, 31 October 1209

It was always hard to justify the crusades along the Baltic shore, because the pagan peoples of north-eastern Europe were not much of a threat to the Germans. Innocent III had already proposed a just cause: that converts in pagan areas had been threatened by their neighbours, so that the 'Church of Livonia' was endangered and must be defended. In this letter he came near to stating bluntly that the Baltic crusade was a missionary war, something that conflicted fundamentally with canon law but was close to the German experience. A curious feature is Innocent's use of the parable of the wedding feast: Augustine had employed it to justify force against heretics, but it was quite another thing to use it as Innocent did to justify force against infidels.

Source: Innocent III, 'Opera Omnia', *PL* CCXVI, cols. 116–17

The *old serpent*, the suggester of crimes, who *as a lion* always *seeking whom he may devour*, swallows *up a river* and does *not wonder, trusting that the Jordan may run into his mouth*, has blinded certain people, who ought to be compared to the senseless asses they resemble, to such an extent that, completely ignoring their maker who clothed them in skin and flesh and after assembling their nerves and bones gave them life and mercy, they show to a creature the reverence they owe their creator and damnably adhere to the worship of idols. They hold in contempt those who profess the Christian name and persecute as evildoers those who preach the word of God to them. Although you have often undergone many labours and expenses in fighting the war of the Lord against barbarian nations of this sort which border on your kingdom, a recent shower of divine grace has again made fruitful the land of your heart, which has been cultivated so diligently by the ploughshare of holy preaching, so that, set on fire with love of divine law, you are planning once more to take up your arms and shield to compel, just as in the parable in the gospel, the *feeble* and infirm, *the blind and the lame* to *come in* to the wedding feast of the highest king. After you have dragged the barbarian nations into the net of the orthodox faith, the *verdure of the reed and the bulrush* will be able to spring up where until now only ostriches have lived. And so, commending your resolution in the Lord, we advise your royal devotion most carefully and encourage and enjoin you for the remission of your sins that, out of love for him who by his power *led* our *captivity captive*, you gird yourself manfully to root out the error of paganism and spread the bounds of the Christian faith. You must not be afraid of *the sufferings of this time, which are not worthy to be compared with the glory to come that shall be revealed in us*, but, with your arm stretched out strongly, you should confound with their idols the filth of the pagans. Fight in this battle of the war bravely and strongly like an active knight of Christ; if you fight properly you will deserve to be crowned in eternal glory, which *hath* not *entered into the heart of man*.

15 Two letters from Pope Innocent III on the proclamation of the Albigensian Crusade

On 17 November 1207, in the first of these letters, Innocent offered King Philip II of France and all who would fight with him against the heretics in Languedoc indulgences similar to those granted to crusaders to the Holy Land. Letters were also sent to all the faithful in France, with special appeals to the leading magnates. From that time the Albigensian Crusade was in train, although the pope may have been thinking more of reinforcing the actions of the king of France in the performance of his traditional duty to extirpate heresy than of arousing all Christendom to war; at any rate Philip, while not refusing the summons, asked for guarantees that the pope was in no position to give. On 14 January 1208, however, the papal legate in Languedoc, Peter of Castelnau, was assassinated by a servant of Count Raymond VI of Toulouse. The news reached Rome in February and Innocent's response was a magnificent letter, again sent throughout France, in which he moved from a hagiographical treatment of Peter as a martyr to the crimes of the count of Toulouse and to a traditional justification of the use of force against heretics because of the threat they posed to orthodox Christianity: in a phrase that would reverberate throughout the thirteenth century he stated that they were worse than Muslims. The version translated here was sent to the faithful in the ecclesiastical provinces of southern France.

i Innocent to King Philip II of France, 17 November 1207

Source: Innocent III, 'Opera Omnia', *PL* CCXV, cols. 1246–7

The perverseness of heresy, which has corrupted men throughout the ages, is constantly on the increase in the region of Toulouse. It gives birth continually to a monstrous brood, by means of which its corruption is vigorously renewed, after that offspring has passed on to others the canker of its own madness, and a detestable succession of criminals emerges. These men, glorying in the inventions of their vanity, reject the dogmas of the true faith and consider that they are exceptional in their false declarations: the more they hear the truth preached to them, the more boldly they pass on to others the false deceptions which they have invented, while *deep calleth on deep and night to night showeth knowledge*. These men *having*, according to the words of the apostle, *an appearance of godliness but* inwardly *denying the power thereof*, entice with sweet words, in the guise of a religion which they alone profess to hold, many unwary people and unite them with themselves in their evil ways. That woman in the Book of Wisdom [sic. Proverbs] was certainly describing them when, after she was in *harlot's attire prepared*, she proclaimed, *I have woven my bed with cords; I have covered it with painted tapestry*. Heretics, indeed, promise their hearers in a wholesome way, weaving in heavenly words and in the painted attire of eloquence, that they are preparing for them a bed on which they may rest from the tumult of vices with free hearts. But in reality they are creating a place of perdition with the threads of sins, with reference to which it is said through the prophet, *The inhabitants of Samaria have worshipped the kine of Beth-aven*. For the heretics lie when they claim to live in Samaria, that is under the protection of the commands of God: they do not understand God's law but attack it, nourishing wanton doctrines of many different kinds of novelty and error. But when now or in the future they suffer the due punishment for their iniquity, *the people* will *mourn over* them. For truly the Lord, according to the word of the prophet, will strike *the summer house* as much as *the winter house: and the houses of ivory shall perish*. It follows from this that the Lord, making their memory perish with the trumpet blast, will strike and scatter as much those who, burning with the heat of licentiousness, devote themselves to the pleasures of the flesh and those who weaken their flesh by abstaining from certain vices, in order that men should think them pious, as those also who with polished speech fashion falsehoods to deceive the simple. But although on many occasions and through many agents we have set ourselves the tasks of correcting these worst of men living in your kingdom, who congregate there in an empty attempt to overthrow the Christian faith, and of reducing to nothing the forms of their many-sided deceit, yet they, given over to false understanding, do not pay attention to the arguments put before them, nor are they frightened by threats, nor can they be softened by flattery.

And so, since wounds that do not respond to the healing of poultices must be lanced with a blade and those who have little regard for ecclesiastical correction must be suppressed by the arm of secular power, we have considered that we ought to call on your aid, most beloved son, to vindicate the injury to Jesus Christ and to seize *the little foxes* who, influencing the simple, are forever destroying the vineyard of the Lord of Hosts. We admonish your royal serenity most carefully and we encourage you in the Lord and enjoin you for the remission of sins to arm yourself strongly and powerfully to root out such degenerate shoots which, after putting down roots into the depths of the soil, produce suckers and not grapes. You must eliminate such harmful filth, so that the purity of your faith, which as a Catholic prince you hold as an ideal, may be revealed in deeds by vigorous action and also so that the perfidious heretical sectaries, worn out by the force of your power, may be brought back amid the sufferings of war at least to a knowledge of the truth. Just as the Lord your God benevolently stood by you in your kingdom's troubles and gave you a glorious solution to them by bringing peace and tranquillity to your land, so now he summons you to go the more strongly to meet his enemies and those of the Church.

Meanwhile we take your land and your men and their goods under the protection of Blessed Peter and ourselves, so that you can aspire to these things that much more confidently, and if anyone, which we do not believe, should wickedly presume to molest you or yours we shall take care to punish with canonical censure such a great injury, which we would consider to have been inflicted mainly on the apostolic see. In addition, we wish all the goods of these heretics to be confiscated and made public property and the remission of sins which we have thought right to grant to those who labour in aid of the Holy Land to be made equally effective for you, whether you are toiling in your own person or lending necessary aid, and for the men of your land who take up arms to overcome the perfidious. But we want you and they to bear in mind the needs of the Holy Land, so that no aid is prevented from reaching her.

ii Innocent to the faithful in the provinces of Narbonne, Arles, Embrun, Aix and Vienne, 10 March 1208

Source: Peter of Vaux-de-Cernay, *Hystoria Albigensis*, eds. P. Guébin and E. Lyon (Paris, 1926) i, pp. 52–65

We have heard of a cruel deed, one that gives rise to grief shared by the whole Church. Our brother of sacred memory Peter of Castelnau, a monk and priest, a man outstanding among other truly virtuous men for his life, learning and reputation, who with others had been sent by us to preach peace and spread the faith in Provence, had laudably made, and was continuing to make, progress in the ministry assigned to him, for he really was a man who had fully learned in the school of Christ what he taught and he could, embracing *that faithful word which is according to doctrine, exhort in sound doctrine and* refute those who contradicted him, being always ready to give a reasoned answer to anyone who asked him; in other words he was a man Catholic in faith, expert in law and eloquent in speech. But then the devil aroused against him his own servant, the count of Toulouse, who had often incurred ecclesiastical censure because of the many and great outrages he had committed against the Church and God and, like the changeable and crafty, slippery and inconstant man he was, had often been absolved for feigned repentance. At length the count could not contain the hatred he had conceived against Peter, because in Peter's mouth was the unfettered word of the Lord *to execute vengeance upon the nations, chastisements among the people*, and he hated him and his fellow-legate the more strongly because he himself was deservedly rebuked for his greater crimes. He summoned the legates of the apostolic see to the town of St Gilles, promising to give full satisfaction on all the matters of which he had been accused. At one moment that count promised, like a truthful and compliant man, those who had assembled in that town that he would follow the salutary advice given him; and at the next moment he absolutely refused, like a deceitful and hard man, to carry it out and he publicly threatened with death those who wanted eventually to leave the town, saying that he would keep a constant watch on them wherever they went by land or sea. At once putting his words into action, he posted his accomplices in carefully chosen ambushes and, when neither the prayers of our beloved son the abbot of St Gilles nor the importunity of the consuls and burgesses could calm his furious rage, they themselves, against the will of the count and much to his displeasure, led the legates out with a small armed guard to a place near the bank of the River Rhône where they rested as night fell. Entirely unknown to them, several attendants of that count were with them and they were after their blood, as became clear in what transpired. And so on the next day, when morning was over and mass had been said as usual and the innocent knights of Christ were preparing to cross the river, one of these attendants of Satan, brandishing a spear, wounded Peter between the ribs from behind. He, founded with immovable firmness upon the rock of Christ, was unprepared for such a great act of treachery and, looking back lovingly on the wicked man who had struck him and following like Blessed Stephen the example of Christ his master, he said to him, 'May God forgive you because I forgive you', repeating over and over again this phrase so full of love and forbearance. Then, pierced in this way by the lance, he forgot the pain of the wound that he had suffered in his hope of heavenly things and, now that the moment of his blessed death had come, he did not cease to arrange with the companions of his ministry matters which promote faith and peace; after many prayers he at length fell asleep peacefully in Christ.

Surely, because he shed his blood for faith and peace – there are absolutely no more praiseworthy causes for martyrdom than these two things – he would, we believe, have given some brilliantly miraculous signs had these not been prevented by the incredulity of those men. One reads about the same sort of people as them in the gospel where it is said that Jesus did not perform *many miracles there because of their unbelief*; because, although *tongues may be for a sign, not to believers but to unbelievers*, when Our Saviour was brought before Herod who, according to Luke, was very glad to see him because he hoped to see some sign wrought by him, he refused to perform a sign and return an answer when Herod questioned him, knowing that there is no inducement to faith in the performance of signs and that Herod wanted the empty pleasure of a spectacle. But, although this corrupt and perverse generation does not deserve to be given a sign relating to its own martyr as soon as perhaps it itself would like, we believe that it is expedient for it *that one man should die for* it, *so that the whole* should *perish not:* this generation infected by the contagion of heretical depravity that will be recalled from its error by the blood of a slain man, which will intercede for it better than any living man could. For this is the ancient device of Jesus Christ, this is the marvellous ingenuity of Our Saviour, that at the very moment when he appears to his followers to have been beaten he is winning that battle more strongly and, with the same strength with which he himself destroyed death by dying, he will cause the very people who have overcome his servants to be overcome by those very men who were first subdued; because, *unless the grain of wheat falling into the ground die, itself remaineth alone. But if it die it bringeth forth much fruit.* This makes us hope that there will be much fruit to come to Christ's Church through the death of this most fertile grain, since he would be really a severely culpable man, and culpably severe, whose soul is not pierced by this sword. Nor are we entirely without hope, for the shedding of his blood ought to bring the same great advantage as did the beginning of his holy preaching throughout the aforesaid Provence, on behalf of which he himself descended into corruption. May God grant the desired increases.

We consider that our venerable brothers the archbishops of Narbonne, Arles, Embrun, Aix and Vienne and their suffragans ought to be advised most carefully and encouraged and we now command them through the Holy Spirit under strict obedience to cause the words of peace and faith sown by Peter to take root by the waterings of their preaching; and they must by their insistent and untiring zeal attack the depravity of heresy and confirm the Catholic faith, root out vices and implant virtues. And they must, on behalf of almighty God, the Father, the Son and the Holy Spirit, and also on the authority of Blessed Peter and Paul, his apostles, and ourselves, denounce throughout all their dioceses as excommunicated and accursed that murderer of the servant of God, all of those people by the help of whose deeds, counsel or favour he has perpetrated so great a crime and also those who have sheltered and defended him. And on the authority of this letter they must cause to lie under ecclesiastical interdict absolutely every place to which they or any of them come, solemnly renewing sentences of this kind each Sunday and feastday, with bells ringing and candles lit, until those men approach the apostolic see and deserve to gain absolution through making fitting satisfaction.

On the other hand, the prelates must promise with assurances the remission of their sins, granted by God and by his vicar, to those who, burning with zeal for the orthodox faith, gird themselves manfully against this kind of pestiferous people, who simultaneously attack both peace and truth, to vindicate the just blood which cries ceaselessly from the earth to heaven, until the Lord sends down his vengeance on the earth to confound the subverted and the subverters. This indulgence shall mean that an undertaking of this kind will make satisfaction for what the faithful have done and for those offences about which they shall have assuredly offered heartfelt contrition and made true oral confession to God. For if pestiferous men of this sort are trying not only to ravage our possessions but also to annihilate us ourselves, they are not only sharpening their tongues to crush our souls but they are also in reality stretching out their hands to kill our bodies: the perverters of our souls have become also the destroyers of our flesh.

That count has already long since been struck with the sharp blade of anathema for many great crimes which it would take a long time to list one by one, but he is presumed to be guilty of the holy man's death on account of reliable evidence. Not only did he threaten publicly to kill him and prepared an ambush for him, but also it is said that he received the murderer with great warmth and rewarded him with valuable gifts; we will pass over the other things he is supposed to have done about which the prelates have notified us more fully. For this reason the same archbishops and bishops must publicly pronounce that man to be anathematized and since, according to the canonical sanctions of the holy fathers faith ought not to be kept with a man who does not keep faith with God, after he has been cut off from the communion of the faithful, like one who ought to be avoided rather than nurtured, they must on apostolic authority denounce all those bound by oaths of fealty or association or any pacts of this kind to him. They must also announce that all men bound in these ways are absolved from their oaths for the time being and that any Catholic man is allowed, saving the rights of the overlord, not only to pursue the person of the count but also to occupy and hold his land, especially on the grounds that through their worthy action the land may perhaps be cleansed of heresy, in so far as until now it has been stained shamefully by his wickedness; for it is right that everyone should raise his hand against a man whose hand has been raised against everyone. If he is not brought to his senses by this sort of harassment we will make it our business to take more serious action against him and when he promises that he really will make amends he must definitely give these sure signs of his repentance: that he dissociates himself from the followers of heretical depravity as completely as he possibly can and that he makes every effort to reconcile himself in peace with his brothers, since he fell under ecclesiastical censure chiefly because of the offences he is known to have committed on both counts, although if the Lord wishes to *mark* his *iniquities* he will scarcely be able ever to make appropriate satisfaction, not only on his own behalf, but also on behalf of the host of other people whom he has *brought into a net* of damnation.

And, because according to the judgement of truth we must not be afraid of those who kill the body, but of him who can send the body and soul to hell, we trust and hope in him who died and rose on the third day so as to take away the fear of death from those who believe in him. And we hope that not only will the death of that man of God fail to strike fear in the hearts of our venerable brother the bishop of Couserans and our beloved son the abbot of Cîteaux, legates of the apostolic see, and other followers of the orthodox faith, but also that it will so inflame them with love that, following the example of him who blessedly purchased eternal life for us by his earthly death, they will not be afraid to lay down their lives for Christ if need be in so glorious a struggle. We have considered, therefore, that we should give counsel to those same archbishops and bishops by advising them, reinforcing our prayers with commands and our commands with prayers, to try to put into effect the sound warnings and orders of the legates themselves and to assist them like strong companions in war in everything they think ought to be enjoined on them on this account, in the knowledge that we have ordered the sentence they themselves have published not only against the rebels but also against the inactive to be held firmly and carried out without fail.

So rouse yourselves, knights of Christ! Rouse yourselves, strong recruits of Christian knighthood! May the groans of all Holy Church move you and may the fire of devotion set you alight to vindicate such a terrible injury to your God! Remember that your Creator did not need you when he made you. He does not need your service. It is not so much that he is distressed or his omnipotence is in need of your obedience in doing what he has willed in this affair; it is rather that he is giving you an opportunity of serving him in an acceptable manner in this crisis. And since the Church in that region sits in sadness and grief with no one to comfort her after the death of that just man and it is said that the faith has disappeared, that peace has perished, that the plague of heresy and the fury of the enemy have grown stronger and stronger and that, unless she is strongly supported against such a new attack, the ship of the Church will seem to have been wrecked in that place almost completely, we advise all of you most urgently, encourage you fervently and in so great a crisis of need enjoin you confidently in the strength of Christ, granting you remission of sins, not to delay in making haste to combat so many evils and to make it your business to bring peace to those people in the name of him who is *the God of peace and of love.* You must try in whatever ways God has revealed to you to wipe out the treachery of heresy and its followers by attacking the heretics with a strong hand and an outstretched arm, that much more confidently than you would attack the Saracens because they are worse than them. But if perhaps harassment shall bring to his senses the aforementioned count, who does not consider his own *death* as though he had *entered into a league* with it, and if he begins to *seek* with his face full of *shame* the *name* of God, you must not fail to bring to bear on him the full weight of persuasion so that he may make satisfaction to us and to the Church, but most important of all to God, by expelling him and his followers from the castles under his lordship and taking their lands where, after the heretics have been banished, Catholic inhabitants must be put in their place, who, according to the teaching of your orthodox faith, must serve in holiness and justice before God.

16 Pope Gregory IX and Pope Urban IV justify crusades against the Staufen

In 1240 Gregory IX proclaimed a crusade against the Emperor Frederick II, who had advanced on the city of Rome. As the first of these letters show, he permitted the commutation of vows made for the crusade to the East to that against the emperor and he ordered money collected from crusade redemptions to be used in the same cause. In his eyes this crusade ranked with those in aid of the Holy Land; indeed at this stage it was of more importance because the mother church was herself imperilled. This theme was taken up by Urban IV when he was organizing a crusade, to be led by King Louis IX of France's brother, Charles of Anjou, against the Staufen forces in southern Italy and Sicily under Manfred, Frederick's illegitimate son. In his letter, from which we have omitted the final section, Urban also justified this crusade in traditional terms as a response to a threat posed to the Church and therefore to all Christendom.

i Gregory IX authorizes his legate in Hungary to commute crusade vows to the crusade against Frederick II, 14 February 1241

Source: A. Theiner, *Vetera monumenta historica Hungariam sacram illustrantia* (Rome, 1859) I, pp. 178–9

Since we thought it right to charge you to preach the cross in the kingdom of Hungary against Frederick, called emperor, the son of perdition, and since several people in that kingdom have received the sign of the cross to aid the Holy Land – on which matter you make the point that a great difficulty arises – we, considering that it would be more beneficial to help the apostolic see in such a crisis of need as this, since the mother herself and the head of the faith is assailed, more seriously imperilling the Christian name, concede to your devotion by the authority of the present letter the unrestricted power to commute effectively the vows of these crusaders to the defence of the Church against the same Frederick, if they agree to it, and to grant that indulgence which was given in the general council to those going to the aid of the Holy Land to them and to any others who redeem their vows, provided that you forward for this defence of the Church the money which they would have spent going to the Holy Land, staying there and returning from there and which they assign into your hands and into those of our beloved son the abbot of Pöls of the Cistercian Order and Benedict, canon of Gran.

ii Urban IV explains to King Louis IX of France why a crusade must be launched against Manfred, 3 May 1264

Source: Urban IV, *Registres*, ed. J. Guiraud (Paris, 1901) II, pp. 395–6

See, most beloved son, how Manfred, once Prince of Taranto, not content with the innumerable injuries and vexations with which he has so far damaged the Roman Church, assails the Church herself more roughly and more harshly than usual with continuous attacks using as a pretext the business of the kingdom of Sicily which is engaging us and our beloved son the nobleman Charles, count of

Anjou and Provence, your brother. He strikes her with unremitting persecution, divides her with tyrannical frenzy and incessantly afflicts her with various other kinds of tribulation to such an extent that the same Church, afflicted by so many evils, exhausted by so many molestations, oppressed by so many scourges, can scarcely breathe under oppressions of this kind. For this Manfred, who has embraced the rites of the Saracens and adheres to them particularly in his daily prayers and, to the dishonour of the Catholic faith, gives them precedence over Christian rites, attacks the Church, especially helped by the advice, aid and favour of these Saracens. He also detains, or damnably has had detained and occupied, archbishoprics, bishoprics and other churches and monasteries of the kingdom of Sicily by forcing into some of them false and pernicious ministers or by wickedly cherishing those already forced upon them, by actually commandeering some of them for his pleasure and converting their revenues most dangerously to his own uses. On account of these things heresies crop up nearly everywhere in Italy, the worship of God is diminished, the orthodox faith is borne down, the state of the faithful is thoroughly depressed and oppressed, the liberties of the Church are enslaved and the rights of the Church are trampled upon. And prelates and other men who hold distinguished positions in the clerical army are forced to undergo the penalties of exile, are seized and treated ignominiously and are thrust into dreadful prisons and condemned to most shameful deaths. Sacred and holy places, whether in the hands of religious or others, are despoiled of their possessions and other goods and, although they are dedicated to divine worship, are given over to illicit and profane uses, are despised and are defiled by abominable practices. Several clerics are also forced to celebrate divine services in places on which an ecclesiastical interdict has been imposed, in contempt of the keys of the Church, and to give the Church's sacraments to wicked, excommunicated and impious persons. Episcopal authority and power is counted for little, ecclesiastical censure is despised, souls perish, bodies are slaughtered, cities are burnt, castles are destroyed, the security of the roads is disrupted, travellers are robbed, Saracens and schismatics are set over orthodox Christians, heretics are defended to such an extent that in several places we dare not take action against them. In fact in some lands those who preach the truth of the gospel are forbidden to put the word of God to the faithful and in certain places heresies are publicly preached. Very many other detestable and abominable things are committed, moreover, which offend the eyes of divine majesty, generate scandal in the Church and weaken and abuse the dread force of ecclesiastical censure. Since the forces of this persecutor have grown strong, the

Church herself cannot employ a suitable remedy for these things, especially because recently this Manfred, putting savage hands into her vitals, presumed to send certain Germans, the particular agents of his persecution, into the patrimony of Blessed Peter in Tuscany, where we reside with all our curia, to the disgrace of ourselves and the Church herself, the disorder of the province and the injury of the faithful in it. He has also arranged to send other large forces of knights into the duchy of Spoleto so that, confining us and the aforesaid Church as if in a net, he is so pressing in on the roads from all sides and fencing in the passes that no one can reach us nor can we send out any men from our curia.

Because by the counsel of heaven on high the liberation of the aforesaid Church has been reserved for you and your most Christian house and it appears to be God's desire that the yoke of the same Church's burden and the dominion of her taskmaster should be surmounted by means of the power of your kingdom, you should know that we, with the advice of our brothers, send our beloved son Simon, cardinal priest of the title of St Cecilia, to whom we have given fully the office of legation, to your most Christian kingdom to promote under the Lord's guaranty the business of the said kingdom of Sicily – it is in fact this kingdom which is the source of all the evil afflicting the same Church and is the cause of such great perils – and to treat with the person of the said count to whom we have looked, having weighed the merits of his devotion and vigour. And so we think that your serenity ought to be asked most carefully and encouraged – and we urge you no less for the remission of your sins – to assist that cardinal with all diligence and the ready giving of counsel and favour, out of reverence for the holy see and ourselves, receiving with royal kindness the cardinal who is assuredly relying on your benevolence. And you ought to treat with him on the serious matters which concern the honour of the Church and the more willingly entrust him with the promotion of those necessary arrangements for the same business which its nature requires. And because we know that your most devout and most kind heart is full of abundant mercy and the richness of divine grace and in its great humanity has compassion on the aforesaid Church in her so many calamities, tribulations and pressures, we, proclaiming the clemency of your grace with many inscriptions of praise and offering many acts of thanksgiving to your greatness, pray to the Highest, who gives salvation to kings, that he will keep you safe and sound for a greater length of time for us and for the Church. May he add *days to the days of the king* and extend your life in a prosperous reign and give you peaceful and abundant times to the praise of his name. And so, most

Christian prince, we ask you to show powerfully and willingly the feeling of this your compassion in the advancement of this business, by means of which we hope, with the favour of the Lord, to liberate the Church from her enemies who surround her; so that even after your body has been destroyed, at no time will the memory of the renown of so pious and so wholesome a work die, but on its account the glory of your name will last through generations of ages.

C Right Intention

17 An anonymous poet writes of the love of God expressed by the crusader (*Vos qui ameis de vraie amour*), 1150–1200

Crusading was regarded as an act of Christian love. The idea that the crusader expressed love of God was a feature of ecclesiastical writing, but it also impressed itself upon the popular mind, in which it became particularly associated with the feelings vassals had, or ought to have had, about their lords and the obligation that love of his lord enjoined on a man not to desert him in need. Innocent III was to exploit this idea in his encyclicals **(26)**. The beautiful song translated here is anonymous and undated, but it has been suggested on grounds of style that it must have been written *c.*1189.

Source: J. Bédier and P. Aubry, *Les chansons des croisades* (Paris, 1909), pp. 20–2

> You who love with true love, awake! Sleep no more!
> The lark lets us know that day is here
> And tells us in her songs
> That the day of peace has come
> Which God, in his great tenderness,
> Will give to those who for love of him
> Take the cross and for their burden
> Suffer pain both night and day.
> Then he will see who truly love him.
>
> Anyone deserves to be condemned
> Who has deserted his lord in need.
> So will he be, remember it well.
> He will have much pain and much insult
> On the Day of our Last Judgement
> When God his sides, palms and feet
> Will show bleeding and wounded.

For even he who has done his best
Will be so sore afraid
That he will tremble, whether he wants to or not.

He who was put on the cross for us
Did not love us with a simulated love.
He loved us like the finest friend
And lovingly for us
Carried with so much anguish
The holy cross very gently
Between his arms, before his breast,
Like a gentle lamb, simple and devout.
Then he was nailed with three nails
Painfully through his hands and through his feet.

I have heard it said proverbially,
'A sensible merchant spends money from his purse;'
And, 'He has a very fickle heart
Who sees what is good and chooses what is evil'.
Do you know what God has promised
To those who wish to take the cross?
God help me, a very fair wage:
Paradise, by firm promise.
He who can gain his prize
Is mad if he waits until tomorrow.

For us there is no tomorrow,
We can be sure of that.
Many a man imagines that he has a very healthy heart
And four days later he can no longer prize
Either all his goods or his knowledge
When he sees that death holds him on a rein,
So that neither foot nor hand
Can he move to shake it off or remove it.
He leaves his feather-bed and takes to the straw litter,
But he realizes his mistake too late.

18 Pope Innocent III, writing to Duke Leopold VI of Austria, associates love of God with the service of the cross, 24 February 1208

To love God is to follow him. In his sermon at Clermont Pope Urban II may well have referred to Christ's injunction that a man should deny himself, take up his cross and follow him: it was cited in two of the reports of the sermon (3 ii, iv), in a letter to the pope by the leaders of the crusade and in the opening passage of an eyewitness account of the expedition. It was to be referred to regularly by preachers throughout the history of the movement, including Pope Innocent III in his great encyclical *Quia maior* **(26)**. In this letter to Leopold VI of Austria, who had been on the Third Crusade, had taken the cross again in 1198 and was to crusade yet again in Spain, Languedoc and the East, Innocent movingly expounded the cross's significance for this world and the crusader's denial of self. To be noted also is the reference to the need for a follower of Christ to leave home and family, on the basis, of course, of another of Christ's precepts favoured by crusade preachers.

Source: Innocent III, 'Opera Omnia', *PL* ccxv, cols. 1339–41

We have learned through experience that you have not heard and left unheeded the words that were spoken in the gospel to those who wanted to follow the Lord, since you have pondered with a religious mind how to repay the Lord for all the things he himself has given you and you have disposed yourself humbly to imitate Christ, who made himself *obedient* for you *unto death, even to the death of the cross*; and for love of him you are going to leave your beloved wife, your sweet children, your delightful fatherland, dear relatives, copious riches and worldly honours, so that in the end by denying yourself, together with your fleshly desires, you may the more freely follow him. You wish, we have heard, to carry your cross and you are girding yourself to hurry with a burning desire to the place where your salvation hung on the cross, so as to place yourself under the banner of the victorious cross to oppose the endeavours of the perfidious men whom we have already seen banish the Crucified One from part of the cross's heritage and who are striving to expel him altogether. This intention is a very devout one and a heavenly inspiration, because by taking the cross you intend to repay in your turn Christ, who on it bore your *infirmities and carried* your *sorrows*. But, although your devotion is great, this is a very uneven exchange because, apart from the seeming disparity of grace in the redeemed servant bearing for the Lord Redeemer just what the Lord Redeemer bore for the redeemed servant, there is yet much more merit in the gibbet of Christ's cross than in the little sign of your cross: although the glory of the cross is the same, its cost for you and for the Lord is not equivalent. For you accept a soft and gentle cross; he suffered one that was bitter and hard. You bear it superficially on your clothing; he endured his in the reality of his flesh. You sew yours on with linen or silken threads; he was fastened to his with hard, iron nails. Therefore, however much you might be ready to expose yourself to great and hard experiences in the hope of eternal reward, *sufferings* of this kind *are not worthy to be compared with the glory to come that shall be revealed in* you, even when one takes into account the sincerity of your devotion and when one regards the most urgent need of the Holy Land.

We entrust your intention to the Lord and we ask and encourage your nobility most carefully in the Lord Jesus Christ himself to go to the aid of that same land in accordance with his good inspiration, which he is known to have poured into you. You must gird yourself swiftly and prudently in divine service, not knowing what the morrow may bring, and in this way you must strive to serve God, with his help, by directing your attention more zealously to the defence of that land: it is known to be badly in need of your help and that of others of the faithful, placed as it is in dire necessity. We hope that the result may be fully realized in you, in accordance with this kind of pious desire, so that God may not appear to have inspired this plan in you with nothing to show for it and so that you may not appear to have left in vain all the glory as it were of this world, in which you are known to be pre-eminent, for this business. We also send you, as you requested, the sign of the living cross, to be invested by our beloved son Nicholas, prior of the house of St John of the Carthusian Order. We are sending, nevertheless, the indulgence for which you asked by letters carried by bearers.

19 Pope Innocent II and Pope Alexander III expatiate on the crusaders' love of their neighbours

Love of neighbour as an expression of Christian charity was a theme in crusading propaganda. It nearly always took the form of love shown for brothers oppressed by pagans, rarely – an exception is to be found in a sermon of James of Vitry **(9)** – love of enemy, even though necessary love of enemies was stressed in the writings of contemporary theologians. The extract translated here from Innocent II's charter to the Templars cited the famous description of neighbourly love in John xv, 13, and the passage from Alexander III's encyclical *Inter omnia* also contained references to the crusade as an expression of love of God, who, as St Bernard had written **(20)**, was putting Christians to the test.

i Innocent II to the Templars (*Omne datum optimum*), 29 March 1139

Source: R. Hiestand, *Papsturkunden für Templer und Johanniter* (Göttingen, 1972), pp. 205–6

Every best gift and every perfect gift is from above, coming down from the

Father of lights, with whom there is no change nor shadow of alteration. And so, beloved sons in the Lord, we praise almighty God because of you and for you, since your Order and venerable institution is famous throughout the whole world. For *by nature* you were *children of wrath*, given up to the pleasures of the world, but now through the inspiration of grace you have become receptive to the message of the gospel and, having left behind worldly pomps and your own possessions and also *the broad way that leadeth to* death, you have humbly chosen the hard road that *leadeth to life*; and to prove it you have most conscientiously worn on your breasts the sign of the living cross, because you are especially reckoned to be members of the knighthood of God. In addition to this, like true Israelites and warriors most versed in holy battle, on fire with the flame of true charity, you carry out in your deeds the words of the gospel, in which it is said: *Greater love than this no man hath, that a man lay down his life for his friends.* And, following the command of the chief shepherd, you are not at all afraid to lay down your lives for your brothers and to defend them from the pagans' invasions and, as you are known by name to be knights of the Temple, you have been established by the Lord as defenders of the Church and assailants of the enemies of Christ. But although with endeavour and praiseworthy devotion you are toiling with all your hearts and all your minds in so sacred an undertaking, nevertheless we exhort all the members of your Order in the Lord and we enjoin both you and those serving you for the remission of sins, by the authority of God and Blessed Peter the Prince of the Apostles, to labour intrepidly, calling upon the name of Christ, to protect the Catholic Church and, by fighting the enemies of the cross, to rid that part of the Church which is under the tyranny of the pagans from their filth.

ii Alexander III to the Christian faithful (*Inter omnia*), 29 July 1169

Source: Pope Alexander III, 'Opera Omnia', *PL* CC, cols. 559–600

Among all the means in the course of temporal affairs which divine wisdom has disposed for the exercise of charity, it is not easy for us to think of anything in which that charity may be exercised more gloriously in terms of virtue and more fruitfully in terms of rewards than the relief of the eastern Church and the Christian faithful and so their defence against the onslaught of the pagans, in order that the worship of the divine name should not cease in those parts and that all should praise the resplendence of the strength of brotherhood. Since it depends entirely upon the nod of celestial goodness whether the works of the faithful are destroyed or the ferocity of the barbarians is repressed, for the moment God is pretending that he does not hear the groans of those who call on him and he allows brothers to be afflicted in the sight of their brothers, so that he may see if there be *any that understand and seek God* and whether the image of divine piety is to be found stamped on anyone's soul. For if the creator of men and of angels *bowed* his *heavens and came down* and did not despise to undergo the gibbet of the cross for the salvation of a useless servant, it is now the case *that* he *also who* lives *may not now* live *to* himself *but unto him who died* for us *and rose again*, he who *hath delivered himself for us, a sacrifice to God for an odour of sweetness*. The Christian faithful have toiled often and hard for the defence of that land and by much shedding of their blood have managed to preserve in that place the cult of the Christian faith through the favour of divine grace. When long ago, moreover, the land had fallen under the power of the Saracens because of the people's sins, men of virtue rose up, brought the land back to the faith of Christ after wiping out or routing the heathen and, after setting up the standard of faith there, returned to Christendom the Lord's Sepulchre, which was famous because much frequented by the people. But now, because this land is seen to have been de-populated, worn down by constant troubles and weakened by the variable outcomes of wars, so that if brotherly love does not help her she fears the most extreme danger, she asks again for the usual aid from the western regions; and through our venerable brothers the archbishop of Tyre and the bishop of Banyas and our beloved sons Gilbert, commander of the Hospital, and the nobleman Arnulf of Landast, she humbly begs you, with our encouragement, as though God were exhorting you through us, to bring her aid. She hopes that she will gain the kind of result from the present help that she does not believe she would receive through the efforts of any other peoples. She is aware that the most extreme dangers threaten her if the aid of brotherly love is taken away or delayed. She appears to be at a turning point, whence either her enemies will gain such great strength that she will not be able to resist invasion or the power of the Christians will be so invigorated that each man will sit in peace beneath his tree and your posterity will be able to rest in peace, with no demands for help. And so, terrified by so great a danger and at the same time excited by the prospect of so great a service, we warn and exhort all of you in the Lord and we enjoin you for the remission of sins, out of love for him who in that land wished to bring about the salvation of all men, by being born there, by dying and by rising again, to gird yourselves manfully to come to his aid; and you who are prepared to go personally – I am aware that others have offered their money – do not allow anything to delay you but do your best to put yourselves at risk for the salvation of your brothers, so that the land which is known to have been acquired to the glory of the Christian name by the shedding of so much of your fathers' blood may by your labour and industry be conserved and fortified effectively.

20 In two of his letters St Bernard treats crusading as a meritorious act that will lead to salvation

The letters St Bernard wrote when he was in charge of the preaching of the Second Crusade are among the most beautiful of all crusade documents. We have translated an extract from one and the whole of another. They are full of optimism and joy and present the crusade as a test put by God before laymen, an opportunity for them to set aside considerations of this world and gain merit and the indulgence.

i St Bernard to the eastern Franks and the Bavarians, 1146

Source: Bernard of Clairvaux, 'Epistolae', *PL* CLXXXII, cols. 565–7

Strong men, what are you doing? Servants of the cross, what are you doing? By your delay will you not give a thing which is holy to dogs and cast pearls before swine? How many sinners have obtained forgiveness in Jerusalem, confessing their sins with tears, after the filth of the pagans was banished by your fathers' swords! The wicked man sees and begrudges the fact; he gnashes his *teeth and* pines *away*. He stirs up the vessels of his iniquity and will leave no single sign or trace of such devotion if, which God forbid, he ever manages to reoccupy that holy of holies. This really would be an inconsolable sorrow to all succeeding ages, because it would be a loss that could never be recovered; but it would be a boundless cause of shame to this ungodly generation in particular and an eternal disgrace.

But what is in our minds, brothers? Has the hand of the Lord been shortened or has it been made powerless to save, just because he has called poor little worms to guard his inheritance and restore it to him? Can he not send *more than twelve legions of angels* or simply say the word and the land will be set free? It is completely within his power to do so when he wishes it. But I say to you that the Lord is putting you to the test. He is looking down on the children of men, to see if there be any that understand and seek him and grieve over his plight. For the Lord has pity on his people and is providing a saving remedy for the gravely fallen. Consider how much skill he uses to save you and be astonished. Look at the depth of his love and trust him, sinners. He does not desire your death, but that you should turn from your way and live, because this is his way of offering you a favourable opportunity, not of destruction but of salvation. For what is this other than a most excellent chance, and one that is within your reach, of the salvation that God alone can give? For the almighty has deigned to summon to serve him murderers, robbers, adulterers, perjurers and those involved in other crimes, *just as a nation that hath done justice*. Do not despair, sinners: the Lord is kind. If he wanted to punish you he would not seek your service in any way nor would he even accept your offer of it. I repeat that you ought to consider the riches of the most high God and listen to the counsel of his mercy. He puts himself into a position of necessity, or pretends to be in one, while all the time he wants to help you in your need. He wants to be thought of as the debtor, so that he can award to those fighting for him wages: the remission of their sins and everlasting glory. It is because of this that I have called you a blessed generation, you who have been caught up in a time so rich in remission and are found living in this year so pleasing to the Lord, truly a year of jubilee. This blessing is poured out on the whole world and all are hurrying eagerly to the sign of life.

The whole world praises you and the renown of your strength has gone to the ends of the earth, because there is an abundance of strong men in your land and it is known to be full of vigorous young men. So gird yourselves manfully and take up arms joyfully with zeal for the Christian name. You should not desist from your earlier militarism, but you should desist altogether from your malice, with which you are accustomed to kill one another, destroying one another in such a way that you are bringing one another to ruin. What mad desire drives these miserable men to run through their neighbours' bodies with swords? Their souls might perish in the process. But the man who glories over an act of this sort will not escape: a sword will pass through his soul just at the moment when he is rejoicing over killing his enemy. It is not strength, it is insanity to surrender oneself to such a risk; and it is not to be ascribed to boldness, but rather to madness. But now, strong soldier and man of war, you have a battle you can fight without danger; in which to win will be glorious and to die will be gain. If you are a prudent merchant, if you are a man fond of acquiring this world's goods, I am showing you certain great markets; make sure not to let the chance pass you by. Take the sign of the cross and you will obtain in equal measure remission of all the sins which you have confessed with a contrite heart. If the cloth itself is sold, it does not fetch much; if it is worn on a faithful shoulder it is certain to be worth the kingdom of God. Those who have already taken the heavenly sign have done well; and the rest will do well and will not be acting foolishly if they hurry to seize what is also there for their salvation.

ii St Bernard to the duke and people of Bohemia, 1147

Source: Bernard of Clairvaux, 'Epistolae', *PL* CLXXXII, cols. 652–4

I have something to say to you about the business of Christ, in which lies true salvation. I hope that the authority of the Lord, the consideration of how useful it will be to you and our charitable intention will plead with you as an excuse for the unworthiness of the person who writes this. I am a very ordinary man, but I am not ordinary in my desire for *you all in the bowels of Jesus Christ*. I am urged by this zeal to write to you what I would prefer to try to inscribe in your hearts with my voice and I would do that if I had the means: the spirit is willing but the flesh is weak; the corruptible body cannot be controlled by the desires of the soul, nor can earthly bulk keep pace with the swiftness of the spirit. But the part of me about which I have been complaining is not with you; the part which will be of more use to you, my heart, is brought straight to you, in spite of the distance which separates our burdensome bodies. And so I want you all to hear the good word, to hear the word of salvation and to embrace with your souls the wealth of indulgence offered to devout men. This age is like no other that has gone before; a new abundance of divine mercy comes down from heaven; blessed are those who are alive in this year pleasing to the Lord, this year of remission, this year of veritable jubilee. I tell you, the Lord has not done this for any other generation before, nor has he lavished on our fathers a gift of grace so copious. Look at the skill he is using to save you. Consider the depth of his love and be astonished, sinners. He creates a need – he either creates it or pretends to have it – while he comes from heaven to help you in your necessity. This is a plan not made by man, but proceeding from the heart of divine love.

The earth has been shaken and has trembled, because the Lord has caused his land to lose territory. His land, I repeat, where he was seen and in which he lived among men for more than 30 years. His land, which he honoured by his birth, embellished by his miracles, consecrated with his blood and enriched by his burial. His land, in which the voice of the turtle-dove was heard when the Son of the Virgin praised the life of chastity. His land, where the first flowers of his resurrection appeared. Evil men have begun to occupy this land of the new promise and unless someone resists them they will be feasting their eyes upon the sanctuary of our religion and will try to stain that very bed, on which for our sake slept our life in death; they will profane the Holy Places, the places, I say, purpled with the blood of the immaculate lamb.

I have something else to say which ought to move a Christian man's

97

heart, however hard it is. Our king is accused of treachery; it is said of him that he is not God, but that he falsely pretended to be something he was not. Any man among you who is his vassal ought to rise up to defend his lord from the infamous accusation of treachery; he should go to the sure fight, where to win will be glorious and where to die will be gain.

Why are you delaying, servants of the cross, why are you deceiving yourselves, you who have great physical strength and many worldly goods? Take the sign of the cross and the supreme pontiff, the vicar of him to whom it was said, *Whatsoever thou shalt loose on earth, it shall be loosed also in heaven*, offers you this full indulgence of all the crimes you confess with contrite hearts. Take the gift that is offered to you and race one another to be the first to take advantage of the irrecoverable opportunity of the indulgence. I ask you and advise you not to want to put your own business before the business of Christ, nor to leave undone a duty, which you cannot take up again later, for the sake of those things which could or can be done at other times. And listen to a few more words to learn when, by what means and how you ought to go. The army of the Lord will set out next Easter and a large section of it has resolved to go through Hungary. It has also been laid down **(5)** that no one should wear multi-coloured clothing or minivers or silken garments. The crusaders must not attach anything of silver or gold to the horses' trappings, but only to the shields and the wood of the saddles used; when they march out to battle those who want to wear gold or silver may do so, so that the sun may shine upon them and fear may melt the courage of the pagans. I would have expanded further on this matter and gone into it in more depth if you did not have with you the lord bishop of Moravia, a holy and learned man. We want him to be asked to take care to encourage all of you most diligently about this, according to the wisdom given him by the Lord. We have also sent a copy of the lord pope's letter **(5)**: you ought to listen to his appeal very attentively and obey his orders.

21 Nivelo announces that as a crusader he is going on pilgrimage to Jerusalem to expiate his crimes, *c.*1096

This charter illustrates better than most the feelings of guilt aroused in the eleventh-century knightly class by the preaching of the First Crusade. But it is also an example of the way in which crusaders approached religious houses for money for their journey, and in the phrase 'peregre proficiscenti ad Jerusalem' it witnesses to the fact that the crusade was regarded even before its departure as a pilgrimage, although this element may not have been as pronounced as it was to become.

Source: Cartulaire de l'abbaye de Saint-Père de Chartres, ed. B. E. C. Guérard (Paris, 1840) II, pp. 428–9

Anyone who is the recipient of pardon through the grace of heavenly atonement and who wants to be more completely freed from the burden of his sins, whose weight oppresses the soul of the sinner and prevents it from flying up to heaven, must look to end his sins before they abandon him. And so I Nivelo, raised in a nobility of birth which produces in many people an ignobility of mind, for the redemption of my soul and in exchange for a great sum of money given me for this, renounce for ever in favour of St Peter the oppressive behaviour resulting from a certain bad custom, handed on to me not by ancient right but from the time of my father, a man of little weight who first harassed the poor with this oppression. Thereafter I constantly maintained it in an atrociously tyrannical manner. I had harshly worn down the land of St Peter, that is to say Emprainville and the places around it, in the way that had become customary, by seizing the goods of the inhabitants there. This was the rough nature of this custom. Whenever the onset of knightly ferocity stirred me up, I used to descend on the aforesaid village, taking with me a troop of my knights and a crowd of my attendants, and against nature I would make over the goods of the men of St Peter for food for my knights.

And so since, in order to obtain the pardon for my crimes which God can give me, I am going on pilgrimage to Jerusalem which until now has been enslaved with her sons, the monks have given me 10 pounds in *denarii* towards the expenses of the appointed journey, in return for giving up this oppression; and they have given 3 pounds to my sister, called Comitissa, the wife of Hugh, viscount of Châteaudun, in return for her consent; 40 *solidi* to Hamelin my brother; with the agreement of my son Urso and my other relatives, whose names are written below. If in the course of time one of my descendants is tempted to break the strength of this concession and is convicted of such an act by the witnesses named below, may he, transfixed by the thunderbolt of anathema, be placed in the fires of hell with Dathan and Abiram, to be tormented endlessly. And so, to reinforce my confirmation of this, I make the sign of the cross with my own hand and I pass the document over to my son called Urso and my other relatives and witnesses for them to confirm by making their signs. And everyone ought to note that I make satisfaction to St Peter for such abominable past injuries and that I will forever desist from causing this restless trouble, which is now stilled.

22 Pope Alexander III grants the fully developed indulgence (*Cor nostrum*), 16 January 1181

The first recognizable indulgence for Christian fighters was granted by Pope Alexander II in 1063. Urban II gave an indulgence to the first crusaders, but it is not at all clear what he intended by it, since sometimes he seemed to exempt the faithful only from the performance of penances imposed by priests in the confessionals **(1, 2 ii)** and sometimes he seemed to go further, referring to the remission of sins rather than of penances **(2 i, 2 iv)**. Ordinary Christians were convinced from the start that an indulgence remitted all the penalties imposed by God for sin, but the Church did not make up its mind for over 80 years. St Bernard **(20)** and Pope Eugenius III **(5)** went quite a long way towards meeting the aspirations of the faithful, but the final decision seems to have been made by Alexander III. His first two crusade encyclicals followed the line taken by Eugenius, but this may have worried the pope's advisers, because in the bull *Inter omnia* of 1169 the indulgence was defined merely as 'that remission of penance imposed by the priestly ministry'. Over the next 12 years the curia made up its mind. *Cor nostrum*, from which the extract translated here is taken, was modelled partly on *Inter omnia*, but now the indulgence granted was wide and it stands at the head of a long line of unequivocal definitions of the indulgence as a remission of all or part of the punishment imposed by God in this world or the next. The terminology was not yet precise: the developed *formulae* appeared in the indulgences of Pope Innocent III **(15, 26, 27, 34)**.

Source: Alexander III, 'Opera Omnia', *PL* CC, col. 1296

Trusting in the love of Jesus Christ and the authority of the blessed apostles Peter and Paul, we give to those military men, who are fit to defend the Holy Land and go to those Holy Places with the fervour of devotion and fight there for two years against the Saracens in defence of the Christian name, absolution from all their crimes of which they make confession with contrite and humble hearts, unless perhaps they have stolen the goods of others or extorted interest or committed thefts, in which cases they ought to restore all goods to their former owners; even if it is not in their power to correct their offences, they will still get their remission as we have said, for the sins they have committed. Those who stay in the East for a year may obtain, as we have said, indulgence of half the penance enjoined on them and remission of their sins. We allow all those willing to visit the Lord's Sepulchre with the intention of answering to the present need, whether they die on the journey or reach that place, to count the toil of this journey as penance and an act of obedience to the Church and for the remission of all sins, so that they may leave the penitentiary of this present life for that blessedness, if the Lord grants it, which *eye hath not seen, nor ear heard; neither hath it entered into the heart of man* what God has promised to those who love him.

23 Pope Gregory VIII accords the Church's protection to the crusader Hinco of Žerotjn, 21 October–17 December 1187

Like pilgrims, crusaders enjoyed the protection of the Church for themselves, their families and properties. The Church assumed this duty during or soon after the First Crusade, although in some areas, notably thirteenth-century England, the crown also acted as a guardian. The principles of ecclesiastical protection were confirmed by the First Lateran Council in 1123 and the encyclical *Quantum praedecessores* of 1145–6 (5) and they were constantly repeated thereafter.

Source: A. Boček, *Codex diplomaticus et epistolaris Moraviae* (Olmütz, 1836) I, pp. 320–1

In her performance of her office of habitual affection the most holy Roman Church is accustomed to love more readily devout and humble sons and to foster them like a loving mother by defending them with her protection, so that they are not disturbed and harassed by vicious men. Since, therefore, you, fired with the zeal of devotion of faith and having assumed the sign of the life-giving cross, have proposed to go to the aid of the Holy Land, we, agreeing to your just requests with gracious approval, take under the protection of Blessed Peter and ourselves your person together with your family and those goods which at present you possess fairly and we strengthen this with this present letter as a guarantee, establishing that once you have set out overseas in the first general passage appointed by the apostolic see these should all remain undiminished and united until your return or death is most certainly known.

24 St Bernard treats the soldier of Christ as a potential martyr, comparing him to the old, selfish knight, 1128–37

The treatise 'De laude novae militiae' was composed for the Templars, but what St Bernard wrote here applied with equal validity to crusaders. Written between the Council of Troyes of 13 January 1128 and the death on 24 May 1136 or 1137 of Hugh of Payns, the first

Master and perhaps a relative of Bernard's – probably after 1130 because Bernard wrote that Hugh had asked him for the treatise three times since the council had met – it is an evocation of the glories of the new knighthood and of martyrdom.

Source: Bernard of Clairvaux, 'De laude novae militiae', *Sancti Bernardi Opera*, ed. J. Leclercq *et al.* (Rome, 1963) III, pp. 214–15

The knight who puts the breastplate of faith on his soul in the same way as he puts a breastplate of iron on his body is truly intrepid and safe from everything. Undoubtedly defended by both kinds of armour he fears neither demon nor man. And a man who desires death surely cannot dread it. What in fact is there to fear for the man, whether he is living or dying, for whom to live is Christ and for whom it is gain to die? He remains in this world faithfully and willingly for Christ; but his greater desire is to be dissolved and to be with Christ; this in fact is better. And so go forward in safety, knights, and with undaunted souls drive off the enemies of the cross of Christ, certain that neither death nor life can separate you from the love of God which is in Christ Jesus, repeating to yourselves in every peril, *Whether we live or whether we die, we are the Lord's.* How glorious are the victors who return from battle! How blessed are the martyrs who die in battle! Rejoice, courageous athlete, if you live and conquer in the Lord, but exult and glory the more if you die and are joined to the Lord. Life indeed is fruitful and victory glorious, but according to holy law death is better than either of these things. For if those are *blessed who die in the Lord*, how much more blessed are those who die for the Lord?

Indeed, whether a man dies in bed or in battle, no doubt the death of his saints will be precious in God's sight; but if in battle certainly his death will be that much more precious because that much more glorious. Oh, a life is free from care where there is a pure conscience! Oh, I say, a life is free from care where death is looked forward to without fear and indeed is desired with sweetness and is accepted with devotion! Oh, this is a truly holy and secure knighthood and it is certainly free from that double peril which often and habitually endangers one sort of man, in so far as he fights for some other cause than Christ. For how often do you who fight the knighthood of the world come to grips with a most dread situation, in which either you may kill the enemy in body while in fact killing your own soul, or by chance you may be killed by him and die in body and soul simultaneously. To be sure, it is not from the accident of war but from the disposition of the heart that either peril or victory is allotted to the Christian. If the cause for a fight is good, evil cannot result from the fight, just as an end cannot be judged to have been good where the cause was not good and where it was not preceded by right intention. If it happens that when you want to kill another man you are killed yourself, you will die a homicide. And if you prevail and when you want to overcome and have revenge upon another man you happen to kill him, you will live a homicide. It is not profitable to be a homicide, whether in death or life, whether in victory or defeat. Unhappy victory by which, overcoming man, you succumb to vice and, ruled by anger or pride, you glory vainly over the man you have overcome. There is also the man who kills another not out of zeal for revenge nor out of pride of conquest but rather as a means of escaping from him; but I would not have said that even this was a good victory, since of the two evils it is less serious for the body to die than the soul. The soul, however, does not die because the body is killed, but *the soul that sinneth, the same shall die.*

D Apologetics

25 Humbert of Romans answers critics of the crusades to the East, *c.*1272–4

Humbert of Romans, who had been Master General of the Dominican Order and the author of *De praedicatione crucis*, a treatise on crusade preaching, wrote the 'Opus tripartitum' at the request, direct or indirect, of Pope Gregory X before the Second Council of Lyons met in 1274. The passage in which he replied to objections to crusading to the East provides important evidence for the kinds of criticism then being put forward. Fundamental criticism of crusading certainly existed, but it is important to add that it was much less widespread, even in the later thirteenth century, than is often believed. Humbert's arguments ought also to be studied for the positive points he made in defence of crusading. His apologia would certainly not convince anyone today, but in the context of the time it was a closely argued *tour de force*, written by one of the most experienced crusade preachers. In it the ideological appeal of crusading was restated and it culminated in a magnificent passage on the importance of man's resignation to the mysterious workings of divine providence.

Source: Humbert of Romans, 'Opus tripartitum', ed. E. Brown, *Fasciculus rerum expetendarum et fugiendarum* (London, 1690) II, pp. 191–8

There are seven kinds of men who condemn the action the Church is taking against the Saracens.

There are some men given over to leisure who avoid all labour for

Christ and are in the habit of condemning the measures the Church has undertaken against the Saracens, like people, to use Jerome's words, who always pass judgements on everything and can think of nothing to do themselves. These people are like those spies who disparaged the task of gaining the Promised Land and frightened the people and therefore were destroyed in the desert. And they are also like the scribes and pharisees, of whom it is said, *Woe to you, scribes and pharisees, hypocrites,* who *shut the kingdom of heaven against men: for you yourselves do not enter in, and those that are going in, you suffer not to enter.* By this attitude of opposition, these people are, in fact, holding back many from the road which leads to heaven, that is to say the holy pilgrimage, and are causing them to stay behind with them, sharing their own idleness. There are also, which is worse, men like the heretics, who are always making great mockery of people going on and returning from and suffering misfortune on this kind of pilgrimage, through which false prophets, as it is written, *the way of truth shall be evil spoken of.* This *way* is the way of the holy pilgrimage against the Saracens, which is truly good and of which these people speak evil.

The reply to the first kind of condemnation:
There are some of these critics who say that it is not in accordance with the Christian religion to shed blood in this way, even that of wicked infidels. For Christ did not act thus; rather, *When he suffered, he threatened not, but delivered himself to him that judged him unjustly,* as Peter says. Nor did Christ teach this, but he said to Peter when the latter wanted to defend him, *Put up thy sword into the scabbard.* The apostles did not act in this way; indeed *they went from the presence of the council rejoicing that they* were *worthy to suffer reproach for the name of Jesus.* They did not even teach this doctrine. On this subject Paul says to the Romans, *Revenge not yourselves, my dearly beloved.* How much more ought you not to launch attacks? And Peter says, *Not rendering evil for evil, nor railing for railing, but contrariwise, blessing.* The holy martyrs did not act in this way either, for Maurice with his whole legion of soldiers did not resist his murderers. In the same manner countless other martyrs also died; indeed they even ran to martyrdom and were put to death for God's sake and were *counted as sheep for the slaughter.* The saints of old did not teach this either. Jerome says, 'A man who lives according to the flesh will persecute a spiritual man, but in fact a spiritual man will never persecute a carnal man'. And there are countless authorities – holy writers and popes and councils – by which these wars seem to be condemned, as is clear in Gratian's *Causa XXIII* in many places. One should conclude, therefore, that the

Christian religion, which ought to adhere to the example and teaching of Christ and the saints, ought not to initiate wars of any kind whatsoever, through which so much blood may be shed.

When replying to a condemnation of this kind it ought to be noted that sometimes in human affairs something is brought into existence and at other times it is kept in being. For instance, a vineyard planted by a householder grows as it should with the help of the dew and the rain and the warmth of heaven, but if perhaps enemies were to desire to root it up, it is preserved by the sword. Sometimes, moreover, a man is weak in what he does, sometimes he is strong. And he gets along when he is weak by behaving humbly, but when he is strong by behaving sternly. In the same way every workman works with the tool he has, not one he does not possess; and when he lacks a particular implement, he uses whatever is to hand. Christianity operates in the same way. It is promoted by the miracles and sufferings of the saints and holy teaching and not by any earthly power, lest its advance be attributed to man rather than to divine force alone. But once what has been promoted in this way is established it must be defended when necessary from its enemies by the sword. In its primitive state the Lord had not yet given it earthly authority nor had he subjected the powers of the world to it as he did afterwards and so then it functioned like a weak man. But afterwards it advanced like a powerful man by exercising earthly power. For what purpose had divine providence given it secular power if God did not wish it to use it? Otherwise it would bear the *sword in vain*, contrary to the words of St Paul to the Romans. And so, just as then it did not have earthly power, but miracles and *diverse kinds of tongues* and the Holy Spirit teaching all things, of which it then made use, so now it does not have those things, but it has earthly power. Since it is without those things, it uses what it has, that is to say earthly power, just as the workman uses the implement to hand. Therefore I beseech those critics to consider that they themselves are not willing to be poor, as Christians were in the early Church, but they want to be rich; nor lowly, as Christians were then, but to be held in honour; nor in want of food, as Christians were then, but to live in luxury. And since these matters have changed in a way that suits them and they do not declare that there is anything wrong with them, they should not be displeased by the change that has resulted in the use of arms by the Christian religion for the benefit of the faith.

The fact that Christianity can and ought to use arms against infidels and evil-doers is clear in countless arguments to be found in many writings. For who is so stupid as to dare to say that, were infidels or evil men to desire to kill every Christian and to wipe out the worship of Christ from the world, one ought not to resist them? Did not the Maccabees decide to fight on the sabbath day against the enemies who would attack them from then on, although this might seem to have been against the law? This is also clear in the teaching of the saints, much of which is contained in *Causa XXIII*, and it is clear in the teaching of Christ himself, who says, *He that hath* no sword, *let him sell his coat and buy a sword*; according to *The Gloss* this means that sometimes Christians must use the sword. But in answer to the points made in opposition by those critics, to what extent can it really be proved that the Christian religion is now in an entirely similar state to that of the early Church? Because as time has passed and in different circumstances Christianity has been in different states, just as a boy grows through various states before he reaches old age. Similarly, the Church then was poor, but now she is rich – and there are many instances like this – so now she uses arms, but then she did not.

Indeed, in answer to the first point made by the critics, one ought to say this much in explanation of teaching: that what the Lord said to Peter, *Put up again thy sword* etc., applied to Peter on that particular occasion, for the time had not yet come to use the sword. These words, moreover, were applied to him as a person, for, although the Church has the sword, not every one of its members has the right to use it: just as in a man it is not every limb, but only the hand, that wields the sword, so in the body of the Church only lay persons may use the sword. One ought to say about the other idea contained in the teaching of the apostles that these things were said in the context of that time. If, on the other hand, they are applicable in all ages, it is to be understood that those actions must not be performed with a heart bent on revenge or with any other evil intention or in any other irregular manner. Augustine says on this subject when writing against the Manichees: 'The desire to give hurt, the cruelty of vengeance, the spirit that will not be appeased, the savagery of rebellion, the lust for power and any similar things are the aspects of war which are rightly condemned.' One should answer the point raised about what is contained in the teaching of the saints and councils in this way: that everything they say can be explained in the way I have mentioned before or in some other way. And so it must be held without doubt that it is not inconsistent with the Christian religion to wage war according to circumstances against Saracens, extremely wicked men and particular enemies of Christendom.

The reply to the second kind of condemnation:
There are others who say that although one ought not to spare Saracen blood one must, however, be sparing of Christian blood and deaths. It

is true that on this sort of pilgrimage against the Saracens countless people die, sometimes from sickness at sea, sometimes in battle, sometimes from a lack or excess of food; not only the common people, but also kings and princes and persons who do great service to Christianity. How much harm was done through the death of King Louis, whose life was so beneficial to the Church of God, and through the deaths of many others! Is it wisdom to put at risk in this way so many and such great men of ours, to expose so many to death for the sake of killing Saracens and thus to empty Christendom of so many and such good people? At the end of the Book of Judges the elders of Israel say: *We must use all care, and provide with great* counsel *that one tribe be not destroyed out of Israel.* Why should we not similarly provide with Christian wisdom against the deaths of such a great host of Christians?

I would reply that those who speak like this can only be considering contemporary or recent events. I do not know by what hidden judgement of his God has allowed in our times misfortunes to happen frequently to the Christians who have gone on pilgrimage against the Saracens, just as once the sons of Benjamin killed 22,000 of the children of Israel in one battle and 27,000 in another, although the children of Israel were fighting against the tribe of Benjamin on the express command of the Lord, as is said in Judges xx. But if those critics had read the ancient histories perhaps they would speak differently. For one reads that Charles Martel, going to the aid of the duke of Aquitaine, killed 370,000 Saracens who came against him with very little loss of his own men. One also reads that when Jerusalem was captured in the time of Godfrey of Bouillon the Christians rampaged so uncontrollably against the Saracens that at Solomon's Porch the blood of the slain came up to the horses' knees. Who could, moreover, count how many Saracens the army of Charlemagne killed in Spain? Charles himself attacked Spain twice to liberate it from the grip of the Saracens after Blessed James, whose votary he was, had appeared to him in a vision asking him to do this and summoning him to this task. So I beseech all men like them to read and meditate on the chronicles and various histories and they will find, as they consider the facts about the wars fought in our times between Christians and Saracens, that the outcomes of these events were not disasters that ought to be blamed on the sins of modern Christians, but successes in which many more Saracens were killed by the Christians than vice versa. And so it is not true when they say that the numbers in Christendom are diminished by the Saracens, but rather it is the case that the numbers of Saracens are diminished by the Christians.

Besides, if the Christians had not fought the Saracens, those same Saracens, who once held Sicily and Sardinia and Spain and many coastal places, would have done to countless Christians what they once did to the city of Genoa, a very populous and fine city. They sailed there from Africa with their fleets and not only sacked it, but also killed nearly all its inhabitants. Indeed they have an insatiable thirst for Christian blood. The fact that Christians cross their borders and invade their lands, although at much risk to their own lives, means that Christian blood is spared, blood which the Saracens would spill much more abundantly if the Christians were not to do this. If those critics, moreover, consider it foolish for Christians to risk their lives in this way, arguing that through these actions Christendom may lose useful people, they should also consider to be stupid what the glorious martyrs of old did as they hurried to martyrdom, because by these acts too Christendom was similarly emptied of such great and so many men. And if there is so much fear over the scarcity of people in Christendom, why then Christians ought to be reproached on the subject of virginity and every one ought to be forced to marry in order to increase the number of Christians. But the aim of Christianity is not to fill the earth but to fill heaven. Why should one worry if the number of Christians is lessened in the world by deaths endured for God? By this kind of death people make their way to heaven who perhaps would never reach it by another road.

The reply to the third kind of condemnation:
There are others who say that when our men go overseas to fight the Saracens the conditions of war are much worse for our side, for we are very few there in comparison to their great numbers. We are, moreover, on alien territory, while they are on their own ground; we are in a climate foreign to us, while they are in one to which they are accustomed; we must eat many kinds of food strange to us, while they are used to their diet; they are familiar with dangerous passes and hiding-places, while we are not; we are often short of supplies there, while they have plenty. And so it looks as though we are putting God to the test or we are showing a great lack of faith when we enter into such a contest. Therefore, since discretion is the most necessary attribute in wars, it seems that Christians ought never to undertake wars of this kind.

I would reply that although using the above arguments, which are concerned with human wisdom, the Saracens are in a better position, considering many other matters, which are concerned with divine wisdom, the Christians have the advantage. For the Christians are fighting for justice: it is this that does much to make them fight well, as can be seen in the contestants. The Saracens, on the other hand, have an unjust cause. Also the Christians have God as their helper, except when their sins prevent it. David said about this: *We will push down our enemies with the horn: and through thy name we will despise them that rise up against us.* Similarly the Christians hope that they have holy angels to aid them, just as Elisha showed to his servant. They have not only the angels, but also the saints, according to what was revealed to Judas Maccabaeus about Onias and Jeremiah. Similarly they have the prayers of the whole of Christendom on their behalf. They have precedents to lend them great strength; for just as *one* of the faithful pursued *after a thousand and two ten thousand,* so a few Christians frequently put a great host of Saracens to flight. We read that after the fall of Jerusalem, when the Saracens had renewed their forces and gathered together a countless host and attacked the Christians, the Christian army, made up of no more than 5,000 horse and 12,000 foot, killed 100,000 Saracens, and 2,000 of them were drowned in the port of Ascalon where they were fleeing. The number of those who perished in the sea and died among the thickets is not known for certain. And many similar instances can be read about in various histories. And anyway, even on the level of human wisdom we have many advantages in waging war against the Saracens. For our men, as everyone knows, are more able and better trained and generally stronger and better equipped with arms. We never encourage them to enter into battle against the Saracens unless they have a king or emperor or well-known prince as commander and lord of the army, each of whom *alone* is *accounted for ten thousand,* as was said of David. The Christians, with such a leader, have never engaged in battle unless they have considered that they have had a likely hope of victory. And so it is not, as those critics suggest, putting God to the test or imprudence to engage in this kind of battle, since according to both divine and human wisdom we are in a better position by far for making war than are the Saracens.

The reply to the fourth kind of condemnation:
There are others who say that, although we have a duty to defend ourselves against the Saracens when they attack us, it does not seem that we ought to attack their lands or their persons when they leave us in peace. It does not seem, moreover, that this can be done without committing an injury.

I would reply that the Saracens are so hostile to Christians that they do not spare them whenever they have a chance of defeating them.

This is why the Christians attack them on their own territory to weaken their power, by means of which they aim to harm Christians whenever they can. If the Christians had not done this, the Saracens would already have overwhelmed almost the whole of Christendom: the Christians could not easily offer resistance to the invaders unless they had first subdued them to a certain extent and had attacked them on their own ground. There is also the fact that in the land which they occupy the worship of Jesus Christ has been driven out and a different one introduced. If all the thorn trees are uprooted in thorny lands so that there may be cultivated lands bearing good fruit, how much more ought we to eradicate those worst of men and throw them out of the lands of God, so that the worship of God may be established in them? Whoever does not resist wickedness to the best of his ability apparently consents to it. How, therefore, can Christians be without fault if they are at peace with the Saracens and do not resist their deeds, which are so evil, especially since the Lord commanded the children of Israel never to make a treaty with the gentiles who lived among them? And so when the Christians attack the Saracens even on their own territory they do so justly and with good reason; in the first place to undermine their strength, by which they overwhelm us when they can; in the second place to banish their filthy practices and establish the worship of God in their lands; in the third place so as not to be a party to their sins by tolerating such great crimes.

It is not against God and apostolic teaching for Saracens to be killed by Christians, because they have a law which forbids them ever to hear Christ spoken of, so that they may never perhaps be converted to him and go over to his service. It is Christ himself who says in Luke xix, *But as for those my enemies, who would not have me reign over them, bring them hither and kill them before me.* For they are the cockle intermingled with the wheat and who would not decide that where there is nothing but cockle it must be entirely uprooted? Do not, Christ says in Matthew, root up the cockle, *lest perhaps you root up the wheat also together with it.* But when it is not mixed in with wheat, as in this case, perhaps it ought to be uprooted. They are also the fig-tree from which there is no hope of bearing fruit, because they do not receive the benefit of dung or anything else to make them bear fruit, since the divine word cannot reach them as they themselves prevent it. And so, if such a fig-tree ought to be cut down, according to the saying, it is obvious that those people ought to be removed from the world. They are also like those most evil men of Sodom, who consented to men abusing their wives as they pleased and did all sorts of other foul deeds, thinking it would be enough for them to wash themselves with water in the morning. If men like these were consumed with heavenly fire, how can we possibly consider that this enemy ought to be spared when it practises just such filthy deeds and allows such things to be done. God, *reducing the cities of the Sodomites and of the Gomorrhites into ashes, condemned them to be overthrown, making them an example to those that should after act wickedly*. Similarly, the beast *that toucheth the mount* shall be stoned to death. So, because those bestial men are touching the mount of the Holy Trinity by blaspheming against it and by often cursing in their Koran all those who believe it in God, surely they deserve to die? Similarly, in the epistle to the Hebrews: *A man making void the law of Moses dieth without any mercy under two or three witnesses: How much more, do you think he deserveth worse punishments, who hath trodden underfoot the Son of God and hath offered an affront to the Spirit of grace?* The Saracens, in fact, do this more than everybody else when they persecute Christ and, sinning against the Holy Spirit, do not allow his grace to reach them: in other words by rejecting his preaching. It is obvious, by these arguments and many others, that they must be removed from this world, not only according to human law but also according to the teaching contained in the gospels and epistles, although in a proper manner in accordance with the Church's authority.

But it must be said in addition to what I have already said about their territories, that the lands the Saracens now hold were in the hands of Christians before the time of Muhammad; they seized the opportunity of taking them away from the Christians and they never had a just cause to occupy them. So when Christians invade the lands in which they live, they are not invading other peoples' territory but rather intending to regain their own. In the time of Godfrey of Bouillon, when Pope Urban had sent an army to the Land of Promise, our people recovered it: the land had once belonged to the Jews by the gift of God and had passed to the Christians on their conversion. Saladin in particular and other Saracens later violently took most of it away from us. It is quite clear from this that as far as that land is concerned we have a perfect right to it. And even if we had no right to their lands they should still be taken away from them, because of the fault they are committing and have committed against the Lord of all the earth, as the saints say, and especially Augustine, quoting these phrases from the gospel: *The Kingdom of God shall be taken from you and shall be given to a nation yielding the fruits thereof*; and this one: 'The just shall consume the works of the unjust'; and this one: 'All things belong to the just', in *Causa XXIII*, quaestio 7, chapters 1–3. So it is clear that as long as there are no truces we are not, as those critics vainly think, injuring the Saracens with respect to their lands or their persons by invading their lands and attacking their persons.

The reply to the fifth kind of condemnation:
There are others who say that, if we ought to rid the world of the Saracens, why do we not do the same to the Jews and why do we not treat the Saracens who are our subjects in the same way? Why do we not proceed with the same zeal against any other idolaters who still exist in the world? Why do we not mete out similar treatment to the Tartars and barbarian nations of this kind who are all infidels?

I would reply that, as far as the Jews are concerned, it has been prophesied that in the end the remnant of them will be converted; as far as the conversion of the Saracens is concerned, no one has any reason to expect it, according to the judgement of hell, because no man can reach them to preach the gospel to them. Again, the Jews are so abject, because they are in our power and are our servants and cannot molest us as the Saracens do. Also, if they were removed from the world, what the scriptures say about their rejection would not be so clearly apparent as it is now; and so their existence is an aid to our faith. Therefore they must be tolerated because there is hope that they may be converted, just as one does not immediately cut down a tree from which there is still hope of fruit; because of the fact that we must take care that we are not cruel, and we would be acting very cruelly if we were to kill people subject to us when they were not rising up against us; and because of the help their existence gives to the Christian faith, all of which factors are absent as far as the Saracens are concerned. The same reasons for forbearance apply to the Saracens who are subject to us. For they, whether they like it or not, can be forced to listen to preaching, by which some are sometimes converted. And so there is not such a great reason for despair concerning them as there is concerning the other Saracens outside Christendom. They do not trouble us and they cannot trouble us in the way the other Saracens can. Also they are a help to us, at least in temporal things, because they pay tribute and give us aid in war and perform many other services for their lords. And so, as long as they do not stage a rebellion or commit any other outrage against Christians, they are to be tolerated like the Jews. One ought to add that there is still hope that the idolaters living in the northern regions – the Prussians and their like – can be converted, as were many of their neighbours such as the Poles, the Danes, the Saxons, the Bohemians and many others, who were converted a long time after the apostles. They are not accustomed, moreover, to make war on us, nor are they much able to do so. One must also say the same thing about the Tartars, the Cumans and other barbarians, as far as the hope of converting them goes, since it has been prophesied that every tongue shall serve the Lord Jesus Christ. Moreover, they are very far away from us, especially the

Tartars, and between them and us lie our enemies, that is to say the Saracens. And neither the Tartars nor the Cumans have fixed dwelling-places in which they can be found. And so it would be stupid to try to attack them in such far-flung regions and in places where we would not be sure of finding them and with our enemies stationed in the lands that lie in between. And so it is enough for Christians to defend themselves manfully against them when they attack them.

The reply to the sixth kind of condemnation:
Other people are asking, what is the point of this attack on the Saracens? For they are not roused to conversion by it but rather are stirred up against the Christian faith. When we are victorious and have killed them, moreover, we send them to hell, which seems to be against the law of charity. Also when we gain their lands we do not occupy them like colonists, because our countrymen do not want to stay in those regions, and so there seem to be no spiritual, corporeal or temporal fruits from this sort of attack.

I would reply that, just as honour is due to a king when he has at his disposal a great army to launch against his enemies whenever he wishes, so is honour due to Jesus Christ, the King of Kings, when he has at his disposal the Christian army, ever ready to attack those enemies of his cross. And in that fight the faithful amass for themselves the merits of good works and acquire indulgences for themselves through which they are absolved from their sins. And when we get possession of the lands of the Saracens the filthy practices of their damnable worship are driven out and the true veneration of God, the Holy Trinity, Jesus Christ and his saints is introduced in them. And this is spiritually fruitful in three ways: it leads to the honour of God, the salvation of Christians and the extension of the Church in so far as God is more worshipped. The Saracens, moreover, bear such malice towards Christians that they would have killed all Christians everywhere, just as they have done in many places, if they had not been prevented by the resistance of the Christians. So just as a worthy knight invades his enemy's personal property to prevent him from rampaging over his own ground, so in this instance do the Christians. Also the Saracens are so proud that, thrusting themselves everywhere in days of old, they wanted to subject the whole world to themselves, just as Nebuchadnezzar, king of the Assyrians, planned to subject the whole universe to his sway, as is told in the Book of Judith. But because we are prepared for their invasion and even attack them ourselves they are forced down from their position of pride and humiliated in their very selves on account of the boldness and power of the Christians. Also it usually happens that when any knight allows any other knight to abuse him everyone feels the more emboldened against him. But when he defends himself manfully and crushes the other man everyone fears him the more. In the same way, when the Christians make a spirited attack on the Saracens it causes them to be feared the more, not only by the Saracens themselves, but also by the Tartars and other enemies of Christianity, who would otherwise have attacked them the more boldly. And so it will be corporeally fruitful in three ways: the Saracens will be restrained through the death of our men, they will be dismayed and the hearts of all the enemies of the Christian faith will be struck with fear. And when we happen to gain their lands we will win great spoil into the bargain and the produce of those lands will come to us from then on; and the Saracens themselves, when they are spared, will remain our slaves and tributaries and will be very useful in many ways to their overlords. So it will be temporally fruitful in three ways. And so this kind of attack is not, as those critics say, without any fruitfulness, but rather great fruitfulness, spiritual, corporeal and also temporal, frequently follows from it.

The argument which is put forward concerning the conversion of the Saracens must be answered thus: that although an attack on them may not be able to produce an immediate result of this kind directly it can, however, produce the other spiritual fruits I have mentioned before; and the Saracens may even be brought to conversion indirectly by being scourged, just as men are sometimes taught by illnesses and are forced to come to a greater knowledge of themselves. It follows from this that it is possible that if the Saracens were well shaken they would not place so much trust in their Muhammad. In reply to the point made about sending them to hell, it should be said that it is not the Christians' intention to do this but to deal with them, as is just, like a judge dealing with a thief. May they see for themselves where they are going when they leave this world. Nevertheless divine providence treats them kindly, because it is better for them to die sooner rather than later on account of their sins which increase as long as they live. Augustine says about the children of Sodom that it would have been better for the same reason for them to have died than to have lived long. In answer to the other point one should say that, although we do not have people at the moment who can inhabit the lands which have been gained, it is to be hoped that in a little while Christians will go there in numbers for various reasons, if they become overlords in those lands. When our men held strongholds, moreover, the Saracens themselves and many Greeks and others of that kind remained willingly under our dominion and cultivated the lands and were our tributaries; and the same is true of the Greeks in Achaea. And in this situation there was more hope that those Saracens who were under our rule would be converted more quickly than their fellow Saracens.

The reply to the seventh kind of condemnation:
Others say that it does not appear to be God's will that Christians should proceed against Saracens in this way, because of the misfortunes which God has allowed and is still allowing to happen to the Christians engaged in this business. For how could God have allowed Saladin to retake from us almost at a blow nearly all the land which had been won with so much Christian blood and toil; and the Emperor Frederick to perish in shallow water as he hurried to bring it aid; and King Louis of happy memory to be captured in Egypt with his brothers and almost the entire nobility of France; and, when he had started out afresh on this business, to die with his son when he had reached Tunis; and then when their remaining ships were withdrawing, so many of them to be wrecked in a storm off Sicily; and so great an army to have achieved nothing, and countless other such events, if this kind of proceeding had been pleasing to him?

I would reply that it should be said that people who speak like this do not understand at all well how God acts. For there is no place in this world for divine reward in the sense of good being always rendered here for good by the Lord or evil for evil, but quite the reverse. Just as he causes the sun of his prosperity to rise on the good and the evil alike, so adversities here fall not only on the evil but also on the good. It is said in Ecclesiastes: *There are just men to whom evils happen, as though they had done the works of the wicked: and there are wicked men who are as secure as though they had the deeds of the just.* Not only do trials befall good and evil men alike; no, sometimes, what is more extraordinary, they befall more frequently the good rather than the evil. For it is written about the wicked, *They spend their days in wealth* etc., but about the good it is said, *All that have pleased God, passed through many tribulations, remaining faithful.* And this is not only true of the adversities sent by God, but also of those inflicted by man. It is said in Habakkuk: *the wicked prevaileth against the just.* It is on this account that one reads that the Egyptians afflicted the Israelites; the king of the Assyrians carried away 10 tribes beyond the Caspian mountains; the king of Babylon took off two tribes in captivity to Babylon. And so it is clear from these examples that the misfortunes that befall some people are not a sign that their deeds displease God, but rather they are signs of the reverse, since in this world calamities befall more often those who do good than those who do evil. Besides, who could count how many and how great are the men, even great men and saints, over whom the devil has triumphed? Should it be said because of this that it does not please God that we should still fight against the devil or that the battles already waged against him have not pleased God? We read in the Book of Judges that in the first battle the sons of Benjamin killed 22,000 of the 300,000 of the children of Israel who had gone out against the tribe of Benjamin on the advice of the Lord to avenge the crime committed against the Levite's wife; but in the second, when the Israelites returned to the fight according to the will and with the advice of the same Lord, they killed 27,000. Did that misfortune happen as a sign that the hostile encounter of the children of Israel with the tribe of Benjamin did not please the Lord, when the Lord himself had advised and ordered it? We also read that in the fight which the children of Israel began against the Philistines, Israel was defeated and even the Ark of God was taken. And in another place we read that Saul, the first king of Israel, and Jonathan his son and the strong men of Israel were overcome by the Philistines and were killed in the mountains of Gilboa. Ought it to be said because of those misfortunes that those wars of Israel were not pleasing to God, when the Lord had ordered the children of Israel to attack those gentiles and never to enter into a treaty with them? Those critics ought to be silent and they should know that the Lord sometimes allows misfortunes of this kind to befall our countrymen not for the reason they ascribe to them – that this kind of action against the Saracens is displeasing to him – but for various other reasons.

It would help us to understand this if we took note of the fact that sometimes these misfortunes happen to our men on account of our sins. For our sins have deserved whatever we suffer, as the judgement of Judith says: Let us esteem *these punishments to be* what *our sins deserve.* She said this when the Israelites were besieged by Holofernes and had come to the final straits, for they had no water. Sometimes misfortunes befall us for our good so that we deserve more not only through our good deeds but also through our suffering, like the martyrs and other saints, who both did good deeds and suffered for justice's sake. For we have it on authority that this is the life of the saints, to do good and suffer evil. They say that when King Louis of good memory was captured by the Saracens he boasted greatly about it, saying that he would be able to reply to the Lord, who would say on the Day of Judgement that he had been ill-treated for our sake, that he himself had been captured and ill-treated for Christ's sake, just as Christ had been for him. But sometimes misfortunes occur because we are incautious and rash, as happened to Judas Maccabaeus who, although he had only 800 men with him and his companions tried to dissuade him, wanted to fight against 20,000 warriors and 2,000 horse and said, *God forbid that we should do this thing and flee away from them.* And there are other hidden reasons flowing from the vast depths of the judgements of God, on account of which Habakkuk says: *Why holdest thy peace when the wicked* crushes *the man that is more just than himself?* We ought to consider all of these most just, since they come from God, saying with Daniel, *To thee, Oh Lord, justice: but to us, confusion of face, as at this day.*

But these considerations ought not to give rise to the criticism I mentioned before, but to other good things. One of these is that we should have recourse to God with a cry, as did the children of Israel almost throughout the Book of Judges, where one reads that when they were hard-pressed by their enemies they cried continually to the Lord to send them help; as is sung in the psalm: *And they cried to the Lord in their tribulation.* Another thing is that we should be humble, following the example of the children of Israel, about whom it was said, after they had been defeated the first and second time by the sons of Benjamin, *Wherefore the children of Israel came to the house of God, and sat and wept before the Lord. And they fasted that day till the evening, and offered to him holocausts, and victims of peace offerings* etc. And one should notice that after this they were victorious in the third battle. Another thing is that we should correct evildoers, as was done to Achan: the children of Israel stoned him when they discovered that he was the man in the army of the Lord who had stolen something under the ban against the Lord's command and that because of his crime they had been defeated. And another thing is that we should grieve over the abasement of the name of the Lord, as Joshua grieved when the people he had sent against Ai were defeated, about which we read, *Joshua rent his garments, and fell flat on the ground before the Ark of the Lord*; and later, *My Lord, what shall I say, seeing Israel turning their backs to their enemies? The Canaanites will hear of it*; and later, *And what wilt thou do to thy great name?* Another thing is that we should peacefully accept the divine will, as did Judith: *As for us therefore let us not revenge ourselves for these things which we suffer. But esteeming these very punishments to be less than our sins deserve, let us believe that these scourges of the Lord, with which like servants we are chastised, have happened for our amendment, not for our destruction.* And this refers to the most severe siege of Holofernes. Another thing is that we should persevere in good works. For the hammer of this kind of adversity does not usually destroy good men, but instead makes them stand more firmly, as is sung by the psalmist: *All these things have come upon us: yet we have not forgotten thee: and we have not done wickedly in thy covenant. And our heart hath not turned back,* etc.

III The Experience of Crusading

We have chosen texts to illustrate what it was like to take part in a crusade, giving examples of the sources for the various stages in the planning of a crusade and the campaign that followed: proclamation, preaching and recruitment, for which we have taken most of our material from the sources for the Fifth Crusade; an occasional side-effect of preaching, the appearance of peasant bands led by demagogues; the raising of money; the appointment of temporal and spiritual leaders; preparations for departure and the distress it caused; the journey with its regulations for participants en route, its cults and penitential processions; fighting, looting and death.

A Proclamation

26 Pope Innocent III proclaims the Fifth Crusade (*Quia maior*), 19–29 April 1213

During the second half of April and early May 1213 almost all the provinces of Latin Christendom were sent copies of Innocent's greatest crusade encyclical. This justly famous letter marks the apogee of papal crusading propaganda. It contains references to many of the themes we have already encountered – charity, the crusade as a divine test, the Holy Land as Christ's patrimony – together with a list of privileges and prohibitions and liturgical instructions. Included in it is an important new statement on the enforcement of vows. Until Innocent's pontificate the papacy had regularly stressed that crusade vows should only be taken with full deliberation and advice. Innocent, however, while insisting on strict enforcement, had already laid down that he could also grant deferment, commutation (the performance of another penitential act in place of the one originally vowed) and redemption (dispensation in return for a money payment): the amount spent to redeem a vow should equal the sum that would have been spent had the crusader actually departed. The announcement in *Quia maior*, Innocent's advice in a letter to a preacher (28 ii) and the activities of his legates in France at this time, which caused a scandal, revealed a new policy according to which everyone, whatever his or her suitability, was to be encouraged to take the cross; the vows of the unfit could then be redeemed for money payments which would benefit the crusade financially. *Quia maior* also ended temporarily the Spanish and Albigensian crusades. The encyclical was issued in conjunction with a summons to a general council of the Church (the Fourth Lateran Council), because in Innocent's eyes reform and consequent Christian renewal and the success of the crusade were inseparably linked. At the same time the pope established an elaborate system for the preaching of the cross. *Quia maior* was itself, of course, a preaching document and was used as a guide for preachers **(29)**. At least one of them, Abbot Rainer of Rommersdorf in the province of Trier, seems to have carried it around with him. We have translated the copy sent to the province of Mainz.

Source: G. Tangl, *Studien zum Register Innocenz' III* (Weimar, 1929), pp. 88–97

Because at this time there is a more compelling urgency than there has ever been before to help the Holy Land in her great need and because we hope that the aid sent to her will be greater than that which has ever reached her before, listen when, again taking up the old cry, we cry to you. We cry on behalf of him who when dying *cried with a loud voice* on the cross, *becoming obedient* to God the father *unto the death of the cross,* crying out so that he might snatch us from the crucifixion of eternal death. He also cries out with his own voice and says, *If any man will come after me, let him deny himself and take up his cross and follow me,* as if to say, to put it more plainly, 'If anyone wishes to follow me to the crown, let him also follow me to the battle, which is now proposed as a test for all men.' For it was entirely in the power of almighty God, if he had so wished, to prevent that land from being handed over into hostile hands. And if he wishes he can easily free it from the hands of the enemy, since nothing can resist his will. But when already wickedness had gone beyond all bounds and love in the hearts of many men had grown cold, he put this contest before his faithful followers to awaken them from the sleep of death to the pursuit of life, in which he might try their faith *as gold in the furnace.* He has granted them an opportunity to win salvation, nay more, a means of salvation, so that those who fight faithfully for him will be crowned in happiness by him, but those who refuse to pay him the servant's service that they owe him in a crisis of such great urgency will justly deserve to suffer a sentence of damnation on the Last Day of severe Judgement.

Oh, how much good has already come from this cause! How many men, converted to penance, have delivered themselves up to the service of the Crucified One in order to liberate the Holy Land and have won a crown of glory as if they had suffered the agony of martyrdom, men who perhaps might have died in their wicked ways, ensnared in carnal pleasures and worldly enticements! This is the ancient device of Jesus Christ, which he has deigned to renew in these times for the salvation of his faithful. For if any temporal king is thrown out of his kingdom by his enemies, when he regains his lost kingdom surely he will condemn his vassals as faithless men and for these bad men will devise unimagined torments, with which he will bring them to a bad end, unless they risk for him not only their possessions but also their persons? In just such a way will the King of Kings, the Lord Jesus Christ, who bestowed on you body and soul and all the other good things you have, condemn you for the vice of ingratitude and the crime of infidelity if you fail to come to his aid when he has been, as it were, thrown out of his kingdom, which he purchased with the price of his blood. So you must know that anyone who fails to serve his Redeemer in this hour of need is blameworthily severe and severely to be blamed.

For how can a man be said to love his neighbour as himself, in obedience to God's command, when, knowing that his brothers, who are Christians in faith and in name, are held in the hands of the perfidious Saracens in dire imprisonment and are weighed down by the yoke of most heavy slavery, he does not do something effective to liberate them, thereby transgressing the command of that natural law which the Lord gave in the gospel, *Whatsoever you would that men should do to you, do you also to them*? Or perhaps you do not know that many thousands of Christians are being held in slavery and imprisonment in their hands, tortured by countless torments?

The Christian peoples, in fact, held almost all the Saracen provinces up to the time of Blessed Gregory; but since then a son of perdition has arisen, the false prophet Muhammad, who has seduced many men from the truth by worldly enticements and the pleasures of the flesh. Although his treachery has prevailed up to the present day, we nevertheless put our trust in the Lord who has already given us a sign that good is to come, that the end of this beast is approaching, whose *number*, according to the Revelation of St John, will end in 666 years, of which already nearly 600 have passed. And in addition to the former great and grave injuries which the treacherous Saracens have inflicted on our Redeemer, on account of our offences, the same perfidious Saracens have recently built a fortified stronghold to confound the Christian name on Mount Thabor, where Christ revealed to his disciples a vision of his future glory; by means of this fortress they think they will easily occupy the city of Acre, which is very near them, and then invade the rest of that land without any obstructive resistance, since it is almost entirely devoid of forces or supplies.

So rouse yourselves, most beloved sons, transforming your quarrels and rivalries, brother against brother, into associations of peace and affection; gird yourselves for the service of the Crucified One, not hesitating to risk your possessions and your persons for him who laid down his life and shed his blood for you, equally certain and sure that if you are truly penitent you will achieve eternal rest as a profit from this temporal labour. For we, trusting in the mercy of almighty God and the authority of the blessed apostles Peter and Paul, by that power of binding and loosing that God has conferred on us, although unworthy, grant to all those submitting to this labour personally or at their own expense full forgiveness of their sins, of which they make truthful oral confession with contrite hearts, and as the reward of the just we promise them a greater share of eternal salvation. To those who do not personally campaign, but at least send out suitable men at their own expense according to their means and station in life and similarly to those who go personally although at another's expense we concede full forgiveness of their sins. We also wish and concede that all those who donate a fitting proportion of their goods to the aid of that land should share in this remission of sins, according to the amount of their aid and the depth of their devotion.

We also take under the protection of Blessed Peter and ourselves the persons and goods of those same people from the time they take the cross; in fact they are to remain under the protection of the arch-bishops and the bishops and all the prelates of the Church of God and we decree that these goods are to remain untouched and rest unmolested until it is known for certain whether they have died or have returned home. If anyone dares to defy this he must be restrained by the prelates of the churches with ecclesiastical censure and with no right of appeal.

And if any of those setting out to that place are strictly held by oath to repay usuries we order with the same strictness that their creditors be compelled by the prelates of the churches to refrain from enforcing the oaths that had been made to them and to stop exacting usuries. And if any of their creditors forces them to pay usuries we command him to be compelled by a similar censure to restore them. We command Jews to be compelled by means of the secular power to remit usuries to the same people; and all contact of any kind, whether in commercial dealings or in anything else, with all the Christian faithful should be denied them by sentence of excommunication until they have remitted them.

But so that the aid to the Holy Land may be given more easily if it is shared by many, we beg each and every one of you through the Father and the Son and the Holy Spirit, the one only true, the one eternal God – and we speak as Vicar of Christ for Christ – for an adequate number of fighting men with expenses for three years, to be provided by archbishops and bishops, abbots and priors and chapters, whether of cathedrals or other conventual churches, and all clergy, and also cities, villages and castles, according to their own means. And if there are not enough fighting men for this in any particular company, several groups must be joined together. For we certainly hope that manpower will not be insufficient if the means are not lacking. We ask the same thing from those kings and princes, counts, barons and other magnates, who themselves perhaps are not going personally to the service of the Crucified One. We also demand naval help from maritime cities.

And so that we should not seem to be laying on others *heavy and insupportable burdens* which we are not willing to *move with a finger of our own*, we declare truthfully before God that we ourselves will do with a willing heart what we have demanded others to do.

We give special licence to the clergy for their needs in this business; for this matter and without any contradiction they may pledge the returns of their benefices for up to three years.

Because in fact it would mean that aid to the Holy Land would be much impeded or delayed if before taking the cross each person had to be examined to see whether he was personally fit and able to fulfil a vow of this kind, we concede that anyone who wishes, except persons bound by religious profession, may take the cross in such a way that this vow may be commuted, redeemed or deferred by apostolic mandate when urgent need or evident expediency demands it.

And for the same reason we revoke the remissions and indulgences formerly granted by us to those setting out for Spain against the Moors or against the heretics in Provence, chiefly because these were conceded to them in circumstances which have already entirely passed and for that particular cause which has already for the most part disappeared, for so far affairs in both places have gone well, by the grace of God, so that the immediate use of force is not needed. If perchance it were needed, we would take care to give our attention to any serious situation that arises. We concede, however, that remissions and indulgences of this kind should remain available to the people of Provence and the Spaniards.

And because corsairs and pirates hinder exceedingly aid to the Holy Land by capturing and despoiling those travelling to and from her, we bind them and their principal aiders and abettors with the bond of excommunication, forbidding, under threat of unending anathema, anyone knowingly to communicate with them in any contract of sale or purchase and enjoining the rulers of their cities and districts to call them back and curb them from committing this iniquity. Otherwise we will take pains to show ecclesiastical severity towards their persons and their lands, since such people are turned against the Christian name no less than are the Saracens, and because to be unwilling to confound the wicked is nothing less than to foster them, and a man who openly fails to challenge a malefactor does not escape the suspicion of being in some secret league with him. We renew, moreover, the sentence of excommunication promulgated at the Lateran Council against those who carry weapons, iron and wood for building galleys to the Saracens and who captain the Saracens' pirate vessels, and if these people are captured we judge that they are to be punished by the confiscation of their goods and are to become the slaves of their captors. We order sentence of this kind to be read out publicly each Sunday and feastday in all maritime cities.

We are sure that, since we ought to put much more trust in divine mercy than in human power, we ought to fight in such a conflict not so much with physical arms as with spiritual ones. And so we decree and command that once a month there must be a general procession of men separately and, where it can be done, of women separately, praying with minds and bodies humbly disposed and with devout and fervent prayer, that merciful God will relieve us of this shameful disgrace by liberating from the hands of the pagans that land in which he accomplished the universal sacrament of our redemption and by restoring it to the Christian people to the praise and glory of his holy name; with this wise proviso that during that procession the preaching of the cross which brings salvation should always be offered to the people in a way that is assiduous and encouraging. Fasting and almsgiving should be joined to prayer, so that with these as wings the prayer itself may fly more easily and quickly to the most loving ears of God, who will mercifully listen to us at the appointed time. And every day during the celebration of mass, when the moment has come after the Kiss of Peace when the saving sacrifice is to be offered for the sins of the world or is about to be consumed, everyone, men and women alike, must humbly prostrate themselves on the ground and the psalm *Oh God, the heathens are come into thy inheritance* should be sung loudly by the clergy. When this has been ended reverently with this verse, *Let God arise, and let his enemies be scattered: and let them that hate him flee from before his face*, the priest who is celebrating must chant this prayer over the altar:

> God, who disposes all things with marvellous providence, we humbly beseech thee to snatch from the hands of the enemies of the cross the land which thine only-begotten son consecrated with his own blood and to restore it to Christian worship by mercifully directing in the way of eternal salvation the vows of the faithful here present, made for its liberation, through the same Our Lord etc.

An empty chest must be placed in each church where a general procession gathers. It is to be locked with three keys which are to be looked after faithfully and held, one by an honest priest, another by a devout layman and a third by another religious. The clergy and laity, men and women, should put their alms for the aid of the Holy Land into this chest, to be spent according to the decision of those to whom this concern is entrusted. Nothing ought to be laid down about arranging a fitting place from which the army of the Lord may depart and about its proper and orderly passage and its time of departure until the crusaders have taken the cross. But then, when the circumstances on every side have been taken into consideration, we must decide to take whatever measures seem right with the advice of prudent men.

And so we are committing the task of carrying this out to our beloved sons the abbot of Salem and the former abbot of Neuburg and Conrad the dean of Speyer and the provost of Augsburg, men of entirely proven integrity and faith, who, after they have admitted to their company men of foresight and integrity, must on our authority lay down and determine whatever arrangements they consider advantageous to promote this business. And they must see to it that their decisions are faithfully and carefully carried out in each diocese by suitable men especially appointed for this task. And so we ask, advise and beseech all of you in the Lord, commanding you by means of apostolic letters and enjoining you in the power of the Holy Spirit, to take pains to show them that you are the kind of people through and in whom they may produce the much desired result, supplying them with necessities inasmuch as these men are acting in the office of Christ's legation.

27 Pope Innocent III legislates at the Fourth Lateran Council for the Fifth Crusade (*Ad liberandam*), 30 November 1215

This decree carried further the organization of the Fifth Crusade. It repeated some of the provisions of *Quia maior* (**26**), but it is such an important constitution and was treated by future generations with such respect that we feel justified in including it in its entirety. It will be noticed that it decreed a general tax of a three-year twentieth on clerical incomes. This type of taxation had been instituted by Innocent III in 1199 **(34)**, but that decree had caused so many problems that the pope had refrained from imposing it in 1213.

Source: Conciliorum oecumenicorum decreta, eds. J. Alberigo *et al.* (Basel, 1962), pp. 243–7

We desire with an ardent longing to liberate the Holy Land from the hands of the impious. And so, on the advice of prudent men who know fully the circumstances of time and place and with the approval of the Holy Council, we declare that the crusaders should make preparations so that on the first day of June in the year after next all men who decide to travel across by sea should gather in the kingdom of Sicily; some, according to need and convenience, at Brindisi and others at Messina and at places in the vicinity of both towns. We intend to be there in person on that date, God willing, so that the Christian army which is about to set out with divine and apostolic blessing may be organized to its advantage by our counsel and aid. Those who propose to go by land should also take care to prepare themselves within the same time-limits.

In the meantime they should let us know of their plans so that we may give them a suitable legate *a latere* to counsel and help them. Priests and other clerics in the Christian army, whether subordinates or prelates, should devote themselves conscientiously to prayer and exhortation, teaching the crusaders both by word and example, so that they may always have before their eyes the fear and love of God lest they say or do anything which might offend the divine majesty. And if the crusaders should ever lapse into sin, may they soon recover through penitence, being humble in heart and body, observing moderation in food and clothing, completely avoiding quarrels and envy, utterly banishing rancour and anger, so that, armed in this way with spiritual and material weapons, they may do battle with the enemy the more secure in faith, not presuming on their own power, but trusting in divine strength. We permit these clerics to enjoy their benefices in full for three years and, if they are resident in churches and it is necessary for them to do so, they can pledge their benefices for the same term.

Lest anything should occur to impede or delay this holy design, we strictly command all prelates of the Church, each one in his jurisdiction, to advise conscientiously and persuade those who have laid down the sign of the cross to take it up again and to see that these men as well as other crusaders and those who have hitherto taken the cross fulfil their vows to the Lord. If necessary, the prelates should compel them to desist from any subterfuge by excommunication of their persons or sentences of interdict upon their lands, those only excepted who are so hampered by some impediment that this would result in their vows being commuted or deferred with reason, as has been laid down by the apostolic see.

In addition, lest anything be omitted in those matters that touch upon the business of Jesus Christ, we wish and order patriarchs, arch-bishops, bishops, abbots and others who have the cure of souls to preach studiously the cross to those committed to their care. They must entreat kings, dukes, princes, marquises, counts and barons and other magnates, together with the communities of cities, towns and castles, through the Father and the Son and the Holy Spirit, the one only true and eternal God, to see to it that those who cannot go personally to the aid of the Holy Land contribute an adequate number of soldiers with their necessary expenses for three years, according to their means and for the remission of their sins. This has been expressed in the encyclical and is also expressed below for greater security. We wish not only those who provide their own ships, but also those who take the trouble to build ships for this work to benefit from this remission of sins. But to those men who refuse to take part, if indeed there be perchance any men so ungrateful to the Lord our God, we firmly state on behalf of the apostle Peter that they should know that they will have to answer to us on this matter in the presence of the Dreadful Judge on the Last Day of severe Judgement. They should first consider whether they can make their confessions with clear consciences or any assurance of salvation in the presence of Jesus Christ, the only begotten son of God whose *father* has *given all things into his hands,* if they have refused to serve him who was crucified for their sins in this enterprise which is, as it were, particularly his own: it is by his gift that they live, by his maintenance that they are sustained and by his blood that they have been redeemed.

So that we should not seem to be laying on *men's shoulders heavy and insupportable burdens* which we are not willing *to move with a finger of our own,* like men who talk but do nothing, be it known that we concede and give 30,000 pounds to this undertaking from those moneys that we can set aside after necessary and moderate expenses, besides the ship which we grant to crusaders from Rome and its neighbourhood. We assign to the ship 3,000 silver marks, left in our hands from the alms of some of the faithful; the rest of these alms has been distributed in a trustworthy manner for the needs and use of the Holy Land by the abbot of happy memory, the patriarch of Jerusalem, and the masters of the Temple and the Hospital. Desiring that other prelates of churches and also all of the clergy shall participate and share both in the merit and in the reward of this undertaking, and with the approval of the General Council, we decree that absolutely all the clergy, whether subordinates or prelates, should give a twentieth part of ecclesiastical income for three years for the aid of the Holy Land into the hands of those who are entrusted with this task by apostolic foresight, excepting only some religious who have rightly earned release from this said tax, and similarly those who are going in person, having taken or taking the sign of the cross. On the other hand, we and our brothers the cardinals of the holy Roman Church will pay a full tithe. All should recognize that they are bound to observe this duty faithfully under sentence of excommunication, which will be incurred by those who knowingly commit some fraud in this matter.

Because it is seemly that those who persevere in obeying the just judgement of the heavenly emperor should enjoy a special right, when the campaign lasts for rather more than a year the crusaders are to be immune from taxes or tallages and other burdens. Once they have assumed the cross we take their persons and goods under the protection of Blessed Peter and ourselves and we decree that they are to be under the protection of the archbishops, the bishops and all the prelates of the Church, even should they have appointed their own protectors specifically for this task, so that their goods are to remain untouched and unmolested until it is known for certain whether they have died or have returned home. And anyone who dares to defy this must be restrained by ecclesiastical censure. If any of those setting out to that place are strictly held by oath to repay usuries, we order with the same strictness that their creditors be compelled to refrain from enforcing the oaths that had been made to them and to desist from exacting usuries. And if any of their creditors forces them to pay the usuries, we command him to be compelled by a similar censure to restore them. And we command Jews to be compelled by means of the secular power to remit usuries; all contact of any kind with all the Christian faithful should be denied them by sentence of excommunication until they have remitted them. Secular princes ought to provide a suitable delay to those who cannot at present pay their debts to Jews, so that after hasty departures they do not incur the disadvantages of usurious debts until it is known most certainly whether they have died or have returned home. The Jews must be made to keep accounts of the yields of the securities they have received in the meantime, after the deduction of necessary expenses according to the capital lent, provided that property pledged in this way is seen not to have too many expenses, which defer payment in such a way that the debt is not repaid. Henceforth prelates of the Church who show themselves to be negligent in giving justice to crusaders and their families should understand that they will be gravely punished.

In addition, because corsairs and pirates hinder exceedingly aid to the Holy Land by capturing and despoiling those travelling to and from her, we bind their particular aiders and abettors with the bond of excommunication, forbidding, under threat of unending anathema, anyone knowingly to communicate with them in any contract of sale or purchase and enjoining the rulers of their cities and districts to call them back and curb them from committing this iniquity. Otherwise we wish and order the prelates of churches to show ecclesiastical severity towards their persons and lands, because to be unwilling to confound the wicked is nothing less than to foster them, and a man who openly fails to challenge a malefactor does not escape the suspicion of being in some secret league with him. And we excommunicate and anathematize those false and impious Christians who carry weapons, iron and wood for building galleys to the Saracens, against the interests of Christ himself and the Christian people; and we judge that those also who sell galleys or ships to the Saracens and who captain pirate vessels for them or give them any counsel or aid in the matter of siege engines or anything else whatever are to be punished by the confiscation of their own goods and are to become the slaves of their captors. We order sentence of this kind to be read out publicly each Sunday and feastday in all maritime cities. To such people the bosom of the Church will not be opened unless they send all such damned property that they have taken and an equivalent amount of their own for the aid of the Holy Land, so that they are punished by a penalty equal to their crime. And in cases in which such people are not in the position to pay, let them be so chastised by another charge that by their punishment others will be prevented from presuming to similar audacity. We prohibit and forbid, moreover, under pain of anathema, all Christians to send or sail their ships to the lands of the Saracens who live in eastern parts for the next four years. This should result in a great many ships being prepared to transport those willing to go to the assistance of the Holy Land and in the withdrawal of the aid which the Saracens have usually received from this traffic; it has not been insignificant. Although tournaments have been prohibited generally in several councils with fixed penalties, we firmly forbid them to be held for three years under pain of excommunication, because at this time they are greatly hindering the business of the cross.

Because it is of the greatest necessity for the fulfilment of this undertaking that the princes of Christian people keep peace with one another, we decree, on the recommendation of the Holy Universal Synod, that peace should be generally observed throughout the whole

Christian world for at least four years, in such a way that by the agency of prelates of churches discords are resolved into unbroken peace or into the inviolable observance of steadfast truces. Those who perhaps treat this order with scorn should be most firmly compelled to acquiesce by the excommunication of their persons and the laying of interdicts on their lands, unless the malice of the injuries they commit is so great that they themselves ought not to enjoy the peace mentioned above. And those who happen to hold ecclesiastical censure in little esteem can fear, not without reason, that by the authority of the Church secular power may be brought in against them as people obstructing the business of the Crucified One.

And so we, trusting in the mercy of almighty God and the authority of the blessed apostles Peter and Paul, by that power of binding and loosing that God has conferred upon us, although unworthy, grant to all those submitting to the labour personally or at their own expense full forgiveness of their sins, of which they freely make oral confession with contrite hearts, and as the reward of the just we promise them a greater share of eternal salvation. To those who do not personally campaign, but at least send out suitable men at their own expense according to their means and station in life and similarly to those who go personally although at another's expense we concede full forgiveness of their sins. We also wish and concede that all should share in this remission of sins who, according to the quality of their aid and the depth of their devotion, donate a fitting proportion of their goods to the aid of the Holy Land or lend suitable counsel and aid. And to all setting forth piously on this common work the Universal Synod imparts the aid of all its good works, so that it may worthily help them to salvation.

B Preaching and Recruitment

28 Three letters from Pope Innocent III to preachers of the Fifth Crusade

At the same time as he issued *Quia maior* (26) Innocent III introduced an elaborate system for the preaching of the cross. He personally oversaw the preaching in Italy; every bishop in Hungary was to preach the crusade; in Latin Syria and Palestine James of Vitry, the new bishop of Acre and one of the great preachers of the day, was to recruit crusaders; in Denmark and Sweden the legate, the archbishop of Lund, was to be assisted by the bishop of Uppsala; and in France another legate, first Robert of Courçon and later Archbishop Simon of Tyre, was to be in charge. But elsewhere for every province of

Christendom the pope appointed small groups of preachers, many of them bishops, with legatine powers in this matter, who could delegate the task of recruitment to deputies in each diocese. The first of the letters translated here was addressed to all the provincial preachers and contained further instructions for them. Our copy was sent to the four preachers in the province of Mainz whom we have already met in *Quia maior*. The second letter, to one of these men, the dean of Speyer, is the most interesting, because the dean had asked for guidance on some of the most difficult problems faced by the preachers of the Fifth Crusade. The pope stressed that the Albigensian Crusade, which in *Quia maior* had been demoted, no longer ranked with the crusade to Jerusalem. He repeated a point he had already made in the decretal *Ex multa* of 1201: that men might freely make and fulfil the vow to crusade without their wives' consent. This radically altered existing canon law, denying wives what canonists had assumed to be their natural right, and commentators on canon law, while never questioning the validity of this exception, were always to be uncomfortable with it. The third issue on which the dean had required clarification was also an Innocentian introduction, the new policy on the commutation, redemption and deferment of vows stated in *Quia maior*. We have omitted from our translation of this letter a passage on the jurisdictional rights of preachers, which is also to be found in the third letter, addressed to the bishop of Regensburg, a preacher in the province of Salzburg. This letter also dealt with a query about the number of mounts Innocent had allowed the preachers to use in the disorderly conditions prevailing after a period of civil war in Germany and with the connected problem of procurations: the charge a preacher could make on the parishes he visited.

i Innocent to the abbot of Salem, the former abbot of Neuburg, the dean of Speyer and the provost of Augsburg, *c.* May 1213

Source: Innocent III, 'Opera Omnia', *PL* CCXVI, col. 822

You can gather plainly from the encyclical the devout and holy plan which with God's inspiration we have conceived to aid the Holy Land for the common welfare and which we are striving to put into effect. And so, since we have the fullest confidence in your sincerity and concern and deem you to be fitted to act in the office of legates for Christ in this matter, we appeal to your devotion and we beg and beseech you in the Lord, strictly commanding you through apostolic letters and enjoining you for the remission of sins to be aflame with zeal for the Christian faith and to carry the message of the cross through the province of Mainz, humble in heart and bearing. And you must faithfully vindicate the injury of the Crucified One himself and must pass on with great care and attention to detail exactly what is contained in the encyclical, transmitting carefully and effectively everything you will see has been included in that letter for the aid of the Holy Land, which we wish you to note most carefully. So that you should show by your actions that you bear in your hearts the wounds of Jesus Christ, we strictly order you to deny yourselves all financial rewards: you must not accept anything from anyone but food and other necessities and even these you must take moderately and modestly; and each of you must have no more than four mounts and six attendants at the most. You must be careful to watch your behaviour and appearance in these and other matters, so that people will find in you no fault that might be taken as a cause of offence against the gospel entrusted to you. You must promote the cause of Christ with such zeal and vigilance that you will share in the many and great benefits we believe will result from it. If, on the other hand, anything is offered to you for the aid of the Holy Land, have it deposited carefully in some religious house with the intention of telling us at the end of the year how your concern has advanced and prospered, so that we will be able to see how you have made progress among the persons and in the matters involved in this salutary business. We ought to reply to you, telling you of our good pleasure and instructing you on how to proceed in future.

ii Innocent to Conrad, dean of Speyer, 9 September 1213

Source: Innocent III, 'Opera Omnia', *PL* CCXVI, cols. 904–5

Because you appear, according to the word of the apostle, not to *be highminded, but fear*, realizing your own imperfections with the prophet, but on the other hand trusting in him who, giving abundantly to all and not reproaching them, makes *the tongue of the* stammering fluent, and because you have humbly undertaken the office enjoined on you of encouraging the people and you have assiduously striven to fulfil it, God commends your discretion to us and, since you are going about this business in a praiseworthy manner, he has entrusted more to you. Therefore we have most kindly taken into consideration your questions and our reply is that those who have taken the sign of the cross and have proposed to set out against the heretics in Provence and have not yet translated their intention into action must be diligently persuaded to take up the labour of the journey to Jerusalem, because this is an action of greater merit. If perhaps they cannot be persuaded, they must be compelled to carry out the vow they have not yet fulfilled. And we consider that you ought to reply in the following way to those who want to take the sign of the cross although their wives are holding them back; you are doubtful whether you ought to prevent them from carrying out their intention. Since the heavenly king is greater than an earthly king and wives' objections cannot in fact prevent the departure of those called to the army of an earthly king, it is clear that those invited to and wanting to join the army of the highest king should not be prevented by this circumstance, since the bond of marriage is not broken because of this, but the co-habitation of husbands and wives is made subject to the needs of the time; this has to occur in many other instances. You can deduce clearly from the encyclical what you ought to do about women and other persons who have taken the cross and are not suitable or able to fulfil the vow. It states expressly that anyone, except a religious, may take the sign of the cross at will in such a way that when urgent need or evident expediency demands it that vow may be commuted or redeemed or deferred by apostolic mandate. And because the Lord has taken your colleague from this world we think that the abbot of Schönau ought to be appointed in his place, according to your request.

iii Innocent to Conrad, Bishop of Regensburg, 10 September 1213

Source: Innocent III, 'Opera Omnia', *PL* CCXVI, cols. 906–7

We rejoice in the Lord and glory in the power of his might, because you have told us to your credit that you are dealing with the business of Christ's cross entrusted to you and that it is progressing well with the co-operation of divine grace. We advise most carefully and encourage your charity to bear in mind heavenly retribution and to follow up the business in such a way that, when you have overcome all difficulties for the name of Christ, you will gather sheaves of joy, with those who *going, went and wept, casting their seeds*. Because we realize that you cannot be content with the number of mounts we have allowed you, seeing that, as you have told us in your letter to us, you would not dare to venture with that number as far as two miles outside your own city on account of the evils of the time, we approve the remedy which your discretion has provided against an impediment of this kind and we command you, brother, in apostolic letters to delegate the task to honest and circumspect men when you cannot personally carry out this business. Consider any decision you reach to be endorsed by our authority. And because we have the greater confidence in the prudence of your wisdom in estimating the number of mounts which seems to you expedient according to the prevailing conditions, both for yourself and for your representatives, we concede to you the free power to act in such a way as the situation will seem to demand, according to the guidelines which you yourself have provided concerning those who pay procurations: that is to say that when you have assembled the people of two or three or even more parishes to hear the word of God, their parish priests must at the same time pay a moderate sum to the preachers of the word of God in those circumstances in which each individual priest does not have enough.

We also allow you to grant the favour of absolution on our authority to incendiaries and those who have laid audacious hands on clergy and other ecclesiastics and then want to take the cross, provided they have made adequate satisfaction for the injuries, unless perhaps the crimes are so serious and enormous that they ought properly to be sent to the apostolic see for consideration. To protect you in this affair, you are allowed, with no right of appeal against you, to punish with ecclesiastical rigour all those of any diocese whatever who rashly invade and disturb the possessions and other goods of your church while you are occupied with this kind of business. And so take pains to show yourself to be wise, careful and discreet in all things, so that through the performance of this task your reputation may grow in the eyes of men and your worth in the eyes of God; and we will bestow on you, brother, ever increasing apostolic grace and favour.

29 In a sermon James of Vitry reminds Christians of their moral duty to take to cross, *c.* 1213–18

This sermon must have been delivered during the period of recruitment for the Fifth Crusade, of which James of Vitry was one of the principal preachers. As Innocent III had urged **(28 i)** it echoed *Quia maior* **(26)**, especially in its use of the image of Christ as a lord who had lost his patrimony and now called on his vassals to fulfil their obligations to him, although it should be noted that James expressly stated that Christians were 'not bound by feudal law' to Christ: as we have already pointed out, churchmen were not happy with the feudal analogy, because a feudal relationship was contractual and involved reciprocal obligations, which was most definitely not the case with man's relationship to God.

Source: James of Vitry, 'Sermones vulgares', pp. 421–2

I saw an angel ascending from the rising of the sun, having the divine sign.
Upon whomsoever you shall see Thau, kill him not.

Only those who groan and sorrow over the abominations done in
Jerusalem are defended from the striker. For a man who has a heart of
earth and does not mourn over the insults to his father does not
deserve mercy. We read in I Kings iv about the priest Eli, that,
although he was bad on another occasion, as soon as he heard that the
Ark of the Lord had been taken he fell from his stool and died from an
excess of sorrow. What of those who are neither moved by sadness
nor seem to care when they hear that the Holy Land is being trodden
underfoot by the enemies of Christ? The Lord says against them in
Haggai i, *My house is desolate and you make haste every man to his own
house.* Today the mistress of the nations has been forced to become a
tribute payer and the enemies of the cross of Christ stretch out
sacrilegious hands to her noblest limb, to her innermost parts, to the
apple of her eye, oppressing the city of our redemption, which is the
mother of our faith; *for the law shall come forth from Zion: and the word of
the Lord from Jerusalem,* in which the Lord wrought salvation in the
middle of the earth: that is to say the place where he gave his *body to the
strikers* and his *cheeks* to his taunters, where he did not turn his face
away from those railing at him and spitting upon him, where he bore
our sins in his body upon the tree. But now she has been made *the
habitation of dragons and the pasture of ostriches* and all the Christians
living in her are enslaved to the Saracens. Is there anyone consumed
by zeal for the house of the Lord? Where are the groans and anxiety of
Mattathias? Where is the strength of the Maccabees? Where is the zeal
and dagger of Phinehas? Where is Ehud's sharpened sword? Where is
Shamgar's ploughshare; and the jawbone of an ass in Samson's hand?

The Lord really has been afflicted by the loss of his patrimony. He
wishes to test his friends and to see whether his vassals are faithful. If
anyone holds a fief of a liege-lord and deserts him when he is attacked
and loses his inheritance, that vassal should rightly be deprived of his
fief. You hold your body, your soul and everything you have from
the highest emperor; today he has had you summoned to hurry to his
aid in battle and, although you are not bound to him by feudal law, he
offers you so many and such great rewards, that is to say the remission
of all your sins, however much penalty and punishment is due, and
eternal life as well, that you ought to hurry to him of your own free
will.

I remember that when I was preaching the cross one day in a certain
church there was a holy man present, a *conversus* of the Cistercian
Order called brother Simon, who often experienced divine revelation

and received the secret counsels of God. When he saw tearful knights leaving wives and children, fatherland and possessions on taking the cross, he besought God to show him what sort of reward the crusaders would receive. Immediately he had a vision of the Blessed Virgin holding her son and the interpretation of this is that she was giving her son to everyone who was receiving the sign of the cross with a contrite heart. And so you ought not to desert your true friend, who did not desert you but gave himself up to death for you.

30 Oliver, scholastic of Cologne, writes to Count Peter and Countess Jolanta of Namur of miraculous appearances during his preaching of the Fifth Crusade, June 1214

Oliver, the scholastic of Cologne and later bishop of Paderborn, was the most successful of the preachers appointed by Innocent III in 1213. In this letter, written to encourage the count of Namur to take the cross, he described signs that had appeared in the sky during his sermons and boasted of the success of recruitment in the province of Cologne. The judges referred to in the last sentence were presumably hearing cases on crusade vows.

Source: Oliver of Paderborn, *Schriften*, ed. H. Hoogeweg (Tübingen, 1894), pp. 285–6

When I was by the Atlantic Ocean in the diocese of Münster of the province of Cologne on the sixth day before Pentecost in the year of grace 1214 and there were with me in obedience to my lord the pope abbots of the Cistercian, Premonstratensian and Cluniac Orders and many other religious, I had the high mass of the Holy Cross sung. The text of my sermon was: *God forbid that I should glory, save in the cross of Our Lord Jesus Christ.* Many thousands of men and women, who had gathered to hear the sermon, were sitting in a meadow outside the Frisian town called Bedum and there was hardly a breath of wind, when from the north there appeared a shining cloud and on it was a white cross with no human figure; next there appeared in the south another cross of the same colour and shape; thirdly a great cross appeared between and above these, of a medium hue, which had on it the form of a human body, so it seemed, as tall as a man, naked, with his head up above and his feet below, his head leaning on his shoulders and his arms not stretched out straight but raised upwards. There were, clearly visible, nails through the hands and feet, which had the same appearance as those portrayed skilfully in a church. Many were hurrying up to take the cross. There was one knight, who until then had refused to do so, but as soon as he had seen one cross, he immediately vowed himself to crusade. One of the local people rushed up to me when he saw this, saying, 'Now the Holy Land has been recovered', as though treating this event as a sure prophecy for the future. As long as the vision lasted, a girl of 11, who had stood up to express her adoration but had been forced to sit down again by the crowd, pointed it out to her mother and grandmother and the many people sitting round her, who were lost in adoration as they looked upwards with great veneration. This vision lasted throughout the length of the whole mass, which took place around the third hour. More than a hundred people saw this miracle.

On a former occasion in another part of that country there appeared a cross without the shape of a human body on it, coloured like a rainbow when viewed against the sun, which was seen by the abbot of Heisterbach and one of his monks and more people than saw the vision at Bedum. Then in another region, at the Frisian port called Dokkum where Blessed Boniface was crowned with martyrdom, a great cross appeared on St Boniface's day [5 June]; there were in that part of the country more than 10,000, so it is believed. The cross was white and it moved a little in the air as if it were being pulled by a cord, as though to show the way to the pilgrims who were about to set sail for the Promised Land between Europe and Africa. In that gathering were counted 50,000 who were affected by these things and took the cross, 8,000 esquires and . . . [lacuna in MS] thousand armed men.

You ought to know that so many ships are being prepared for the expedition of Jesus Christ that we believe that from the province of Cologne alone more than 300 transports are about to set sail, to be filled with fighting men and arms, rations and instruments of war. We have written these things to you because we hope that you have been signed with the cross and have enlisted in the knighthood of Jesus Christ, a step salutary for you and beneficial for the Holy Land. We beseech you urgently to help those who have taken the cross and to be well disposed towards the judges whom we have appointed at Namur.

31 The rite for taking the cross in the Coventry Pontifical, c.1200

The rites for taking the cross developed, as one would expect, out of and as addenda to the ceremonies for blessing pilgrims' insignia; indeed there appears to have been no formal ceremony for the taking of the cross itself until the middle of the twelfth century. The rites varied a good deal from place to place. The one to be found in the Coventry Pontifical, written in an early-thirteenth-century hand, has some unique elements and although it is similar to other English rites, these form a distinct group. It was, however, probably the rite of the English Midlands at the time of the Fifth Crusade and it may have been used when some of those who answered the summons of Pope Innocent III took the cross.

Source: J. A. Brundage, 'Cruce signari: the rite for taking the cross in England', *Traditio* XXII (1966), pp. 306–7

TO BLESS THE PILGRIMS

Hear us, almighty and merciful God, and favourably accompany the journey of thy servants; and, just as thou art everywhere, vouchsafe to be everywhere present so that when they have completed this necessary journey with prosperous passage they may find everyone safe and deliver due thanks to thy name. Through Our Lord Jesus Christ, thy son, who is God, and liveth and reigneth with thee in the unity of the Holy Spirit, world without end.

℞ Amen

HERE HOLY WATER MUST BE SPRINKLED OVER THEM, AND THEN:

Lord, have mercy

℞ Christ, have mercy

Lord, have mercy

Our Father, who art in heaven, hallowed be thy name; thy kingdom come; thy will be done on earth as it is in heaven. Give us this day our daily bread; and forgive us our trespasses, as we forgive them that trespass against us.

℞ And lead us not into temptation, but deliver us from evil. Amen

℣ *I said: Oh Lord, be thou merciful to me.*
℞ *Heal my soul, for I have sinned against thee.*
℣ *Blessed are the undefiled in the way:*
℞ *Who walk in the law of the Lord.*
℣ *May the Lord show you his ways.*
℞ *And teach you his paths.*
℣ *Oh that your paths may be directed*
℞ *To keep the justifications of the Lord.*
℣ *Arise, Oh Lord: Help us.*
℞ *And redeem us for thy name's sake.*
℣ *Hear, Oh Lord, my prayer*
℞ *And let my cry come unto thee.*

The Lord be with you

℞ And with thy spirit

A PRAYER FOLLOWS:

God of infinite mercy and immense majesty, whom neither distance nor time can separate from those whom thou protectest, be at hand for thy servants trusting everywhere in thee, and vouchsafe to be their leader and guide on every journey they undertake. May no misfortune harm them. May no difficulty stand in their way. May everything be beneficial and prosperous for them and may they obtain whatever they ask with just desire of heavenly things through the power of thy right hand. Through Our Lord Jesus Christ, thy son, who is God, and liveth and reigneth with thee in the unity of the Holy Spirit, world without end,

℟ Amen

BLESSING OF THE SCRIP AND PRAYER OVER THE STAFF:

God of invincible might and immense love, who has given thy servants conquering arms, vouchsafe, we beseech thee, to bless this scrip and staff, so that the sign of the venerable cross, the form of which is traced upon them, may be a most invincible source of thy servant's strength. May it be a defence against all the temptations of the ancient enemy on the road, a protection when indoors; and may it be a guard throughout the outward journey and the return. And may he proceed where he desires to go with thy grace. When he has finished his journey may he be worthy to return to his own home with benefit to mind and body. Through Our Lord Jesus Christ, thy son, who is God, and liveth and reigneth with thee in the unity of the Holy Spirit, world without end,

℟ Amen

TO BE SAID WHEN THE SCRIP IS GIVEN:

Receive this scrip, to wear on thy pilgrimage, in the name of the Father and of the Son and of the Holy Spirit.

℟ Amen

TO BE SAID WHEN THE STAFF IS GIVEN:

Receive this staff, to bear thee on the journey of thy pilgrimage in the name of the Father and of the Son and of the Holy Spirit.

℟ Amen

BLESSING OF THE CROSS TO BE GIVEN TO THOSE GOING TO THE HOLY
LAND OR GOING TO ANOTHER LAND TO FIGHT THE ENEMIES OF THE CROSS:
We beseech thee, Lord, holy Father, almighty, eternal God, to
vouchsafe to bless this sign of thy cross, so that it may be to this
thy servant N. an especial means of assistance, a support of faith,
the consummation of his works, the redemption of his soul and
a protection and safeguard against the fierce darts of all his
enemies. Through Our Lord Jesus Christ, thy son, who is God,
and liveth and reigneth with thee in the unity of the Holy Spirit,
world without end.
℟ Amen

TO BE SAID WHEN THE CROSS IS GIVEN
Receive for the remission of thy sins the sign of the holy cross in
the name of Jesus Christ who suffered on the cross for our
redemption, with the help of the same Our Lord Jesus Christ
who with the Father and the Holy Spirit liveth and reigneth God.
℟ Amen

32 Matthew Paris records Thomas of Sherborne's account of the Crusade of the Shepherds, 1251

Popular crusading fervour regularly showed itself in eruptions from
below, outbursts of peasant and artisan piety whipped up by popular
preachers like Peter the Hermit in 1095–6, the Cistercian Radulph in
1146 and Nicholas, the boy preacher of the Children's Crusade, in
1212. One of the most curious of these occured after news had
reached Europe of the failure of King Louis IX's crusade and his
capture by the Egyptians. It developed in northern France, its leader
being a demagogue known as the master of Hungary. Speaking with
great eloquence and carrying in his hands a letter he claimed to have
been given by the Blessed Virgin Mary, he denounced the pride of
French knights and churchmen generally and proclaimed that just as
shepherds had first heard the news of Christ's Nativity, so it was to
them, in their simplicity and humility, that the Holy Land would be
delivered. Gathering an army of the poor, he led them to Amiens,
where they had a rapturous reception. They then went on to Paris,
where they were well received by Queen Blanche, the king's mother
and regent in his absence: in spite of the master of Hungary's eccentric
behaviour the movement was still a peaceful one and the devotion of
the shepherds to the imprisoned king must have appealed to the queen
mother. But in Paris violence broke out, before the shepherds moved
on in several companies. At Rouen, Tours and Orleans the clergy
were violently attacked, and at Bourges, where the master also

preached against the Jews, their fortunes changed. Blanche now outlawed them, and the master, who had murdered a man who had publicly contradicted him, was killed; there were, in fact, conflicting stories about how he died. His movement soon disintegrated.

There is better evidence for the Crusade of the Shepherds than for most of these popular uprisings. Among the sources for it are a letter from a Franciscan in France included in the Annals of Burton (*Annales monastici*, ed. H. R. Luard (London, 1864) I, pp. 290–3) and this account in the *Chronica majora* of Matthew Paris, based on what an English monk, Thomas of Sherborne, who had been held prisoner for eight days by the shepherds, reported in Matthew's hearing in July 1251. Matthew assumed wrongly that the master had been a child preacher of the Children's Crusade.

Source: Matthew Paris, *Chronica majora*, ed. H. R. Luard (London, 1880) V, pp. 246–52

There was a 60-year-old Hungarian, who had been from his earliest years a most evil apostate from the Christian faith. He had drawn most fully all the deceitful devices of sorcery from the sulphureous well of Toledo and had also become a slave and disciple of Muhammad. He had firmly promised the Sultan of Cairo, whose servant he was, to deliver to him a countless number of Christians to be taken captive, so that, with France emptied and bereft of her king, the Saracens would have easier access to Christian climes. And so this imposter, who could speak French, German and Latin, wandered about everywhere preaching without papal authority or the licence of any prelate, falsely claiming that he had received an order from Blessed Mary, the mother of the Lord, to summon shepherds and herdsmen of other animals. He said that heaven had granted them in their humility and simplicity the privilege of recovering the Holy Land from the power of the infidels together with all those enslaved by them; for the pride in arms of the French had not pleased God. His eloquence lent credibility to his words and so did his tightly closed fist, in which he lyingly said that he held a charter and mandate from the Blessed Virgin. And he summoned all sorts of shepherds and they gradually began to follow him, leaving their flocks, herds and studs without asking their lords or relatives and without bothering about what they would eat. He was using, of course, that kind of evil practice which he had employed once before, when about 40 years earlier, while still a beardless youth, he had made a fool of all the French people and had assembled a countless host of little boys, who had followed in his footsteps singing; and what was extraordinary was that neither bars nor bolts could hold them back; nor could the commands of fathers and mothers, soft words or inducements recall them . . .

This scoundrel and all his followers took the cross. There were many who gave them their support and also their help, saying that often *the weak things of the world hath God chosen, that he may confound the strong*, nor does the almighty *take pleasure in the legs of a man*, nor does he accept those who trust in their arms and strength. For this reason Blanche, the regent and queen of the French, hoping that they would take possession of the Holy Land and avenge her sons, gave them her grace and favour. And so their numbers greatly multiplied to such an extent that, mustering a hundred thousand and more, they made themselves military standards and a lamb bearing a flag was drawn on the banner of their master; the lamb as a sign of humility and innocence; the flag with the cross as a sign of victory . . .

And so thieves, exiles, fugitives and excommunicates swarmed to join them, men who were all commonly called rogues in France, and they swelled the very great numbers of the army, so that they now had 500 standards, all resembling the banner of their master and leader. They carried swords, battle-axes, heavy spears, poniards, daggers, so that they looked more and more like worshippers of Mars rather than of Christ; and as they got wilder they had illicit marriages contracted among themselves. And their leaders and masters, who dared to preach although they were only laymen, deviated widely in their preaching from the tenets of the Christian faith and the rules of revealed truth. And if anyone opposed them they savagely attacked him with arms, rather than with reasoned arguments or reference to authorities. And when their supreme leader preached, surrounded on every side by armed men, he severely condemned all orders other than their own conventicles. Most of all he condemned the Dominican and Franciscan friars, calling them vagabonds and hypocrites. He claimed that the monks of the Cistercian Order were very greedy men who loved flocks and lands; that the Benedictines were gluttonous and proud; that the canons lived half in the world and were men who devoured meat; that bishops and their judges only loved money and abounded in every kind of filthy practice. He preached unspeakable abuse about the Roman curia, saying that its members appeared quite plainly to be heretics and schismatics. But when the people heard these ravings, spoken in hatred and contempt of the clergy, they encouraged them and applauded them and, what was very dangerous, gave them a hearing.

On the Feast of St Barnabas [11 June] the shepherds arrived with great display and strength at Orleans and entered the city against the wishes of the bishop and all the clergy but with the assent of the people. And when their leader, as though he were a miracle-working prophet, got a herald to announce that he would preach, although in truth he decreed it more like a tyrant, infinite numbers of people came to him. The bishop of the city was terrified of this deadly danger and forbade under penalty of anathema any cleric to listen to his speeches or follow in his footsteps, declaring that all these things were snares of the devil. But his lay people were already ignoring his threats and orders; and indeed some of his clerics who were scholars, rashly infringing the bounds set by the bishop's prohibition, could not keep themselves from lending wanton ears to such an unheard of novelty; they did not really want to adopt the errors of the shepherds, but only to witness this insolence. For it was novel and ridiculous for a layman, and a common man at that, to spurn the authority of a bishop and preach in public so boldly and in such a great city, in which there was a thriving university of scholars, and move the hearts and ears of so many people in favour of his deceits. Because there were 500 standard-bearers, the wiser clergy hid in their houses, firmly bolting and barring the doors, not without fear of disturbances. And when that master got up to preach in an open square, he began to bellow many unrepeatable abuses, not basing his sermon on any text. Then one of the scholars stood up, boldly walked nearer and burst out as follows: 'Oh most evil heretic and enemy of the truth, your lies be on your own head! You are ensnaring the innocent with your false and deceiving sermons!' He had scarcely finished saying this when one of those vagabonds rushed on him and, raising a beaked axe, split his head in two, battering him to stop him from uttering another word. Then a tumult broke out and those people, whom up to now we have called shepherds but now ought to call imposters and forerunners of Antichrist, leaped up and attacked the clergy of Orleans in every place and rushed armed upon the defenceless; they broke doors and windows and pillaged and burned precious books. And they butchered many and drowned many in the Loire, while the citizens shut their eyes to it and pretended that they did not know what was happening, but really consented to it, because of which they deserve to be called dogs. And they wounded others and despoiled many. When those who were hiding in their houses saw this they fled in a body secretly by night. And so the whole university was thrown into a tumult and it was learned that about 25 clerics perished, not to mention those suffering from wounds and various other kinds of injury. The bishop and his men, moreover, who also hid so as not to be caught up in similar disasters, suffered many abuses and injuries. But the shepherds withdrew, fearing that the citizens might rise up in arms, fall upon them and fight them. The bishop put the city under an interdict, so that he should not be compared to a dog which has lost its bark, because the citizens had behaved in a criminal and infamous way through their connivance, consent and co-operation.

The outcry and complaint about all this reached the ears of Lady Blanche and the magnates, but most of all the bishops. The queen gave a simple answer. 'The Lord knew I believed that they would take possession of all the Holy Land in their simplicity and holiness; but because they are deceivers they must be excommunicated, imprisoned and executed.' And so all those knaves were excommunicated and denounced as such. But before this sentence was publicly announced those deceivers came to Bourges where the city gates were opened to them with the consent of the people in disobedience to the archbishop, who had forbidden it. The greater part of them entered the city and the rest stayed beneath the vineyard walls outside: there were so many of them that no other city could receive them properly and therefore many armies of them went in separate directions through different provinces, so that even Paris suffered the evil effects of them. When the greatest of these deceivers had promised to preach publicly at Bourges and also to perform astounding miracles, a great multitude gathered there from every region to hear things which had never been heard from the beginning of time and to see things which they had never seen before. And as that trickster was making nonsensical assertions and the miracles which he had promised had been found to be frauds, one of the people, a butcher carrying a hatchet, struck him on the head and sent him to hell deprived of his brains; he was stretched out unburied at the crossroads to be gnawed to pieces. And when the rumours had spread that all of them and their abettors and those who had listened to them were going to be excommunicated, they dispersed and like mad dogs were cut down wherever they went.

C Raising and Spending Money

33 The ordinance of the Saladin Tithe in England, 1188

Crusades, especially crusades to the East, were very expensive and the costs were far too heavy for most participants to bear alone. Various official measures for providing finance soon came into existence, among the earliest of which was taxation of their subjects by those kings who intended to crusade themselves. In 1146 King Louis VII demanded an aid from France to raise money for the Second Crusade; and in 1166 and 1185 taxes for the Holy Land, based on assessments of income and movable property, were levied by the kings of France and

England. They were followed over the years by several measures of this kind. The most famous of them was the Saladin Tithe of 1188, levied by King Henry II of England and King Philip II of France after the disastrous news of Saladin's victories in the previous year had reached the West and both kings had taken the cross.

Source: W. Stubbs, *Select charters*, 9th ed., ed. H. W. C. Davis (Oxford, 1913), p. 189.

I   Each person will give this year in alms for the aid of the land of Jerusalem a tenth of his income and movable goods, except for his arms, horses and clothes in the case of a knight; likewise except for his horses, books, clothes, vestments and any sort of church furniture in the case of a cleric; and except for precious stones belonging to both clergy and laity.

II   In each parish this money is to be brought into the presence of the parish priest and the rural dean and one Templar and one Hospitaller and a servant of the lord king and a clerk of the king and a servant of the baron and his clerk and a clerk of the bishop. But first of all excommunication must be pronounced in each parish on behalf of the archbishops, bishops and each rural dean upon anyone who does not lawfully give the appointed tenth in the presence and with the knowledge of those who ought to be there, as has been said. And if anyone gives less than he ought according to their reckoning, four or six law-worthy men must be chosen from the parish and these jurors must assess the amount he ought to have declared; and then he will be obliged to pay in addition the amount he did not pay.

III   But clerics and knights who have taken the cross will give nothing of that tenth, except what they give for their personal property and for their demesne lands; and whatever their men have owed must be collected for the crusaders' enterprise by the men mentioned above and the whole sum rendered to them.

IV   The bishops will write letters and have it announced in every parish of their dioceses on Christmas Day, St Stephen's Day and St John's Day that each parishioner must gather together in his house the appointed tenth by the time of the Feast of the Purification of the Blessed Virgin [2 February] and on the next day and from then on each person must pay it in the presence of the said men at that place to which he has been summoned.

34   Pope Innocent III begins the taxation of the Church for the crusades (*Graves orientalis terrae*), 31 December 1199

The greatest financial contribution to crusading in the thirteenth and fourteenth centuries came from the direct taxation of the Church by the popes, a form of taxation begun by Innocent III in this letter. The fortieth of clerical incomes he asked for on this occasion proved to be very difficult to raise – there was always to be resistance to these taxes – and it was not until 1215 that he decreed another general levy (**27**). But from that time onwards an elaborate system of taxation developed, with papal collectors in more or less continual operation throughout Europe; by 1274 Christendom was divided into 26 districts administered by collectors and sub-collectors. At first the proceeds were paid to local crusaders or were sent directly to the Holy Land, but by 1220 the pope himself was overseeing the transmission of money and it became normal for the yields of the taxes to be paid directly to kings or magnates who had promised to go on crusade.

This copy of the encyclical was sent to the archbishop and clergy of the province of Magdeburg. We have omitted the opening passage, in which the pope gave news of events in the East and explained the needs of the Holy Land, and a final section granting privileges to crusaders.

Source: Innocent III, 'Opera Omnia' *PL* CCXIV, cols. 829–31.

We have been discussing the subject of aid to the Holy Land with our brothers; and because we do not want to appear to *lay heavy burdens* on the *shoulders* of our subjects, which we are not willing to move even *with a finger of* our *own*, only talking but doing very little, we have, with the approval of the bishops and other religious men residing at the apostolic see, arranged that a tenth part of all our revenues in money and in kind is allotted for the aid of the eastern province. We have subtracted not a little from this tenth because of our needs, for which our means are not enough since the present circumstances are more serious than usual and because of this demand heavier expenditure; our intention is to give you, and through you the laity, an example of generosity, following the example of him who *began to do and to teach*, and, although we cannot give anything that is ours, at least to return a little of his own to him who in his mercy has given us everything. And so as to assign necessary aid to the Holy Land in men as well as in goods, we propose to send there our beloved sons the cardinals Soffred, priest of the title of St Praxedis, and Peter, deacon of St Maria in Via Lata, on whom we have already placed the sign of the cross. They will go before the army of the Lord, acting in our stead, so that everyone may have recourse to them as though to one head.

Because we feel very strongly that this is in no way enough, for it is little, really very little, to answer to the so very many needs of that province, we command you all by apostolic letters, and we order each of you strictly under the threat of divine judgement on behalf of God almighty in the strength of the Holy Spirit, to render at least a fortieth part of all his ecclesiastical revenues in money and in kind for the aid of the Holy Land, after deducting the usuries which he cannot avoid paying. We, trusting in the mercy of almighty God and the authority of the blessed apostles Peter and Paul, relax a quarter of the penance imposed on all clergy, both subordinates and prelates, who pay this fortieth willingly and faithfully, as long as they practise no deceit and support the payment with pious devotion. But you should also know that anyone who refuses in so great a need to give such trifling aid to his Creator and Redeemer, from whom he has received body and soul and every good thing he has, is blameworthily severe and severely to be blamed; and we who, although unworthy, act in God's stead on earth can in no way hide the seriousness of this fault. Nor must you in any way believe that we are intending to use this to impose a law on you to your cost, thinking that from now on a fortieth may be exacted from you as if it were a duty or a custom. We do not wish you, moreover, to be damaged in any way on account of this and, grieving that a crisis of such great need has come upon ourselves and you, we pray that a similar crisis will not occur again. Nevertheless, if it is not possible for this aid to be levied in Magdeburg on account of hostility to it or some other obvious impediment, we wish and command you, our brothers the archbishop and bishops in the metropolitan church, to arrange to meet without delay in two or three places in the province of Magdeburg and discuss amongst yourselves the terms of the apostolic mandate concerning the rendering of aid to the Holy Land. After his return each of you should call a council in his diocese immediately and order on our authority the abbots and priors, both of exempt houses and others, archdeacons and deans and the entire clergy living in the diocese to assess their revenues in money and in kind by just reckoning. They must send without delay, within three months of the announcement being made to them, a fortieth part of their value to a suitable place in the same diocese, with the bishop himself and several religious as witnesses; some faithful and discerning laymen must also be summoned as a safeguard. And we order you to do this, our brothers the archbishop and bishops, with the same strictness.

But we exempt from this general rule Cistercian monks, Premonstratensian canons and Grandmontine and Carthusian hermits, to whom we are sending a special injunction on this matter. We do not wish those who take pains to assess their revenues in money and kind diligently to run the risk of transgressing the aforementioned order if perhaps they do not pay the full fortieth through ignorance rather than with full deliberation; but they must pay in full once they have realized that they have paid too little mistakenly. If, God forbid, anyone deliberately withholds any part of the fortieth he owes, he should be completely immune from the penalty for his fault once he has made due satisfaction. No one should be amazed or even disturbed that we have ordered this under such threats, since the greatest necessity demands it; for, although service to God ought to be offered voluntarily, we read in the gospel about the guests at the wedding feast whom the Lord ordered to be forced to enter. We command you, moreover, our brothers the archbishop and bishops, to have the same fortieth urgently exacted and faithfully collected throughout your dioceses, according to the plan mentioned above, to have it deposited in a safe place and to send an account of it all to us as quickly as possible by means of your letters and special envoys.

In addition to all of this we order that an empty trunk be placed in each church, locked with three keys; the first is to be put in the charge of the bishop, the second in the charge of the priest of the church and the third in the charge of some devout laymen. All the faithful should be advised to put their alms in it for the remission of their sins – the amount will depend on what the Lord inspires them to give – and this ought to be publicly and repeatedly announced once a week at mass in all churches, for the remission of sins and especially for the remission of the sins of those who make offerings. We allow you, our brothers the archbishop and bishops, to substitute the gift of alms for the performance of penance imposed on those who are willing to come to the assistance of the Holy Land with their goods, with the advice of men of good judgement who have considered the station in life of the persons involved and the value of the offerings and have also taken into consideration the warmth of their devotion.

In addition to this we want you to summon to your side two brothers, when you can find them, one of the Hospital of Jerusalem and the other of the Knighthood of the Temple, and two other devout laymen and knights of good judgement or other fighting men who have taken the sign of the Lord's cross. If crusaders cannot afford the journey you should make suitable grants to them from the same cash, after receiving a sufficient assurance from them that they will remain to defend the eastern land for a year or more, according to the amount of the grant, and that if, God forbid, they should die on the way, the aid they have received will not be converted to other uses but must rather be made over for the upkeep of fighting men. And when they return they must not be released from the assurance they made until they have shown you letters from the king or patriarch or masters of the Hospital of Jerusalem or the Knighthood of the Temple or our legate giving you evidence of their stay.

Because the critical situation demands and the common good requires the Christian people to hurry to the Holy Land without delay, bringing aid not only in material goods but also in person against the pagans, we order you our brothers, and we command you by means of this apostolic letter, to press on wisely and conscientiously, in person and with the help of other suitable men, with the task of encouraging and persuading the faithful, so that those who are in a position to fight the war of the Lord take the sign of the cross in the name of the Lord of Hosts, while the rest piously donate alms according to their means. For we, trusting in the mercy of God and the authority of the blessed apostles Peter and Paul, by that power of binding and loosing that God has conferred on us, although unworthy, grant all those submitting to the labour of this journey personally and at their own expense full forgiveness of their sins, for which they have repented in their hearts and by word of mouth, and as the reward of the just we promise them a greater share of eternal salvation. To those who do not personally campaign, but only send suitable men to stay there for at least a year at their own expense according to their means and station in life and to those similarly who personally fulfil another's vow to pilgrimage, although at another's expense, we concede full forgiveness of their sins. We also wish all to share in this remission of sins who, according to the amount of their aid and the depth of their devotion, donate a fitting proportion of their goods to the aid of that land.

35 The accounts for part of King Louis IX's first crusade, 1250–3 (copied *c*.1328–50)

Two fourteenth-century fragments, probably dating from the reign of Philip VI (1328–50), contain details of Louis's expenses on his first crusade. The fragment translated here covers three years, from the summer of 1250, after Louis had been released by the Egyptians, to the summer of 1253. Louis was in Palestine during this period; indeed he was not to leave the Holy Land until 24 April 1254. The figures, probably expressed in French *livres parisis*, are not entirely consistent, but the few discrepancies can be attributed to the clerks rounding up fractions.

Source: 'Dépenses de Saint Louis', *Recueil des historiens des Gaules et de la France* (Académie des Inscriptions et Belles-Lettres, Paris, 1855) XXI, pp. 513–15.

These are the costs of King St Louis and the queen while living overseas and expenditure on war and shipping, the king's ransom, building works and the ransoming of captives, as is shown below, for 1,120 days, which is 3 years and 25 days; that is to say from the Octave of the Ascension 1250 to the Octave of the Ascension 1253.

The costs of the household of King St Louis and the queen, while living overseas, and expenditure on war and shipping, from the Octave of the Ascension 1250 to the Octave of the Ascension 1251; for 384 days, which is 1 year and 19 days.

	L.	s.	d.
Costs of food, with the provisions and wages of the men of the household	28,990	15	8
Mantles of knights and clerks	331	5	0
Clothes and furs for the king	228	15	2
Armour and clothes of knights and clerks	9,367	4	2
Gifts of clothes and silver	1,410	15	8
Alms	1,689	16	8
Crossbowmen and sergeants-at-arms of the household	3,507	12	6
For 136 war-horses, pack-horses and mules and 15 camels bought for the household	3,032	10	3
TOTAL SUM of the costs of the household during the aforesaid period	48,558	15	1
Expenditure on war and shipping in the aforesaid period			
Pay of knights serving for wages	50,195	5	9
Gifts and subsidies promised to knights serving for a year without wages	23,213	14	8
Mounted crossbowmen and sergeants	17,170	0	6
Replacements and purchases of war-horses	22,383	5	10
Crossbowmen and sergeants on foot	30,164	12	4

	L.	s.	d.
Carpenters, miners and other labourers	2,010	15	9
Common expenditure (including L.3,914 5s. 2d. for the ransoming of captives)	72,907	3	6
Loans made against wages	2,096	6	4
Payments of cash	402	19	6
Spent on shipping	20,258	16	6
TOTAL SUM for war and shipping during the aforesaid period	240,803	0	8
TOTAL SUM of the costs of the household, war and shipping during the aforesaid period	289,361	15	9
Item, there was paid in this period for the king's ransom	167,102	18	8

Similar expenditure on the household, war and shipping from the Octave of the Ascension 1251 to the Octave of the Ascension 1252, 351 days, in the Holy Land.

	L.	s.	d.
Costs of food	31,595	11	10
Clothes and furs for the king	104	12	9
Mantles for knights and clerks	312	10	0
Armour and clothes for the same	12,910	8	11
Gifts of robes and silver	771	10	0
Alms	1,515	3	9
Crossbowmen and sergeants-at-arms of the household	4,494	6	6
For 115 war-horses, pack-horses and mules bought for the household	1,916	18	11
TOTAL SUM of the costs of the household of the king and queen during the aforesaid period	53,621	2	8

Expenditure on war and shipping during the aforesaid period

	L.	s.	d.
Pay of knights serving for wages	57,093	17	10
Gifts and subsidies promised to knights serving without wages	23,253	18	4
Mounted crossbowmen and sergeants	22,242	13	6
Replacements for 264 war-horses	6,789	17	0

	L.	s.	d.
Crossbowmen and sergeants on foot	29,575	0	6
Carpenters, war-engineers and other labourers	689	12	3
Common expenditure (including L.41,366 14s. 9d. for labourers in several towns overseas and L.967 13s. 9d. for the ransoming of captives)	66,793	19	6
Spent on shipping	5,725	15	0
TOTAL SUM for war and shipping during the aforesaid period	212,164	13	11
TOTAL SUM of the costs of the household of the king and queen and of war and shipping during the aforesaid period	265,785	16	7

Similar expenditure on the household and on war and shipping from the Octave of the Ascension 1252 to the Octave of the Ascension 1253, which is a period of 385 days or 1 year and 20 days.

	L.	s.	d.
TOTAL SUM of the expenditure on the king's household	60,678	10	10
TOTAL SUM of the costs of war and shipping	270,547	15	5
TOTAL of the two last sums	331,226	6	3

The aforesaid days totalled 1,120 days or 3 years 25 days.

	L.	s.	d.
Sum of the wages of knights serving for pay during the 3 years and 25 days aforesaid	177,938	15	7

And be it known that if, as appears in the aforesaid accounts, each of the said knights took each day in wages only as much as 7s. 6d., one can therefore estimate the number of the aforesaid knights serving each day at 424, whose wages each day were valued at L.158 17s. 6d.

	L.	s.	d.
Total of gifts and payments made to knights serving without wages during the aforesaid period	65,189	8	6

These gifts and payments, if estimated with reference to the common wages of the knights as above, that is to say 7s. 6d. a day for each knight, would be enough to support 155 knights each day during the whole of the aforesaid period. That is L.58 4s. 1d. a day or thereabouts.

TOTAL SUM, estimated as common wages as rendered above, for the aforesaid knights whom the king could have in his company each day during the whole of the aforesaid period: 579 knights; and the sum in silver comes to

	L.	s.	d.
	243,128	4	0

That is L.217 1s. 7d. a day or thereabouts.

	L.	s.	d.
TOTAL SUM of the costs of the household for the whole period of 3 years and 25 days aforesaid; for the king and the queen alike	162,858	8	7
That is L.145 8s. 2d. a day or thereabouts			
TOTAL SUM for the king's ransom	167,102	18	8
TOTAL SUM for the war during the aforesaid period	594,600	4	10
That is L.530 17s. 10d. a day			
TOTAL SUM for shipping during the whole of this period	32,026	2	8
TOTAL SUM for works built overseas during the whole of this period	95,839	2	6
TOTAL SUM for the ransoming of captives	1,050	0	0
TOTAL SUM of all these expenditures during the 3 years and 25 days aforesaid; that is to say the costs of the households of the king and queen, the expenditure on the king's ransom, war, shipping, building works and the ransoming of captives	1,053,476	17	3

36 Adam of Jesmond draws up a contract of service on crusade between the Lord Edward of England and himself, 20 July 1270

Because crusading was so expensive, leaders had to help their followers with subsidies and the accounts for King Louis IX's first crusade (35) refer to knights serving under contract in exchange for grants of cash. Here is an example of a contract of this kind taken from the sources relating to the English contingent on Louis's second crusade. Several agreements made in 1269 and 1270 by Edward and his brother Edmund survive.

Source: H. G. Richardson and G. O. Sayles, *The Governance of Mediaeval England* (Edinburgh, 1963), pp. 464–5

All must know that I am in the company of my lord Edward, the eldest son of the king of England, in order to go with him to the Holy Land with four knights besides myself. I will remain in his service for a whole year, beginning at the time of the next crossing to the East in September. And in return for undertaking this, he has given me 600 marks in money and transport to cover everything, that is to say the rental of the ship and water for as many persons and horses as befit knights. And if it happens that through sickness or for any other reason I have to stay behind, which God forbid, a knight who will go in my place and my aforesaid knights will perform their service entirely for the year, or I will allow them as much of the funds as is needed for them to complete the remainder of the year, and this will be at my discretion. And if it happens by chance that God summons the aforesaid my lord, the Lord Edward, from this life, I will be bound to the man he shall leave or send in his stead just as I am to him according to the arrangement written above. And in testimony of this fact I have had this document sealed with my seal.

D The Appointment of Leaders

37 Geoffrey of Villehardouin describes the election of Boniface of Montferrat as commander of the Fourth Crusade, September 1201 (written *c.*1208)

When a crusade was not led by a king or a king's son like Edward of England, it seems to have been normal for a commander to be elected by the leading figures in the army; even regional contingents elected their own leaders when there was no outstanding person taking part. Count Thibault of Champagne, who had been the first French magnate to take the cross for the Fourth Crusade and had been regarded as one of a triumvirate of leaders with the counts of Flanders and Blois, died in late May 1201. In the extract that follows, Geoffrey of Villehardouin described how, after two French nobles had refused to take Thibault's place, the command of the whole army was offered to Boniface of Montferrat.

Geoffrey of Villehardouin, marshal of Champagne, played a large part in the preparations and the course of the crusade, becoming marshal of the Latin Empire that was founded in Greece by the crusaders. He does not seem to have returned to the West.

Source: Geoffrey of Villehardouin, *La conquête de Constantinople*, ed. E. Faral (2nd ed., Paris, 1961) I, pp. 38–44

After the count of Champagne had been buried, Matthew of Montmorency, Simon of Montfort, Geoffrey of Joinville, who was seneschal, and Geoffrey the marshal went to Duke Odo of Burgundy and said this to him: 'My lord, you can see the misfortune that has befallen the land overseas. We wish to beseech you for God's sake to take the cross and go in the count's place to help the land overseas. And we will put you in possession of all his resources and we will swear to you on relics, and make others swear it to you, that we will serve you in good faith, just as we might have served him.' The duke's will was such that he refused; you must know that he could have done much better. They entrusted Geoffrey of Joinville with a message containing another similar offer to Count Thibault of Bar-le-Duc, who was a cousin of the count who had died. And he also refused. That death of Count Thibault of Champagne was a very great source of distress to the pilgrims and all those who had to go in the service of God.

At the end of the month they held a parliament at Soissons to decide what to do. Among those present were Count Baldwin of Flanders and Hainault and Count Louis of Blois and Chartrain, Count Geoffrey of Perche, Count Hugh of Saint-Pol and many other men of worth. Geoffrey the marshal told them about the speeches and offers they had made to the duke of Burgundy and the count of Bar-le-Duc and how these men had refused them. 'Hear me, my lords,' he said, 'I will give you a word of advice if you will allow me. The Marquis Boniface of Montferrat is a man of great worth and one of the most esteemed men alive today. If you were to send word to him to come here and take the sign of the cross and put himself in the place of the count of Champagne and if you were to give him the lordship of the army he would take it at once.' Many arguments were bandied back and forth, but the outcome of the discussion was such that everyone, great as well as small, was in agreement. And the letter was written and the messengers chosen. And he was sent for and he came, on the day which they had set, travelling through Champagne and across France, where he was shown great honour. He was also honoured by the king of France, whose cousin he was.

So he came to a parliament which was called to Soissons, and thither came very many counts and barons and crusaders. When they heard that the marquis was coming they went to meet him and did him great honour. And so in the morning the parliament met in an orchard at the abbey of My Lady Saint Mary of Soissons. There they begged the marquis to do what they had asked him and they beseeched him to take the cross for God's sake, to receive the lordship of the army, to take the place of Count Thibault of Champagne and to take his money and his men. And they fell at his feet with many tears; and he fell at their feet and said that he would undertake it right willingly. And so the marquis did what they had begged and accepted the lordship of the army. And straight away the bishop of Soissons and my lord Fulk of Neuilly, the holy man, and two Cistercian abbots whom Boniface had brought with him from his country led him to the church of Our Lady and fixed the cross on his shoulder. And so ended this parliament. And the next day Boniface took his leave to return to his country to put his affairs in order; and he said that everyone else was to put theirs in order too and that he would rejoin them at Venice.

38 Pope Innocent IV formally appoints Cardinal Odo of Châteauroux legate, 21 July 1248

Large bodies of crusaders were invariably accompanied by papal legates. The powers of Adhémar of Le Puy on the First Crusade have been the subject of dispute, but it is generally agreed that all legates exercised spiritual leadership with the duty to exhort, advise and arbitrate and with excommunication as a sanction at their disposal. They were not supposed to be generals, however closely one or two of them came in practice to holding military command. A late example of the formal appointment of a spiritual leader of a crusade is this letter to Odo of Châteauroux, a well-known preacher who, like so many of the legates, was also responsible for preaching the cross before the crusade began.

Source: Innocent IV, *Registres*, ed. E. Berger (Paris, 1887) II, p. 108

For such a long time now the faithful of Christ have worked anxiously for the liberation of the Holy Land, not without the spilling of much blood. But this kind of labour has not resulted in the liberation we desired, perhaps because the sins of the Christian people demand it, and there has been no help in it, not the slightest; there has been only hindrance, except in so far as it is seen to have been a means of the salvation of souls, because that land is a great ladder to the heavenly kingdom. And so the ineffable wisdom of God the Father, that is his only begotten son, God and man, the Lord Jesus Christ, perceiving how to fulfil his design, appears to have chosen from among all the princes of the world to liberate this land our most beloved son in Christ the illustrious king of France, a man truly resplendent with purity of heart and body and filled with a wealth of virtues, who is powerful in works of mercy and is known to possess many knights and much riches. Marking himself with the sign of the life-giving cross and desiring to conclude successfully and speedily the labour he has undertaken, this king has through the grace of God equipped himself in such royal state, in provisions befitting so great a prince and profitable for such an important matter, that we hope that he will be the means of bringing the desired conclusion to this business.

Because it rests with us to join the spiritual sword to the temporal sword crossing the sea, in order to reinforce its strength and power, following the example of him whose vicar we, although undeserving, have been made – for he sent the disciples he had chosen throughout the whole world to preach the gospel to every created thing – and distributing tasks among those whom we have summoned to share the burdens of this responsibility and taking counsel, just as Jethro did, in committing to each according to his own ability what is demanded in various circumstances, we have taken care, on the advice of our brothers, to send you to those parts with the king to stay by his side like the angel of great counsel. And we have committed to you the office of full legation which extends as much over the army of the king and of other crusaders making the passage there as over all who set out to aid that land; and this power also extends over all Christian provinces and lands established there and in addition over all kingdoms and regions overseas and all races and the islands that lie beyond Sicily, so that you may root out and destroy, scatter and disperse, build and plant as seems to you profitable. Once you have assumed this kind of burden humbly and faithfully, we order you to apply yourself to the execution of the office of legation committed to you carefully and prudently to the praise of the Crucified One, in such a way that thereafter you can rightly earn the commendation of God and men.

E Preparations and Departure

39 Duke Henry I of Brabant and Lorraine settles a dispute with the priory of Forest before going on crusade, 1197

The cartularies of European religious houses are scattered with documents in which crusaders raised mortgages, settled ancient disputes or made endowments for prayers for them before their departure. The number of these documents is evidence for the crusaders' very real expectation of death and their desire to have their affairs properly in order before they left and adequate arrangements for intercession for their souls. Of course the charters were written by clerics, but they do show a different side to the crusaders than is usually presented: one of devout and anxious men rather than of swashbuckling adventurers. The reference in this charter to the fight against invisible Saracens reflects the conviction that a good crusader made an 'interior journey' at the same time as he travelled to Jerusalem.

Source: Cartulaire d'Afflighem, ed. E. de Marneffe (Louvain, 1894), pp. 306–7

Because as St Augustine says the enemy is never so much oversome as when we are merciful, I, about to go to Jerusalem to overcome Saracens both visible and invisible, wish to show generous mercy with a bountiful hand to the holy nuns serving God and the Blessed Mary at Forest; I wish to honour them and to give them peace of mind and security in the management of all their affairs. For I hope that with the help of their fervent prayers the labour of the journey to Jerusalem will be fruitful for my soul. On account of this I reassign to the same church in free possession the wood of Fronerode, which I have been considering to be rightly mine. So do Henry the *villicus* of Schaerbeek, Reiner, Siger and Henry the *scabinus* of Uccle. Reiner and Henry the foresters have drawn clear boundaries to that wood. The nuns must be given 20 *sous* every year from my annual rents from Uccle to have a mass said on my father's anniversary; and I give in alms 10 *sous* to the church of Forest and 10 to that of Bigard. These arrangements must remain unchanged and established by the validity of this charter with the authority of my silver seal; they are confirmed by the affirmation of suitable witnesses.

40 A crusader laments leaving his love (*Por joie avoir perfite en paradis*)

The sorrow of crusaders at having to leave home, wives, children and loves is often to be found in the sources, and lyrics on that theme constitute a genre in vernacular poetry. This anonymous and undated song is one of the most beautiful.

Source: Bédier and Aubry, *Les chansons*, pp. 283–5

To have perfect joy in paradise
I must leave the land I love so much,
Where she lives whom I thank every day.
Her body is noble and spirited, her face fresh and lovely;
And my true heart surrenders all to her.

But my body must take its leave of her:
I am departing for the place where God suffered death
To ransom us on a Friday.

Sweet love, I have great sorrow in my heart
Now that at last I must leave you,
With whom I have found so much good, such tenderness,
Joy and gaiety to charm me.
But Fortune by her power has made me
Exchange my joy for the sadness and sorrow
I will feel for you many nights and many days.
Thus will I go to serve my creator.

No more than a child can endure hunger –
And no one can chastise him for crying because of it –
Do I believe that I can stay away
From you, whom I am used to kiss and to embrace,
Nor have I in me such power of abstinence.
A hundred times a night I shall recall your beauty:
It gave me such pleasure to hold your body!
When I no longer have it I shall die of desire.

Good Lord God, if I for you
Leave the country where she is that I love so,
Grant us in heaven everlasting joy,·
My love and me, through your mercy,
And grant her the strength to love me,
So that she will not forget me in my long absence,
For I love her more than anything in the world
And I feel so sad about her that my heart is breaking.

Beautiful Isabel, I commend you to God's will.
I cannot stay with you any longer:
Into the land of the paynim, to the race of unbelievers
I must go for the love of God.
I am going there with the good intention of saving my soul;
But remember well, beautiful and noble love,
That if anyone ever died for loving loyally
I do not think I will survive even as far as the sea-port.

For just as the blossom springs from the branch,
Springs from you the great sorrow which torments me;
But if I return, I swear it by the relics,
It will be to serve and honour you.

I sing of loyal love where my thoughts lie,
Nor do I want my heart to repent of it;
But I wish to tell my lord of Gisors
That it is honourable to love loyally.

41 John of Joinville describes his preparations and departure, April–August 1248 (written 1309)

In 1309 John of Joinville presented the future King Louis X with his history of St Louis IX, which contained his recollections of the saint on the first of his crusades, in which John himself had taken part. This extract, in which John looked back 60 years to his own departure from France, is very touching, and in it almost all the experiences of crusaders, which are confirmed in other sources, are brought together in a short narrative: the settling of a crusader's affairs in such a way that if he died no man would have cause to complain of him; the raising of money on his lands; the arrangements for his journey and the transport of equipment; the reception of the scrip and staff; sorrow at leaving; and a leave-taking as a pilgrim, bare-legged and simply dressed, who began his journey by paying visits to local shrines.

Source: John of Joinville, *Histoire de Saint Louis*, ed. N. de Wailly (2nd ed., Paris, 1874), pp. 62–4, 68–70

At Easter in the year of Grace 1248 I summoned my men and my vassals to Joinville; and on the eve of that Easter, when all the men I had summoned had come, my son John, lord of Ancerville, was born of my first wife, who was the sister of the count of Grandpré. All that week we feasted and danced and my brother the lord of Vaucouleurs and the other rich men who were there took it in turns to provide food on the Monday, the Tuesday, the Wednesday and the Thursday. On the Friday I said to them, 'Lords, I am going overseas and I do not know whether I will return. Now step forward; if I have wronged you in any way I will make amends to each of you in turn, just as I have always done to anyone who had any demand to make of me or of my men.' I made amends to them according to the judgements of all the men of my land and so that I would not influence them in their decisions I rose from the court and accepted whatever they decided without questioning it.

Because I did not want to take with me a single penny to which I had no right, I went to Metz in Lorraine to raise a mortgage on a large part of my land. And you should know that on the day I left our country to go to the Holy Land I did not hold a thousand pounds' worth of land, because my lady my mother was still living. And so I went to the Holy Land, taking with me nine knights and being myself the third of three bannerets. And I can recall these things to you because if God, who never failed me, had not helped me I would scarcely have been able to endure such a length of time as the six years I stayed in the Holy Land.

At the time I was preparing to go John, lord of Apremont and count of Sarrebruck by marriage, sent to me and told me that he had settled his expenses for going overseas with nine knights besides himself. And he asked if I would like us to share the hire of a ship. And I agreed: his men and mine hired a ship at Marseilles . . . . We agreed, the count of Sarrebruck and I, to send our equipment in carts to Auxonne, to put it there on a boat on the River Saône, in order to go as far as Arles, by way of the Saône and the Rhône.

On the day I left Joinville I sent for the abbot of Cheminon, who was said to be the most upright member of the Cistercian Order . . . This abbot of Cheminon gave me my scrip and my staff. And then I left Joinville, not to enter the castle again until my return, on foot, without hose and in my shirt. And so I went to Blécourt and Saint-Urbain and to other places where there are relics of the saints. And as I went to Blécourt and Saint-Urbain I never once looked back towards Joinville, for fear that my heart would be moved because of the beautiful castle I was leaving and my two children. I and my companions ate at the Fontaine-l'Archevêque before Donjeux. And there Abbot Adam of Saint-Urbain – may God absolve him – gave me and the nine knights I had with me a great number of beautiful jewels. From there we went to Auxonne and we set off from there with all our equipment, which we had ordered to be loaded on boats to go down the Saône from Auxonne as far as Lyons. And our great war-horses were led along the bank beside the boats. At Lyons we embarked on the Rhône to go to Arles-le-Blanc . . . .

In the month of August we embarked on our boats at the Roche-de-Marseille. On the day we embarked the door in the side of the ship was opened and all our horses which we had to take overseas were loaded. And then the door was closed again and well sealed, as is done when one stops up a barrel, because when the ship is in open sea the whole door is below the water level. When the horses were in, our master mariner called to his sailors who were in the ship's prow and said to them, 'Are you ready?' And they replied, 'Yes sir. Let the clerics and priests come forward'. As soon as they were come, he shouted to them, 'Sing, in the name of God'. And they burst out together into the *Veni creator spiritus*. And the master mariner called to his sailors, 'In the name of God, make sail'.

F The Course of Crusading

42 Crusaders draw up regulations for their voyage, 1–19 May 1147

From the first crusading armies drew up codes of practice for themselves, which were always strongly influenced by the devotional nature of the enterprise, containing sumptuary laws and rules on the performance of religious duties. The earliest surviving code is this one, recorded by an English participant and drawn up for the crusaders from England, Scotland, the Low Countries, Normandy and the Rhineland, who left Dartmouth on 19 May 1147 and helped to take Lisbon in Portugal before going on to the East in the following year. The constables referred to in the text were the four commanders of the English crusaders.

Source: De expugnatione Lyxbonensi, ed. C. W. David (New York, 1936), p. 57

Among those people who spoke so many different languages there were the strongest pledges of concord and friendship. In addition to this they enforced the severest laws, for example that a death was to be demanded for a death, a tooth for a tooth. They forbade every kind of display of rich clothes; and women were not allowed to go out in public. The peace was to be kept by everyone unless injuries were suffered on matters included in the decree. The clergy and laity should hold separate assemblies every week, unless perhaps some important matters demanded that they should both meet together. Each ship should have its own priest and the same rules were laid down to be observed as in parishes. No one should keep anyone else's sailor or servant at his own expense. Each person should go to confession once a week and receive Holy Communion on Sunday. And there were other clauses providing for everything that we might need and special rulings for particular cases. And from every thousand people were chosen two elected officers, who were called judges and fellow jurors. Through their offices cases were to be concluded; and money was to be distributed according to the decree of the constables.

43 Two visions of Stephen of Valence

Crusades were marked for the participants by miracles, by signs in nature and by appearances of Christ, Our Lady, angels, saints and dead crusaders, transmitting divine commands and prohibitions. The First Crusade was not unusual in this, but the appearances on it are very well documented. On that crusade the particularly inspired seem to have been a group of visionaries from southern France, many of whom were in the contingent led by Count Raymond of Toulouse. Stephen, a priest of Valence, was one of these. Of his two visions, the first was reported by all the eye-witness narrators of the crusade: his account of it evidently made a great impression on the army, bottled up in Antioch during the greatest crisis of the campaign. The appearance of Our Lady is to be explained by her patronage of the movement, which historians have not yet studied sufficiently; that of St Peter by the fact that Antioch had been his first see. *Congregati sunt* was the introit of a votive mass said in time of war. We have chosen the version in the *Gesta Francorum*, written by a Norman knight from southern Italy who was in Bohemond of Taranto's army. This part of his history appears to have been written before he left Antioch in November 1098. The second vision, in which the dead legate Adhémar of Le Puy confirmed that he had been burnt temporarily in hell for disbelieving in the newly discovered relic of the Holy Lance, passed on instructions about the Lance and about what seems to have been cross reliquary of his that the crusaders had left in Latakia and transmitted commands from the silent figure of Our Lady, is only to be found in the account of Raymond of Aguilers, chaplain to the count of Toulouse and the most detailed chronicler of the experiences of the visionaries. The *Gaude Maria virgo* belongs to the office of Our Lady.

i Stephen's first vision, 10 June 1098, reported in the Gesta Francorum

Source: Gesta Francorum et aliorum Hierosolimitanorum, ed. R. Hill (London, 1962), pp. 57–8

One day a priest came before our leaders and said, 'Lords, may it please you to hear what I have seen in a vision. One night as I lay in the church of St Mary the mother of Our Lord Jesus Christ, the Saviour of the world appeared to me with his mother and Blessed Peter, the Prince of the Apostles. And he stood before me and said to me, "Do you recognize me?" I replied, "No." After this exchange a whole cross appeared above his head. Again the Lord questioned me, saying, "Do you recognize me?" I replied, "I would not recognize you at all except that I see above your head a cross just like that of Our Saviour." He said, "*I am*". At once I fell at his feet, humbly asking him to help us in the tribulation that had come upon us. The Lord replied, "I have helped you much and I will help you henceforward. I allowed you to take the city of Nicaea and to triumph in all battles; and I have led you thus far and I have suffered with you in the distress you have borne during the siege of Antioch. But although I gave you the aid you needed and brought you safe and unhurt into the city, you have made much sinful love with Christian and wicked pagan women. Because of this a great stench rises to heaven." Then the kind Virgin and Blessed Peter fell at his feet, asking and imploring him to help his people in this distress. And Blessed Peter said, "Lord the pagans have held my house for such a long time and they have done many unutterable evils in it. Lord, as soon as the enemies are driven out the angels will rejoice in heaven." And the Lord said to me, "Go and say to my people that they must return to me and I will return to them; and within five days I will send them great aid; and they must sing every day the entire response *Congregati sunt* together with the verse".'

ii Stephen's second vision, mid April 1099, reported by Raymond of Aguilers (written before 1105)

Source: Raymond of Aguilers, *Liber,* eds. J. H. and L. L. Hill (Paris, 1969), pp. 127–8

Stephen of Valence had a vision of the bishop of Le Puy. He struck him with a stick as he was going back to his house at night and said to him, 'Stephen!' And he replied, 'My Lord?' and, looking back, he recognized him. And the bishop said, 'Why have you ignored what I said to you twice about the cross of the Lord and our mother the Virgin Mary? I mention the cross, because I had it sent on ahead so that it might be brought to the army. For what better standard could you have than the cross? Is that bejewelled cross not enough for you? Did it not lead you well, straight to the Lord's Lance? And now the Lady and Blessed Virgin Mary says that unless you have that cross you will receive no counsel.' And straight away the priest asked, 'Oh my dearest lord, where is the Blessed Mary?' And the bishop showed her to him at once. The Blessed Virgin was about 9 or 10 cubits away from him and she was very beautiful in her appearance and dress; and Blessed Agatha and another maiden holding two candles were waiting on her. And then the priest said to the bishop who was attending her, 'My lord, what are all these things they are saying about you in the army; that your beard and hair were burnt in hell and many other things that are not believed? And now I beg you to give me one of those candles as proof of the things you say, so that I may take it to the count [of Toulouse].' Then the bishop said to him, 'Now you can see me, take a look at my face to see if it is burnt'. After that the bishop went up to the Blessed Virgin Mary and when he had found out what she wanted he returned to the priest and said to him, 'You may not have what you have asked for; but that ring on your finger is of no use to you and you ought not to wear it. Go and give it to the count and say, "The most holy Virgin Mother sends you this ring; whenever you need anything remember the Lady who sent it to you and call her and the Lord will help you".' Next, when the priest asked him what he wanted his brother [Hugh of Monteil] to do, the bishop replied, 'He should beseech the bishop–elect [of Albara] to offer three masses to the Lord for the souls of our relatives. Our Mother commands that henceforth the Lance should not be exposed except by a priest dressed in sacred vestments; and the cross must be held in front of him in this way.' And the bishop held out the cross fixed on to a spear and someone dressed in priestly vestments followed him holding the Lance in his hands. And the bishop began this responsory, *Gaude Maria Virgo cunctas hereses sola interemisti*. Countless hundreds of thousands of men began singing and in this way the assembly of saints departed.

44 Peter Tudebode describes the procession round Jerusalem, 8 July 1099 (written before 1111)

Crusades, like all pilgrimages, were liturgical events, marked by solemn ceremonial, fasting, services of intercession and processions, which had, of course, the effect of heightening the devotional awareness of the crusaders. The most famous of the processions, with obvious parallels with the Israelites at Jericho, was organized during the siege of Jerusalem, when things seemed to be going badly for the crusaders. This eyewitness account described how the crusaders visited the holy places that lay immediately outside the walls. The centrepiece was a sermon preached by Arnulf of Chocques, chaplain to the duke of Normandy, who seems to have assumed spiritual leadership of the crusade after the death of Adhémar of Le Puy and became the first Latin patriarch of Jerusalem.

Source: Peter Tudebode, *Historia de Hierosolymitano itinere*, eds. J. H. and L. L. Hill (Paris, 1977), pp. 137–8

Our leaders held a council in which the bishops and priests recommended them to make a procession round the city. And so the bishops and priests went bare-footed, dressed in sacred vestments and bearing crosses in their hands, from the church of St Mary which is on Mt Zion to the church of St Stephen Protomartyr, singing psalms and praying the Lord Jesus Christ to free his Holy City and Holy Sepulchre from the pagans and deliver it into the hands of the Christians, so that they might perform his holy service. The clerics were also dressed in the same way; the knights and their retainers were armed and marched alongside them.

When the Saracens saw this, they proceeded in the same way along the city walls carrying on a spear an image of Muhammad covered with a cloth. When the Christians had reached the church of St Stephen and had made a station there as is the custom in our processions, the Saracens stood on the walls and shouted aloud at it. They made a great din with trumpets and subjected the Christians to every kind of mockery which they could devise. But worst of all, in the sight of all the Christians they struck the most holy cross, on which merciful Christ redeemed the human race by shedding his blood, with a piece of wood and then, to distress the Christians even more, they dashed it to pieces against the wall, shouting 'Frangi agip salip', which in our language means, 'Franks, is it a good cross?'

On seeing this the Christians were moved with great anguish but continued to pray; and they went up in procession to the church on the Mt of Olives, from where Christ ascended into heaven. And here a most distinguished churchman called Arnulf [of Chocques] preached, pointing out to them the mercy God had shown to the Christians, who had followed him as far as that stone from which he had ascended into heaven. Now these Saracens, seeing the Christians standing in a place from which they could see them most clearly, threatened them, running back and forth between the Temple of the Lord and the Temple of Solomon. Then the Christians went on in the same procession to the monastery of St Mary in the valley of Josaphat, from where her most holy body was carried off to heaven. And from there they returned to the Mt of Olives, wanting to enter the church in that place. A cleric, who was walking in the procession to the door of that monastery, was wounded by an arrow in the middle of his forehead and died there. I believe his soul will reign with Christ for all eternity. Amen. Peter Tudebode, the man who first wrote this, should be believed because he was in the procession and saw it with his own earthly eyes.

45 James of Vitry writes to Pope Honorius III, describing events during the siege of Damietta, August 1218–September 1219

The hardest choice facing us was of a passage to illustrate the physical effort, pain and excitement of conflict; the suffering and deprivation endured by large bodies of men operating in an alien environment very far from home; the real sense of spiritual purpose and at the same time the disorder of a military camp. We have chosen a letter written by James of Vitry, a leading preacher of the cross (9, 29) and bishop of Acre, who was an eye-witness of events in Egypt during the Fifth

Crusade. We have left out an introductory passage, but we have translated the whole of his factual account. The letter falls into two parts. The first related what had happened in the winter and spring of 1218–19 and James clearly intended to send it to the pope by a ship returning home on the spring passage. But for some reason it was not sent and before the ships sailed for the West in September he took up his pen again to add what had happened in the summer. The events he described make depressing but typical reading: disease, death, enormous toil, occasional violence, a pointless excursion during which the leaders changed their minds, and in the end little achieved.

Source: James of Vitry, *Lettres*, ed. R. B. C. Huygens (Leiden, 1960), pp. 114–22

Throughout all the summer after we had come with the Lord as our leader to the port of Damietta on the River Nile next to the plain of Tinnis, a great part of the army of the Lord, praying and joyful in the Lord and with hardly any distress, *fell asleep in the Lord* from dysentery, like guests invited to the feast. But as winter drew near we destroyed a very strong tower, situated in the middle of the Nile between us and the city, which in an extraordinary way our men had already taken by assault *with a strong hand and a stretched out arm* and with great toil and spilling of blood: 10 of our men who had entered the tower by means of a ladder killed some of their 250 adversaries and captured the rest. And we broke the iron chains which were stretched from the tower to the city to prevent ships from reaching the upper river. The Saracens, in fact, sank so many ships in the river and threw in so many other things to hinder us that we remained on the sands above the river for the whole winter and could not haul our ships to the upper river, nor could we cross the river to besiege the city from a close position. But with great peril we had a very few vessels brought up between the tower and the city, through showers of spears and arrows and stones and fire and attacks from petraries, although few of them were destroyed. The venerable father the bishop of Albano, legate of the apostolic see, had his cog hauled into the upper river without damage to his goods and men. I had mine hauled up with nearly 200 men on board, but some of them were killed and wounded; and after this I sent my barbote on to the river with 20 men in it, of whom six were captured and the rest killed, fighting courageously. A cog of the Templars was held up by the Saracens when it crossed near the city with nearly 30 men on board. These men resisted courageously and, after they had killed many of their adversaries and when they could no longer withstand the force of the Saracens' attack, they sank about 500 armed Saracens with them in the river with the ship and destroyed, in the manner of Samson, more in death than they had killed in life.

Not many of our men were killed by the sword that winter, but the swords of our men slew many Saracen knights. One day, when many of the Saracens followed their intention of launching their galleys to attack ours, a few of our knights put to the sword some of the 1,000 and more who disembarked on our side; the rest perished in the river. Not long after that, when one day many of the Saracens had made a bridge across the upper part of the river in order to cross to us, a few of our knights charged and killed more than 2,000 of them; as they fled many of the Egyptians *sunk as lead in the mighty waters*, because the Lord was fighting for us. Our men returned in great triumph to the camp, safe and unhurt, except for two who were crowned with martyrdom. But during that winter season, in which we lingered on the sands, it did not please divine providence that we should cross the river without our souls profiting in many ways. For the Lord sent down on us a sickness that no doctor's skill could cure, a contagious disease with no natural causes, divinely sent down on a great part of our army either to cleanse us from our sins or so that we should be more deserving of the crown. For the thighs and legs first swelled up and then festered; also superflous flesh grew in the mouth. For a long while the sick were weak but in no great pain, and they gradually lost heart and, as they talked to their companions and prayed with them to God, closing their eyes as if they were asleep and commending their spirits to the Lord, they sped from their bodies, leaving them behind for the joys of the citizens of heaven. During that period the venerable father Master Robert of Courçon, cardinal of the title of St Stephen-on-the-Coelian, a learned and faithful man, affable, gracious and kind, who had the *zeal of God* and ardently desired the liberation of the Holy Land, blessedly passed over to the Lord, together with the venerable father the bishop of Paris and certain other noblemen who offered themselves and their goods to the Lord and *whose names are written in the book of life*.

Many of our men died because of the severe winter and the dreadful cold, besides the usual river floods and the high tides caused by the swollen sea, many more by far than died at the hands of the Saracens. And when the sea water suddenly and forcefully reached our camp, scarcely any of our men would have escaped if the Lord had not had compassion on his people and had not miraculously turned it aside. Shortly before this, our men, I believe by divine inspiration, had dug a wide ditch in the sands surrounding our camp, not because they were afraid that there would be a high tide, a danger they were now averting, but in order to be able to haul our ships without peril through the ditch from the lower to the upper part of the river. The waters of the raging sea overflowed the dunes one mile from our camp when the tide exceeded its usual limits and everything beyond our ditch was submerged; that is to say the tents and provisions. And although some of our men were drowned, the rest, who retreated within the ditch, escaped by the grace of God. When the waters reached the ditch and flowed through its course to the river channel, the part of the ditch which ran alongside our camp burst in several places. We were nearly submerged, but we escaped such a dangerous and unexpected flood, as the Lord pleased, by tremendous efforts, blocking the gaps with ships' sails, planks, sand and the corpses of drowned animals.

As our men were busying themselves with these things, the venerable father the bishop of Albano, legate of the apostolic see, together with the patriarch of Jerusalem and the archbishops and bishops and all the clergy, proclaimed an immediate three-day fast on bread and water; and on every Saturday the people were to process bare-footed, singing psalms and a litany and with devout prayers. And they encouraged the people to call upon the Lord and implore divine aid, fixing their anchor of hope in him alone who is the salvation of the humble, the comforter of the distressed and the remedy of miseries, *who shall not delight in the strength of the horse: nor take pleasure in the legs of a man*; he who is powerful enough to be able to conquer when he wants and how he wants, with few men as with many. The prudent man, conscientiously carrying out the office committed to him, expelled from the army of Christ, some of them by sentence of excommunication, all prostitutes and those who were going to drink in taverns and also those who were playing at dice and hazard, defiling and corrupting so holy a business in so far as they could.

As Lent approached the Lord had mercy on the suffering of his people. Already with great toil we had dragged the boats through the ditch to the upper river, but we could not possibly cross the river without great spilling of blood. The Lord stung the king and so mighty an army of Egypt with such fear that they fled their camp by night with their tents and left us a great part of their baggage and ships and animals. Most of those who were in the city took to flight when they saw that their lord with all his army had fled at our approach and created such a crush at the gate that nearly 1,000 of both sexes were suffocated in it and died. The rest had intended to flee and leave us an empty city, but our men, hurrying up and crossing the river late in the morning without hindrance from the enemy, encircled the city on every side, besieging it by water and land alike; and they also constructed a very strong bridge of boats so that those who had remained on the sands on the other side to guard the river and the port could, if need be, bring help without delay or hindrance.

King Coradinus (al–Mu'azzam) of Damascus, hearing that his brother the sultan of Egypt had fled in the way I have described, collected a great host of Turks and descended on Egypt to bring speedy help to his brother and the besieged city. When we were confronted by an army consisting of an aggregation of those who lived beyond the River Euphrates and in the regions of Cairo and Alexandria and also in very distant eastern parts, our men did not think there was anything to gain by engaging such a multitude in battle, because a great part of our men were sick and most of our horses had died during the winter and the rest were weak and thin. After taking counsel, we dug a ditch, furnished with ramparts, around our army. The Turks made a very sharp assault on us from their galleys on the river and on land, attacking the ditch in the sands with swords, bows and crossbows. God protected and helped us and they withdrew in disorder to their camp after we had killed or wounded nearly 2,000 of them. Very few of our men were killed, but some were slightly wounded, and our men prevented from reaching our bridge a fiercely burning instrument of war which they had built on ships and had dispatched to set fire to it; no damage was done to the bridge.

From then on the Saracens were planning to attack the other side of our camp should we happen to make an assault on the city, so as to divert us in this way and hinder us from attacking the city. In the meantime we prepared petraries, trebuchets, ladders and other instruments of war and we also dug mines to bring down the towers on the walls or to enter the city through underground passages. We trust that the Lord will soon deliver the city into the hands of the Christians, for few have remained in it and they are suffering very much from a shortage of food. Coradinus, moreover, was compelled to withdraw with a large part of his army, because he had heard that the sultan of Rum and the king of Armenia and one of Saladin's sons had entered his territory in the region of Aleppo and Damascus with a countless host of horse and foot, to fight against him and seize his land. But once our men occupy the city of Damietta, which is the key to all of Egypt, with the Lord's help we will easily subject all the rest of the land to the rule of Christ and so at last we will return with joy and gladness to the Land of Promise, in triumph and thanksgiving, with the Lord as our guide and your prayers directing our steps.

★ ★ ★

We want you to know that we wrote a full report at the time of the Easter passage to tell you how the army of the cross of Christ, fighting for the faith of Christ before Damietta, was faring; how last winter it was exposed to the perils of tidal floods, fire, the climate and an enemy assault from over the river. We are going to describe in this postscript what has happened to the enterprise since then. We want you to know that throughout last summer we have devoted ourselves to the capture of the city, setting up siege engines and assaulting it frequently by land and sea. And whenever we have used the engines, the Saracens, putting their troops in order and preparing themselves for battle, have attacked our palisades in force so violently that on one occasion they entered our ramparts, although we threw them out with great force and massacred many horses and men. And by harassments of this kind they distracted us from our purpose, which was to be put into effect as soon as possible.

When we realized that we were not going to achieve so great a feat without hard fighting, we first discussed for a long time who should remain on guard in our camp, who should accompany us on a sortie and who should be in command of our galleys and vessels, which were to advance by the river to attack the vessels and take the tents of our enemies. Then, on the feat of the Beheading of Blessed John the Baptist [29 August], by the common counsel of the clergy and the greater and lesser knights and to calm the *murmuring of the people* and some of the clerics, we made a bold and powerful sortie from our palisades, with our lines dressed and our men put in battle order. We had made a firm decision that if we overcame the Saracens on the field of battle by the power of the relic of the Holy Cross and our own efforts and were lodged in their camp, which was a league from us, in this way protecting the main body of our army through our occupation of a position between it and the enemy, we could take it upon ourselves to attack the city. When we left our camp in an orderly manner, marching in battle formation, the Saracens also put themselves in battle order and left their camp in such a way that we believed that we would be sure to win, and they retreated as we advanced. When we reached their ditch, which they had dug to allow their galleys access to the sea, they dishonourably left that ditch undefended and when our men crossed it they found no one to resist them, because as they advanced the Saracens withdrew away from us.

The greater men in our army, however, considered that we would have nothing to gain by following them in this way, since we could not lay hold of them and our men, who were on foot, were delayed by thirst and the heat of the sand and were tormented by the weight of their arms. They also considered that it would not do us any good if we advanced to their camp because the tents themselves had been suddenly carried off. With the assent of the lesser men they declared that it would be better for us to return to our tents. And as we returned the Saracens beset us, some from the side, some from before, some from behind, with lances, arrows, maces, spears and Greek fire. Our footmen and even some of our knights could not endure this and they took flight and ran back out of control towards our palisades, abandoning us and depriving us of their help in the thick of the struggle; many of them were killed by heat and thirst as they fled on the sands. After that the Saracens made so violent an attack on our knights that they inflicted intolerable harm on our men and their horses. Some of our knights could not bear this and some then in their anger charged the enemy, but the Saracens closed round them. They were scattered and were not familiar with the oriental way of fighting. The Saracens so tormented them with maces and swords, spears and Greek fire that they were overcome. And so in that struggle we lost 200 knights of the knighthood of the Temple and the Hospital and other pilgrims; some of them were captured, some were killed. They included the noblemen, the bishop-elect of Beauvais, the Lord Walter the chamberlain of the lord king of France, his son the viscount of Beaumont, Lord John of Arcis, Lord Andrew of Espoisse, Lord Andrew of Nanteuil, the brother of the bishop-elect mentioned above, and other noble men. We lost about 2,000 of the common people. The enemies of Christ's cross followed our men right up to our palisades, cutting them down and killing them, and after confounding us in this way they withdrew to their tents with their booty, not without tumult, jeering and mockery; and as they retired they did great damage. Every day they return to our palisades and provoke us with abuse and challenge us with taunts.

In addition, you should know that some pilgrims because they are afraid, some because they have completed their stay of a year in the army, have been getting ready to return home across the sea. This breeds both fear and rancour among those who are left behind. And you should also know that we have learned from some men who have deserted Damietta of their own free will and from others captured in flight that those confined in the city have nothing to eat; they are in such straits from hunger that soon they will have to surrender or make peace in some other way. And once the city is taken we should easily be able to advance into the rest of the land with very little help. And once the land is conquered with God's help, we will return to Judaea to rebuild the walls of Jerusalem our mother and of other fortresses in Judaea: walls, towers and ramparts which are utterly razed to the ground.

46 Gunther of Pairis describes Abbot Martin's part in the sack of Constantinople, 13 April 1204 (written August 1207–June 1208)

This famous description of Abbot Martin despoiling one of the churches in Constantinople of its relics during a sack which the Greeks have never forgotten or forgiven can only be understood in the context of *furta sacra*, thefts of relics which had been going on in the West for centuries and had in the course of time developed a literature of their own, in which a successful stealing was justified as expressing the will of the saint involved. Abbot Martin was not a bad man; indeed he had been shocked by the course the crusade had taken and had sought release from his vow. The sack of Constantinople, where everyone knew there was the greatest store of relics in the Christian world, was among other things a massive *furtum sacrum*. It has even been suggested that the diversion of the Fourth Crusade to Constantinople was at least partly caused by a desire for relics, especially the True Cross.

Source: Gunther of Pairis, 'Historia', pp. 104–6

When the victors were eagerly looting the conquered city they had made theirs by right of war, Abbot Martin began to think about what he himself could take as spoil and, so that he should not remain empty-handed while all the others became rich, he also planned to put his consecrated hands to plunder. But because he thought it unseemly for those same hands to touch worldly booty, he began to plan how to procure for himself some portion of the relics of the saints, of which he knew there was an enormous quantity in that place. So, taking with him one of his two chaplains and with high expectations of some great result, he made for a church which was held in great veneration because it contained a fine tomb of the mother of the most celebrated Emperor Manuel, a fact which, although it seemed an important matter to the Greeks, was considered by our men to be of no consequence. In it was stored a large amount of money, which had been deposited by the people of the surrounding area, not to mention precious relics, which in the vain hope of safety had been collected there from neighbouring churches and monasteries. Before the city was sacked this fact also had been made known to our men by those whom the Greeks had expelled. While many of the pilgrims were breaking into this church and some were greedily turning their attention to other objects such as gold and silver and other precious booty, Martin, thinking it unworthy to commit sacrilege except in a holy cause, looked for a more concealed place, the very holiness of which would lead him to suppose that he could find the things he most desired.

He found there an old man with an agreeable face and a long white beard; definitely a priest, but very unlike our priests in his appearance. Because of this the abbot, supposing him to be a layman, shouted fiercely at him in a terrifying voice, although he was calm enough inwardly, 'Come now, you perfidious old man, show me where you keep the more potent relics you have or rest assured that you will be punished at once by the penalty of death'. The old man, terrified by the shouting, which indeed he heard, rather than by the content of the words, the meaning of which he could not comprehend, and knowing that he could not make him understand his Greek tongue, began to calm Martin down in the *lingua Romana*, of which he knew a little, and to soften his anger, which did not exist, with flattery. At this the abbot just managed with great effort to make the old man understand in a few words of the same language what he was asking of him. Then the old man, studying his face and dress and judging that it was more tolerable for a religious man to lay hands on holy relics with awe and reverence than for worldly men perhaps to pollute them with bloody hands, opened an iron chest for him and showed him the longed for treasure, which Abbot Martin considered to be more welcome and desirable than all the riches of Greece. When the abbot saw it he swiftly and avidly plunged in both his hands and he and the chaplain, briskly tucking up their habits, filled the folds with holy sacrilege. Wisely hiding the things he thought most important, he left at once. Exactly what and how worthy of veneration are these relics, which that holy plunderer snatched for himself, is more fully explained at the end of this little book. And so, as he hurried in this way to the ships, stuffed full, so to speak, he was seen by those who knew and loved him as they too were hurrying from the ships to the plunder. And they asked him joyfully whether he had carried anything off or with what he was so laden. He answered with a smiling face, as usual, and merry words, 'We have done well.' To which they replied, 'Thanks be to God!'

G Illness and Death

7 The wills of two crusaders on the Fifth Crusade

Crusaders' wills are rare. The first of the two translated here was made by a Bolognese citizen seven weeks after the fall of Damietta, although obviously the city had not yet been occupied. Of interest are his dispositions in favour of the crusade itself and religious Orders and houses in the Latin East and his attempt to ensure that his wife did not lose her place in the tent he shared with his comrades. The second is one of two codicils made in October 1221 and October 1222 by the count of Rodez, who must have been seriously ill for more than a year. It also has interesting features. It was made in the great hospital of the Order of St John in Acre, where the count must have been cared for. This explains the dispositions in favour of the Hospital. The count's participation in the crusade presumably accounts for those made in favour of the Order of St John's sister Military Order, the Temple, including the ending of a legal suit in the Templars' favour. The clauses on the count's goods in the East and the reimbursement of his family in southern France by representatives of the Hospitallers are to be explained by his desire to make use of the international facilities of the Order to transfer home the value of his goods in the East.

i Barzella Merxadrus makes his will in the camp at Damietta, 23 December 1219

Source: L. V. Savioli, *Annali Bolognesi* (Bassano, 1789) II, pt 2, pp. 419–20

On 23 December in the year of the Lord 1219, the seventh indiction, Barzella Merxadrus, crusader and citizen of Bologna, being gravely ill in the army of the Christians at Damietta, has made his will in this way. First, he has left 5 besants for the repose of his soul, to be spent on his funeral, burial and for having masses sung, by his executors, the lord priest Giles, his wife Guiletta and Rainald Maldinarus his uncle, whom he has made his executors. He has left all his arms and armour and his coat of mail with one arm plate and a hood to the Hospital of the Germans, where he has wished to be buried.

Item, he has left for the repose of his soul to one man who remains in the army overseas until next Michaelmas 2 sacks of biscuit, 2 measures of flour, 2 *corbae* of wine, the fourth part of a *mezzina* of meat, a pair of breeches, a shirt and 6 besants for sharing bread and wine in the mess, to be taken from the goods he possesses in the aforesaid army.

He has left 1 besant to the priest Giles to sing masses; 2 besants to Rainald Maldinarus; 5 little *solidi* of the empire to Conrad of Pontecchio. He has left 3 besants to all his companions; and he has left his part of the tent and its furniture to the same companions and his wife Guiletta. His companions must not infringe the rights of his aforesaid wife in the tent itself and to its furniture and she should enjoy them fully and peacefully as long as she is in the army, whenever she stays in that tent in the same way as she has stayed in it until now.

Anselm of Ribemont had a glorious death. When he had risen in the morning he called priests to him and, after confessing his omissions and sins, he prayed earnestly for mercy from God and from them, telling them that the end of his life was near. And when they were astonished at this because he looked healthy and sound, he said to them, 'Do not be surprised, but instead listen to me. Last night I saw the Lord Enguerrand of St Pol, who was killed at Ma'arrat. I really was not dreaming, but awake. And I said to him, "What is this? You were dead; and now, are you alive?" And he replied, "Of course those who end their lives in the service of Christ are not dead." When I asked him in return how he had become so beautiful, for he was beautiful beyond measure, he replied to me, "You ought not to be surprised at my beauty, considering that I live in such a beautiful house." And at once he showed me a house in heaven so beautiful that I could not conceive of anything more beautiful. And when I was amazed at the splendour of that house he said to me, "A far more beautiful house is being prepared for you for tomorrow." And after he had said these things he was carried off.' It happened that on the same day that Anselm had spoken of this vision to many, he went out to fight the Saracens, who had made a secret sortie from the castle and wanted to come up to our tents to snatch anything and harm anyone they could. When both sides were engaged in fierce fighting and Anselm was courageously resisting them, he was struck on the head by a stone from a petrary. And so he left this world for the place prepared for him by God.

49 The priory of Aureil records the fulfilment of the last wish of the crusader Bernard Le Baile, *c.*1100

Source: 'Cartulaires des prieurés d'Aureil et d'Artige en Limousin', ed. G. de Senneville, *Bulletin de la société archéologique et historique du Limousin* XLVIII (1900), p. 126

When he died on the way to Jerusalem, Bernard Le Baile gave a bordar's holding at Cisternes to God and St John for the repose of his soul. He said this in the hearing of Boso of La Chèze, who was his companion and brought back word to us of this gift.

Select Bibliography

Bibliographies

H. E. MAYER, *Bibliographie zur Geschichte der Kreuzzüge* (Hanover, 1960)

H. E. MAYER, 'Literaturbericht uber die Geschichte der Kreuzzüge', *Historische Zeitschrift*, Sonderheft 3 (1969) (For works published 1958–67)

H. E. MAYER, Reviews in *Deutsches Archiv für Erforschung des Mittelalters* (For works published since 1967)

H. E. MAYER is compiling the forthcoming bibliographical volume in K. M. Setton (ed.-in-chief), *A History of the Crusades*

General

P. ALPHANDÉRY and A. DUPRONT, *La Chrétienté et l'idée de croisade* (2 vols., Paris, 1954–9)

J. A. BRUNDAGE, *Medieval Canon Law and the Crusader* (Madison, 1969)

W. E. LUNT, *Papal Revenues in the Middle Ages* (2 vols., New York, 1934)

H. E. MAYER, *The Crusades* (Oxford, 1972)

N. PAULUS, *Geschichte des Ablasses* (Paderborn, 1922–3)

J. S. C. RILEY-SMITH, *What were the crusades?* (London, 1977)

J. S. C. RILEY-SMITH, 'Crusading as an act of love', *History* LXV (1980)

J. S. C. RILEY-SMITH, 'An Approach to Crusading Ethics', *Readin* *Medieval Studies* VI (1980)

S. RUNCIMAN, *A History of the Crusades* (3 vols., Cambridge, 1951–4)

F. H. RUSSELL, *The Just War in the Middle Ages* (Cambridge, 1975)

K. M. SETTON, ed.-in-chief, *A History of the Crusades* (2nd ed., 4 vols. s far, Madison, 1969–)

R. C. SMAIL, *Crusading Warfare (1097–1193)* (Cambridge, 1956)

E. SIVAN, *L'Islam et la croisade* (Paris, 1968)

M. VILLEY, *La croisade: Essai sur la formation d'une théorie juridique* (Paris 1942)

M. VILLEY, 'L'idée de croisade chez les juristes du moyen âge *Relazioni del X congresso internazionale di scienze storiche: III, Stor del medio evo* (Florence, 1955)

F.-W. WENTZLAFF-EGGEBERT, *Kreuzzugsdichtung des Mittelalters* (Berlin, 1960)

1095–1187

E. O. BLAKE, 'The Formation of the Crusade Idea', *Journal of Ecclesiastical History* XXI (1970)

J. A. BRUNDAGE, 'The Army of the First Crusade and the Crusade Vow: Some Reflections on a Recent Book', *Medieval Studies* XXXIII (1971)

G. CONSTABLE, 'The Second Crusade as seen by Contemporaries', *Traditio* IX (1953)

H. E. J. COWDREY, 'Pope Urban II's Preaching of the First Crusade', *History* LV (1970)

E. DELARUELLE, 'Essai sur la formation de l'idée de croisade', *Bulletin de literature ecclésiastique*, XLII, XLV, LIV–LV (1941, 1944, 1953–4)

C. ERDMANN, *The Origin of the Idea of Crusade*, tr. M. W. Baldwin and W. Goffart (Princeton, 1977)

E.-D. HEHL, *Kirche und Krieg im 12. Jahrhundert* (Stuttgart, 1980)

J. H. and L. L. HILL, *Raymond IV de Saint-Gilles, 1041 (ou 1042)–1105* (Toulouse, 1959)

J. H. and L. L. HILL, 'Contemporary Accounts and the Later Reputation of Adhémar, Bishop of Puy', *Medievalia et Humanistica* IX (1955)

P. ROUSSET, *Les origines et les caractères de la première croisade* (Neuchâtel, 1945)

R. C. SMAIL, 'Latin Syria and the West, 1149–1187', *Transactions of the Royal Historical Society*, 5th ser., XIX (1969)

R. SOMERVILLE, 'The Councils of Urban II: Decreta Claromontensia', *Annuarium Historiae Conciliorum*, Supplementum I (1972)

R. SOMERVILLE, 'The Council of Clermont (1095) and Latin Christian Society', *Archivum historiae pontificiae* XII (1974)

R. SOMERVILLE, 'The Council of Clermont and the First Crusade', *Studia gratiana* XX (1976)

1187–1274

B. BEEBE, 'The English Baronage and the Crusade of 1270', *Bulletin of the Institute of Historical Research* XLVIII (1975)

J. P. DONOVAN, *Pelagius and the Fifth Crusade* (Philadelphia, 1950)

A. FROLOW, *La déviation de la quatrième croisade vers Constantinople* (Paris, 1955)

W. C. JORDAN, *Louis IX and the Challenge of the Crusade* (Princeton, 1979)

B. Z. KEDAR, 'The Passenger List of a Crusader Ship, 1250: Towards the History of the Popular Element on the Seventh Crusade', *Studi medievali*, 3rd ser., XIII (1972)

M. MACCARONE, 'Studi su Innocenzo III. Orvieto e la predicazione della crociata', *Italia sacra* XVII (1972)

M. PURCELL, *Papal Crusading Policy 1244–1291* (Leiden, 1975)

D. E. QUELLER, *The Fourth Crusade* (Leicester, 1978)

H. ROSCHER, *Papst Innocenz III. und die Kreuzzüge* (Göttingen, 1969)

R. H. SCHMANDT, 'The Fourth Crusade and the Just-War Theory', *Catholic Historical review* LXI (1975)

P. A. THROOP, *Criticism of the Crusade. A Study of Public Opinion and Crusade Propaganda* (Amsterdam, 1940)

The Later Crusades

A. Z. ATIYA, *The Crusade in the Later Middle Ages* (London, 1938)

J. DELAVILLE LE ROULX, *La France en Orient au XIVe siècle: Expéditions du maréchal Boucicaut* (2 vols., Paris, 1885–6)

J. N. HILLGARTH, *Ramon Lull and Lullism in fourteenth-century France* (Oxford, 1971)

N. IORGA, *Philippe de Mézières (1327–1405) et la croisade au XIVe siècle* (Paris, 1896)

A. T. LUTTRELL, 'The Crusade in the Fourteenth Century', in J. R. Hale et al., eds., *Europe in the Late Middle Ages* (London, 1965)

K. M. SETTON, *The papacy and the levant 1204–1571* (2 vols. Philadelphia, 1976–8)

L. THIER, *Kreuzzugsbemühungen unter Papst Clemens V (1305–1314)* (Werl, 1973)

Crusades in Spain and the Baltic region and against heretics and political opponents of the papacy

H. BEUMANN, *Heidenmission und Kreuzzugsgedanke in der deutschen Ostpolitik des Mittelalters* (Darmstadt, 1973)

E. CHRISTIANSEN, *The Northern Crusades* (London, 1980)

J. G. GAZTAMBIDE, *Historia de la Bula de la Cruzada en España* (Vitoria, 1958)

E. GRIFFE, *Le Languedoc Cathare (1190–1210)* (Paris, 1971)

E. GRIFFE, *Le Languedoc Cathare au Temps de la Croisade (1209–1229)* (Paris, 1973)

G. A. HOLMES, 'Cardinal Beaufort and the crusade against the Hussites', *English Historical Review* LXXXVIII (1973)

D. M. LOMAX, *The Reconquest of Spain* (London, 1978)

H. PISSARD, *La guerre sainte en pays chrétien* (Paris, 1912)

M. ROQUEBERT, *L'Epopée Cathare* (2 vols., Toulouse, 1970–7)

A forthcoming book by N. H. Housley promises to become the standard work on the political crusades in Italy.

The Military Orders

M. BARBER, *The Trial of the Templars* (Cambridge, 1978)

F. BENNINGHOVEN, *Der Orden der Schwertbrüder* (Cologne, 1965)

M. L. BULST-THIELE, 'Sacrae Domus Militiae Templi Hierosolymitani Magistri', *Abhandlungen der Akademie der Wissenschaften in Göttingen* LXXXVI (1974)

R. CAVALIERO, *The Last of the Crusaders. The Knights of St John and Malta in the Eighteenth Century* (London, 1960)

J. DELAVILLE LE ROULX, *Les Hospitaliers à Rhodes jusqu'à la mort de Philibert de Naillac (1310–1420)* (Paris, 1913)

M.-L. FAVREAU, *Studien zur Frühgeschichte des Deutschen Ordens* (Stuttgart, 1974)

K. FORSTREUTER, *Der Deutsche Orden am Mittelmeer* (Bonn, 1967)

D. W. LOMAX, *La Orden de Santiago, 1170–1275* (Madrid, 1965)

M. MELVILLE, *La vie des Templiers* (Paris, 1951)

J. F. O'CALLAGHAN, *The Spanish Military Order of Calatrava and its Affiliates* (London, 1975)

H. PRUTZ, *Die geistlichen Ritterorden* (Berlin, 1908)

J. S. C. RILEY-SMITH, *The Knights of St John in Jerusalem and Cyprus, c.1050–1310* (London, 1967)

M. TUMLER, *Der Deutsche Orden im Werden, Wachsen und Wirken bis 1400* (Vienna, 1955)

Index

The following abbreviations are used
abp archbishop; abt abbot; b bishop; c count; card cardinal; d duke; e emperor; k king;
pr prince; prov ecclesiastical province; q queen